THE ASHES OF WAR
THE FIGHT FOR UPPER CANADA, AUGUST 1814–MARCH 1815

Other Books in the Upper Canada Preserved — War of 1812 Series

The Call to Arms

The Pendulum of War

The Flames of War

The Tide of War

A Crucible of Fire

UPPER CANADA PRESERVED
WAR OF 1812

THE ASHES OF WAR
THE FIGHT FOR UPPER CANADA,
AUGUST 1814–MARCH 1815

RICHARD FELTOE

DUNDURN
TORONTO

Project Editor: Allison Hirst
Copy Editor: Natalie Meditsky
Design: Laura Boyle
Cover Design: Jennifer Scott
Printer: Webcom

Library and Archives Canada Cataloguing in Publication

Feltoe, Richard, 1954-, author
The ashes of war : the fight for Upper Canada, August 1814-March 1815 / Richard Feltoe.

(Upper Canada preserved -War of 1812)
Includes bibliographical references and index.
Issued in print and electronic formats.
ISBN 978-1-4597-2283-5 (pbk.).--ISBN 978-1-4597-2284-2 (pdf).--
ISBN 978-1-4597-2285-9 (epub)

1. Canada--History--War of 1812--Campaigns. 2. Canada--History--War of 1812--Treaties. 3. Canada--History--War of 1812--Influence. 4. Canada-- History--1791-1841. I. Title. II. Series: Feltoe, Richard, 1954- . Upper Canada preserved War of 1812.

FC442.F438 2014   971.03'4   C2014-902945-4   C2014-902946-2

1 2 3 4 5   18 17 16 15 14

We acknowledge the support of the Canada Council for the Arts and the Ontario Arts Council for our publishing program. We also acknowledge the financial support of the Government of Canada through the Canada Book Fund and Livres Canada Books, and the Government of Ontario through the Ontario Book Publishing Tax Credit and the Ontario Media Development Corporation.

Care has been taken to trace the ownership of copyright material used in this book. The author and the publisher welcome any information enabling them to rectify any references or credits in subsequent editions.

J. Kirk Howard, President

Printed and bound in Canada.

Unless otherwise attributed, images and maps are the property and copyright of the author.

The publisher is not responsible for websites or their content unless they are owned by the publisher.

Visit us at
Dundurn.com | @dundurnpress | Facebook.com/dundurnpress | Pinterest.com/dundurnpress

Dundurn	Gazelle Book Services Limited	Dundurn
3 Church Street, Suite 500	White Cross Mills	2250 Military Road
Toronto, Ontario, Canada	High Town, Lancaster, England	Tonawanda, NY
M5E 1M2	LA1 4XS	U.S.A. 14150

This book is offered:

First, as a salute to the memory of all those, on both sides of the lines, who served, sacrificed, and died as they loyally obeyed their country's call to arms in the North American War of 1812–1815.

Second, as a mark of respect to the men and women of the military services of Canada, Great Britain, and the United States, who today honourably continue that legacy of service and sacrifice at home and across the globe.

Third, as a thank-you to my fellow "Living History" re-enactors, with and against whom I've "fought" for so many years.

Finally, as a memory from "Bamp" to my grandsons, Anthony, Lawrence, and Daniel.

TABLE OF CONTENTS

ACKNOWLEDGEMENTS

Nothing would be further from the truth than if I tried to take the sole credit for the six books that have made up this Upper Canada Preserved — War of 1812 series. My name may be on the covers as their author, but it is only through the kind and generous support and assistance of a host of other individuals and institutions that the contents were researched, compiled, written, reviewed, amended, edited, printed, and distributed. Unfortunately, unless a separate chapter was attached, there could not be enough space within these published pages to adequately recognize each and every individual or institution by name, and for this I wholeheartedly apologize. However, as in the past, certain people and organizations have made exceptional efforts on my behalf to support this project and it would be remiss of me not to at least recognize as many as possible.

Without any doubt, the first on my list must be my wife, Diane. Not only because she has steadfastly supported this work as well as tolerated my ongoing absences and hermit-like seclusions when I'm upstairs in the "computer" room, writing for hours on end, but also for having taken upon herself the duties of acting as my "frontline" manager in the administration and bookkeeping of the business end of things to do with this effort.

Second, my grateful thanks go to a dedicated cadre of fellow War of 1812–1815 historians and historical enthusiasts. These have included:

An international collection of professional authors and historians such as Donald Graves, John Grodzinski, Brian Dunnigan, and Carl Benn.

A host of dedicated and knowledgeable museum and archive staff members such as Constance

Barone (Sackets Harbor), Peter Martin (Parks Canada), Jim Hill (Niagara Parks), David Webb (Parks Canada), Susan Ramsay (Stoney Creek), Kevin Windsor (formerly Lundy's Lane), Cynthia Van Ness (Buffalo), and in particular for this volume, Craig Wilson and Brian Jaeschke (Mackinac).

A veritable battalion of enthusiastic Living History re-enactors and keen local historians such as David Brunelle, David McMeekin, Pat Kavanagh, Glenn Stott, Dan Pearson, John Harris, Rob Trumble, Betsy Bayshore, Keith Raynor, and Bryan Gibbins.

These few who I have been able to mention, plus a host more, provided me with valuable source information, acted as sounding boards for ideas, and/or reviewed my work and proffered valuable corrections where needed. For these professional, academic, and personal generosities, I will always be grateful. Beyond that, in many cases they have also allowed me the honour to call them not only associates, but friends, and for that I am most humbly and sincerely appreciative.

Nor can I fail to acknowledge the extensive guidance and support provided by my editorial team, Cheryl Hawley and Allison Hirst, as well as my talented designer, Jennifer Scott — all backed by the extensive creative team at Dundurn Press, who turned this idea into a reality.

Penultimately, I wish to thank Barry Penhale and Jane Gibson of Natural Heritage publications and my friend Karen, who, sadly, has now passed away. Collectively, they put my feet on the path that allowed me to become an author.

Finally, I want to once again go on record in expressing my deepest gratitude and thanks to all my readers, who have supported me by buying my books, overwhelmed me by their kind reviews and compliments on the series, and provided suggestions for future works.

PREFACE

In writing a military history and using original quotes, every author on this subject has to deal with a certain set of problems in presenting the material. First, there is the fact that in the original documents one is dealing with historical personalities, each with their own and varied levels of education and skills of writing and spelling, not all of which correspond to our own modern forms. Second, there are the inevitable references to official military formations, regimental affiliations, ranks and appointments, battlefield tactics and manoeuvres, et cetera, that can sometimes appear alien to a modern reader not familiar with the subject. Third, there is the reality that place names have sometimes changed entirely or have gained different spellings over the years.

To address these points, this author has chosen to adopt the following position in the presentation of his accumulated materials.

On the matter of varied spellings in quotes, the material has been repeatedly checked to ensure its accuracy and is presented just as I found it in the original documents. I have therefore not included the highly distracting term *sic* after each variant word, as it drives me to distraction when I see it used in other works and in my opinion effectively destroys the integrity and meaning of the quote to me as a reader. As I see it, in reading works of this kind, either I trust that the author did his job properly and the quote is accurate, or I don't and I go and look it up for myself if I'm so inclined.

On the second point, while generally recognized military terms are presented as is, some of the more archaic or jargon-type words are either followed by a modern equivalent word or referenced in a separate glossary of terms. In a similar manner, maintaining the differential identification of military units from the two principal combatant nations (when both used a system of numbers to designate their regiments) has forced many modern writers to develop a system that will maintain a clear distinction for their readers. I have adopted this convention, and within this work British regimental numbers are shown as numerals (41st Regiment, 89th Regiment) and where required with their subsidiary titles (1st [Royal Scots] Regiment, 8th [King's] Regiment), whilst the American regiments are expressed as words (First Regiment, Twenty-Fifth Regiment).

Finally, where place names appear under a number of variants (e.g., Sackett's Harbour, Sacket's Harbour, Sakets Harbor, or Sacket's Harbor), I have adopted a single format for each case, based upon a judgment of what I felt was the predominant version used at the time. Where names have changed entirely or would cause needless confusion (Newark becoming Niagara and currently Niagara-on-the-Lake), I have generally gone with what would clarify the location and simplify identification overall or included a reference to the modern name (Crossroads becoming Virgil).

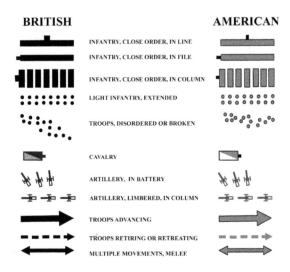

BRITISH		AMERICAN
	INFANTRY, CLOSE ORDER, IN LINE	
	INFANTRY, CLOSE ORDER, IN FILE	
	INFANTRY, CLOSE ORDER, IN COLUMN	
	LIGHT INFANTRY, EXTENDED	
	TROOPS, DISORDERED OR BROKEN	
	CAVALRY	
	ARTILLERY, IN BATTERY	
	ARTILLERY, LIMBERED, IN COLUMN	
	TROOPS ADVANCING	
	TROOPS RETIRING OR RETREATING	
	MULTIPLE MOVEMENTS, MELEE	

CHAPTER 1

Introduction

Between June 1812 and the latter half of 1814, the conflict between Great Britain and the United States had expanded far beyond what either side expected when it began. Across the world's salt seas, warships fought single or multi-ship actions, while closer to home, warships, gunboats, and even bateaux battled for control of the freshwater lakes Ontario, Erie, and Champlain, as well as the strategic St. Lawrence and Champlain Rivers. Similarly, land-based military operations were occurring at all points of the compass in North America, ranging from the southern climes of the Gulf of Mexico and Florida peninsula; eastward along the New England coast; westward across the Missouri, Illinois, and Indiana Territories as far as the Mississippi River and in some places beyond; to the wild northern lands around the strategic junction of Lakes Superior, Michigan, and Huron.

However, the principal focus of fighting in North America during the first seven months of 1814 continued to be the battle to dominate and control the British colonies of Lower and, more particularly, Upper Canada. This part of the story has already been documented in the previous books in this series, but since not all readers may have read those earlier accounts, the following timeline may prove useful to place the events that will be documented below into a proper framework.

TIMELINE

- *January 1814:* Following a series of failed attempts to invade Lower and Upper Canada

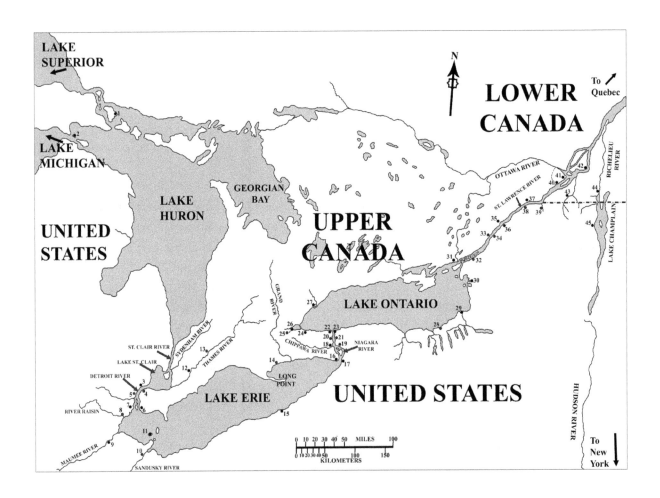

The Northern Frontier of the War of 1812–1815
(Modern Name)   [Fortifications]

1. St. Joseph Island [Fort St. Joseph]
2. Michilimackinac Island (Mackinac) [Fort Michilimackinac/ Fort Mackinac]
3. Detroit [Fort Detroit]
4. Sandwich (Windsor)
5. Monguagon/ Maguaga
6. Amherstburg [Fort Amherstburg (Fort Malden)]
7. Brownstown
8. Frenchtown
9. Perrysburg [Fort Meigs]
10. [Fort Stephenson]
11. Put-in-Bay
12. Moravianstown
13. Longwoods
14. Port Dover
15. Presque Isle (Erie, PA)
16. Fort Erie [Fort Erie]
17. Buffalo and Black Rock
18. Chippawa
19. [Fort Schlosser]
20. Queenston
21. Lewiston
22. Newark (Niagara-on-the-Lake) [Fort George, Fort Mississauga]
23. [Fort Niagara]
24. Stoney Creek
25. Ancaster
26. Burlington Heights (Hamilton, ON)
27. York (Toronto) [Fort York]
28. Sodus
29. Oswego [Fort Oswego]
30. Sackets Harbor [Fort Tompkins, Fort Volunteer, Fort Pike]
31. Kingston [Fort Frederick, Fort Henry]
32. French Creek
33. Elizabethtown/ Brockville (1813)
34. Morrisburg
35. Prescott [Fort Wellington]
36. Ogdensburg
37. Crysler's Farm
38. Hamilton (Waddington, NY)
39. French Mills
40. Coteau-du-Lac
41. Cedars
42. Montreal
43. Châteauguay
44. Île aux Noix
45. Plattsburgh

during 1812 and 1813, an American congressional committee of inquiry requests information from the American secretary of war, John Armstrong, "as may tend to explain the causes of the failure of the arms of the United States on the Northern frontier…."[1] A month later, Armstrong responds with a fifty-page document that includes transcripts of letters and official reports that catalogue numerous American military debacles, but fails to present any real conclusions or recommendations as to how these failures could be remedied. Nevertheless, the Americans are determined to reverse these losses and vanquish Great Britain in 1814. Consequently, Armstrong orders that a new series of campaigns are to be waged on the "Northern frontier."

• *April 11, 1814:* In Europe, Napoleon Bonaparte is finally defeated and forced to abdicate by a coalition of European monarchies spearheaded and substantially funded by Great Britain. Subsequently, the British government orders the transfer of troops and supplies to North America for use against the Americans, while the might of the Royal Navy is directed to expand its blockade of U.S. eastern seaboard ports and capture or sink any American warships that attempt to break out.

• *April 14:* U.S. troops, under Major General Jacob Brown, arrive at Buffalo, on the Niagara frontier, with orders to prepare and train for a springtime invasion of Upper Canada.

- *April 21:* Major General Brown returns to Sackets Harbor, leaving the training of the army at Buffalo to Brigadier General Winfield Scott.
- *May:* At Sackets Harbor, General Brown and the American naval commander, Commodore Isaac Chauncey, meet to plan the Niagara frontier campaign. Following these discussions, Brown believes he has a firm commitment from Chauncey to provide transport for reinforcements, weapons, and supplies as required and consequently bases his entire campaign strategy upon this premise. However, Chauncey's understanding is that he has made no such commitment and that his first priority is to maintain a strike force that could oppose and defeat the British fleet on Lake Ontario (under Sir James Yeo) and not become a subservient transport for Brown's army.
- *May 14–16:* American forces at Presque Isle (Erie, Pennsylvania) make a series of amphibious landings and raids along the Upper Canada shoreline of Lake Erie, looting and destroying property at Patterson's Creek (Lynn River), Charlotteville (Turkey Point), Dover Mills, Finch's Mills, Long Point, and Port Dover.
- *May 23:* Nineteen Upper Canadian renegade turncoats, who had been captured while

THE NIAGARA FRONTIER

Locations Along General Brown's Originally Proposed American Attack Route from Long Point to Burlington Heights

(Modern Name)   [Fortifications]

1. Long Point (Port Rowan area)
2. Turkey Point
3. Dover (Port Dover)
4. Nanticoke
5. Union Mills (Simcoe)
6. Sovereign's and Sayle's Mills (Waterford)
7. Malcolm's Mills (Oakland)
8. Brantford
9. Ancaster
10. Burlington Heights

Locations along the Actual American Invasion Route Following the Niagara River

11. Fort Erie
12. Buffalo
13. Black Rock
14. Scajaquada Creek Navy Yard
15. Frenchman's Creek
16. Weishoun's Point
17. Chippawa fortifications
18. Fort Schlosser
19. Bridgewater
20. Lundy's Lane/Portage Road crossroad
21. Shipman's Corners (St. Catharines)
22. St. Davids
23. Queenston
25. Crossroads (Virgil)
26. Fort Mississauga/Newark/Fort George
27. Fort Niagara

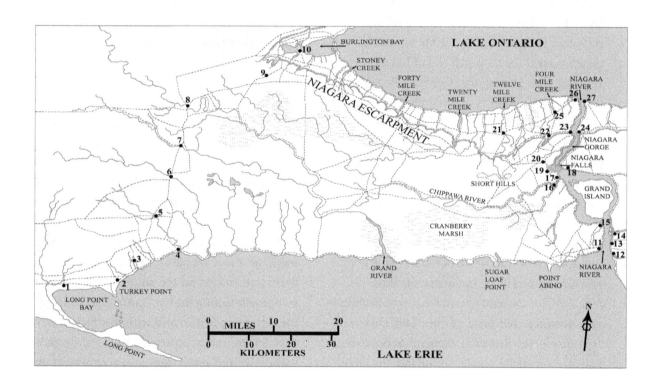

participating in earlier American raids on Upper Canada settlements, are arraigned on charges of high treason at Ancaster. In addition, a further fifty are charged *in absentia.*

- *June:* The U.S. secretary of war, John Armstrong, orders the diversion of the bulk of the American Lake Erie fleet to mount an expedition to recapture the garrison post at Michilimackinac (Mackinac) at the far north end of Lake Huron. Without this transport, General Brown is forced to abandon his original plan to mount an amphibious invasion via Long Point and instead use his limited resources of boat transport to mount his attack through the Niagara River corridor.

    News arrives in North America of the downfall of Napoleon Bonaparte. This creates alarm within the American administration, as the implications of the release of the British troops and naval forces in Europe are recognized.

- *June 7:* Major General Brown returns to Buffalo and assumes command of the "Left Divison." This displeases Brigadier General Scott, who had presumed he would command the invasion force.

    The Ancaster treason trials begin. Of the nineteen men being tried, one pleads guilty and four are acquitted. The remaining fourteen are found guilty and condemned to death.

- *June 26:* The first convoy of British troops transferred from Europe arrive at Quebec City in Lower Canada.

- *July 3:* U.S. troops land at Fort Erie. After forcing the small garrison of 137 British troops and Canadian militiamen to surrender, the Americans secure their bridgehead and prepare to advance north. General Brown's plan is to arrive at the shore of Lake Ontario by July 10th (the supposed date for his rendezvous with Commodore Chauncey's supply fleet).

- *July 4:* The American First Brigade (Brigadier General Winfield Scott), slowly pushes north to the Chippawa (Welland) River in the face of a successful delaying action by the British rearguard (Lieutenant Colonel Thomas Pearson). By the end of the day, the British forces are secure in their main defensive line on the north bank of the Chippawa River, facing Scott's frustrated troops on the south. With the only bridge connecting the two banks dismantled by the retreating British and with insufficient daylight left to mount an attack, the First Brigade withdraws and establishes an encampment on the south side of Street's Creek.

- *July 5:* The Battle of Chippawa. By dawn, the Americans are reinforced by the arrival of the Second Brigade (Brigadier General Eleazer Ripley). During the course of the morning, an

Library and Archives Canada, C-11826.

(Above) Chippawa Village, Sempronius Stretton, artist, 1804. The view looking south across the Chippawa River bridge toward the small village of Chippawa in 1804. Neither the bridge nor the buildings survived the war intact.

(Below) The same view, 2013.

escalating harassment from British Native warriors causes General Brown to order the newly arrived American Third Brigade (Brigadier General Peter B. Porter) to eliminate the threat to the American flank. At the same time, the British commander (Major General Phineas Riall) decides to leave the security of his positions and go on the offensive. While both sides initially commit approximately the same number of troops into action, the Americans have a significant advantage in uncommitted reserves. As a result, during the subsequent Battle of Chippawa (for details see *The Tide of War*), although both sides suffer significant casualties, the American reserves tilt the balance and without any reinforcements to replace their battlefield losses or match the American build-up, the British are eventually defeated and forced to retreat back to their positions on the north side of the Chippawa River.

- *July 8:* U.S. forces attempt to outflank the British right wing at Chippawa by building a pontoon bridge to cross the Chippawa River at Weishoun's Point but are stalled by British fire from the north bank. However, when General Riall receives erroneous reports that his flank has been turned, he orders the abandonment of the Chippawa defensive line and makes a retreat, first to Queenston and then to Fort George.

- *July 9:* U.S. forces advance from the Chippawa River and encamp at Queenston Heights, as British forces dig in at the mouth of the Niagara River around Fort Niagara, Fort George, and Fort Mississauga.

- *July 10:* The U.S. flotilla from Sackets Harbor fails to arrive to rendezvous with Brown's army on the Niagara frontier.

- *July 13:* In order to prevent being cut off in their defensive enclave at the mouth of the Niagara River, General Riall divides his forces, leaving holding garrisons at Forts Mississauga, George, and Niagara, while the remainder of his army retreats toward the Twenty Mile Creek.

- *July 14:* Major General Brown holds a Council of War to discuss campaign strategy in light of the non-arrival of the U.S. flotilla and news of the movement of the British forces.

- *July 15:* U.S. militia forces advance from Queenston to Fort George and skirmish with British picket posts before retiring back to Queenston.

- *July 18:* U.S. militias engage British/Canadian picket positions near Queenston and burn the village of St. Davids.

- *July 20:* U.S. forces advance to Fort George and begin to erect siege works in preparation for an attack on the British garrison.

Native Indian allies from both sides conclude a mutual non-aggression pact and withdraw most of their forces from both the British and U.S. armies on the Niagara frontier.

Eight convicted "traitors" from the trials at Ancaster (Upper Canada) are executed.

On Lake Huron, the U.S. flotilla seeking to retake Michilimackinac (Mackinac) arrives at St. Joseph Island to find the old British military/trading post abandoned. The Americans burn the settlement and also capture the small British supply vessel *Mink*.

- *July 22:* U.S. forces at Fort George abandon their siege and retreat back to Queenston, only to find it occupied by Canadian militias, resulting in a day-long running skirmish between Queenston and the ruins of St. Davids.

  Troops from the U.S. flotilla on Lake Huron occupy Sault Ste. Marie, burning the bateau locks, sawmills, warehouses, and sinking the schooner *Perseverance*.

- *July 23:* General Brown receives word that Commodore Chauncey has no immediate intention of leaving Sackets Harbor with his fleet. Consequently, with no prospect of a rendezvous or reinforcements, Brown orders a general retreat to the Chippawa River to review his campaign strategy and transfers all the army's extra baggage across the Niagara River to Lewiston.

Lieutenant General Gordon Drummond arrives at York (Toronto) from Kingston in order to take over command of the British war effort.

- *July 24:* General Drummond arrives on the Niagara frontier, taking over command from General Riall and orders a major offensive probe on American positions on the U.S. side of the Niagara River. To cover this, a diversionary move is made by British/Canadian Light troops in an overnight march toward Lundy's Lane on the Canadian side of the river.

- *July 25:* The Battle of Lundy's Lane (called the Battle of Bridgewater by some U.S. sources). British/Canadian/Native forces, under Lieutenant General Drummond and Major General Riall, converge on the hilltop at Lundy's Lane in preparation for an assault on the U.S. positions at Chippawa, scheduled for the following day. Late in the afternoon, the American First Brigade (Brigadier General Winfield Scott) advances toward the Lundy's Lane/Portage Road crossroads. Upon reaching the British positions, Scott engages the British, precipitating an unplanned five-hour long battle that draws in reinforcements from both sides in a piecemeal manner and takes place principally after dark. During the battle and under cover of the darkness, elements of the American Second Brigade (Brigadier General

Ripley) capture the central British artillery position and strategically important hilltop. In response, three major counterattacks are made by the British to recapture the position, resulting in significant casualties on both sides. At the end of the fighting, tactically the Americans still hold the hilltop but subsequently abandon it and retire to Chippawa, allowing the British to retain the field and gain the strategic advantage in the overall campaign. (For details see *A Crucible of Fire*.)

- *July 26*: U.S. forces, now under General Ripley, abandon their position at Chippawa and retreat to Fort Erie. British forces, under General Drummond, regain the Lundy's Lane hilltop, but later retire their main force to Queenston/Newark. As a result, only a small advance force shadows the Americans as they retreat.

On Lake Huron, the U.S. squadron, under Commodore Arthur Sinclair, arrives off Michilimackinac Island in an attempt to recapture Fort Michilimackinac.

TROOP MOVEMENTS ON THE NIAGARA RIVER FRONTIER, JULY 26–AUGUST 2, 1814

1. July 26: U.S. forces, under Brigadier General Ripley, advance from their encampment at Chippawa (1) to the hamlet of Bridgewater. From here, only a small reconnaissance force (1a) advances to observe the British positions on the Lundy's Lane hilltop. Convinced that any further offensive would be futile. Ripley orders the return of his units to Chippawa after razing the community of Bridgewater. Subsequently, the British also retire from Lundy's Lane toward Queenston (1b).
2. Notifying Major General Brown of the termination of offensive action, General Ripley orders the retreat of the American army back to Fort Erie (2–2a), where it arrives around midnight on July 26.
3. Following the retreat of the Americans from Chippawa in the late afternoon and the additional movement of the bulk of British units toward Queenston and Fort George (off map), small British detachments, supported by the Incorporated Militia and Native allies, advance to the Chippawa River (3). Crossing the river on July 28, the British detachments concentrate on the south bank at Chippawa (3a) while the Native allies advance to within sight of Fort Erie (3b) and over the following days engage in harassing raids on the American picket positions.
4. July 31–August 2: The reinforced and resupplied British force advances from its positions at Fort George and Queenston (off map), via Lundy's Lane (4) and Chippawa (4a), reaching the ferry dock opposite Black Rock (4b) on August 2.

CHAPTER 2

War on the Niagara Frontier: When Fortune Turns the Wheel

On the afternoon of July 27, 1814, a wounded Major General Jacob Brown, the senior American military commander on the Niagara frontier, was to be found recuperating at the almost deserted settlement of Buffalo, itself still recovering from its fiery destruction the previous December at the hands of the British. General Brown had received his wounds during the latter part of the Battle of Lundy's Lane (or Bridgewater, as the Americans chose to name it) on July 25. (For details see *A Crucible of Fire.*) Under normal circumstances, the military chain of command would have automatically transferred to Brigadier General Winfield Scott, but as he, too, had been seriously wounded at Lundy's Lane, command instead devolved upon Brigadier General Eleazer W. Ripley. Unfortunately, ever since planning had begun for the invasion of Upper Canada that spring, Ripley had questioned or disagreed with Brown's command decisions, to the point of tendering his resignation on the eve of the invasion. At the time, Brown had rejected this resignation, but now it was likely he was regretting that particular decision (for details see *The Tide of War*). In fact, so badly had the personal relationship between himself and Ripley degenerated, that following Lundy's Lane, Brown had sent for Brigadier General Edmund Gaines to take over command instead of Ripley. Brown's thinly veiled enmity toward Ripley had, in fact, just culminated in an acrimonious meeting between the two men, in which Brown had verbally flayed Ripley for proposing the abandonment of the invasion and the withdrawal of all American troops from Upper Canada.

To Brown, this proposal was particularly galling and frustrating, as it was backed by the fact that the army —"his" army — was even then arriving at Fort Erie, directly across the Niagara River, as a savaged remnant of the force that had proudly paraded on that same ground only twenty-five days earlier, thus providing a clear, but bitter, proof that Brown's original grand plans for the conquest of Upper Canada and the defeat — under his exclusive direction — of the otherwise mighty British army now lay shattered and ruined.

Nor were things much better with Brown's remaining subordinate general, Brigadier General Peter B. Porter. As a prominent member of the "War Hawks" in the pre-war period and having been active throughout virtually all of the actions on the Niagara in 1813, Porter had repeatedly expressed his frustration and resentment over the way he and

Brigadier General Edmund Gaines. From the A. Conger Goodyear Manuscript Collections, Vol. 9.

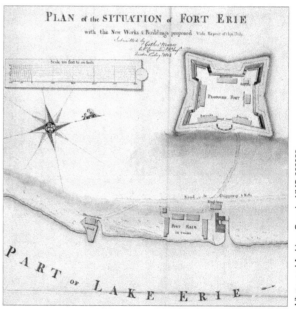

The new Fort Erie, as it was originally planned in 1803, but not completed by the time war began in 1812. It was designed to replace the one previously constructed directly on the riverbank that had been repeatedly damaged by Lake Erie ice driven ashore each spring.

SOME OF THE PERSONALITIES OF THE WAR OF 1812–1815
(Facing page: left to right)

Top row:
1. *Sir George Prevost* (commander in chief, British Forces and governor general, British North America), S.W. Reynolds, artist, date unknown. *Library and Archives Canada, C-19123.*
2. *Lieutenant General Gordon Drummond*, G.T. Berthon, artist, circa 1882. *Archives of Ontario, Acc. 693127.*
3. *Sir James Yeo* (British senior naval commander, Great Lakes). Lossing, Benson. *Pictorial Field Book of the War of 1812. New York: Harper and Brothers, 1868.*

Left to right, middle row:
4. *James Madison* (U.S. president). *Courtesy of the Buffalo and Erie County Historical Society Research Library, Buffalo, NY.*
5. *John Armstrong* (U.S. secretary of war). *Courtesy of the Buffalo and Erie County Historical Society Research Library, Buffalo, NY.*
6. *Commodore Isaac Chauncey* (U.S. naval commander, Northern frontier). *Library and Archives Canada, C-010926.*

Left to right, bottom row:
7. *Major General Jacob Brown*, attributed to J. Wood, engraver. *Courtesy of the Buffalo and Erie County Historical Society Research Library, Buffalo, NY.*
8. *Brigadier General Winfield Scott*. From the A. Conger Goodyear Manuscript Collection, Vol. 9. *Courtesy of the Buffalo and Erie County Historical Society Research Library, Buffalo, NY.*
9. *Brigadier General Eleazer Ripley*. From *Pictorial Field Book of the War of 1812*.
10. *Brigadier General Peter B. Porter*. From the A. Conger Goodyear Manuscript Collection, Vol. 9. *Courtesy of the Buffalo and Erie County Historical Society Research Library, Buffalo, NY.*

his militia had been treated as "inferior" troops during this 1814 campaign. Consequently, upon hearing of Brown's determination to supersede Ripley as second-in-command of the army with an "outsider," instead of devolving the authority on him, Porter promptly resigned his commission. In response, Brown not only refused to accept Porter's resignation, but also issued a series of glowing reports about the general and his militia command in an effort to salve that officer's pride. He also reacted to new reports, indicating that following his acrimonious meeting with Ripley, that officer had continued to voice his determination not to be held responsible for what he considered would be the certain loss of the army if it remained at Fort Erie and was demanding that his orders to maintain that post be provided in writing. Without delay, Brown penned the required orders and had them delivered to Ripley. With these unequivocal dictates, the area of Fort Erie became one massive construction site, as the troops worked around the clock to repair and augment the old fortifications at Fort Erie and erect a new line of batteries and palisades around their encampment that would hold the British at bay once they arrived.

> After it fell into our hands, on the third of July, and until the twenty-sixth, when we returned to it, the American garrison

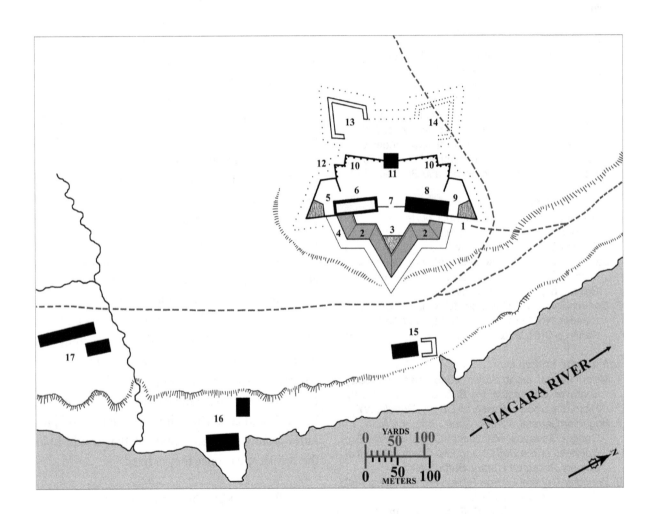

FORT ERIE, AS IT APPEARED AT THE TIME OF ITS SURRENDER ON JULY 3, 1814.

1. Main entrance to the fort and outer gateway (no gate)
2. Eastern ravelin earthwork
3. Eastern ravelin artillery platform (designated for a 9-pounder gun)
4. Eastern ravelin ditch
5. Southeast demi-bastion with artillery platform (designated for a 12-pounder gun)
6. South two-storey stone mess house and barracks (a burnt-out shell and unroofed)
7. Stone curtain wall with a closable gate
8. North two-storey stone mess house and barracks (partially repaired and roofed in)
9. Northeast demi-bastion with an interior artillery platform (designated for a 12-pounder gun)
10. Western wooden stockade or "picket" wall
11. Western wall wooden blockhouse
12. Exterior ditch trace line from pre-war period (only minor excavation and development construction work begun by this time)
13. Southwest bastion foundation from pre-war period (consisting of only a partial stone foundation raised to ground level)
14. Northwest bastion trace from pre-war period, partially excavated, and trace line of proposed ditch and bastion
15. Derelict lime-kiln foundation and small warehouse building
16.–17. Civilian and military warehouses

had been engaged in improving and completing its defences, as a mere fort; but of course, without any idea of the neighbouring ground being occupied by the army at large; nor had any works with reference to such an occupancy, been laid out or contemplated in the labors of the garrison. The Fort Erie of the siege … was rather an entrenched camp, having the proper fort, indeed, for one of its strong points, but extending for more than half a mile from it, along the lakeshore, with numerous other redoubts and batteries; and embracing an area sufficient for the accommodation of two or three thousand men…. On the twenty-eighth and following days of the month [of July] … the works of intrenchment were commenced …

— Lieutenant David B. Douglass[1]

The continued existence of the American army on the Niagara now hung in the balance and if the British had been in hot pursuit and had attacked, they could probably have swept the Americans from the Niagara frontier with relatively little effort or additional loss.

No such attack took place. Instead, a wounded General Drummond had effectively broken contact with the Americans on July 26 by retiring the bulk of his army from Lundy's Lane to positions at Queenston and the mouth of the Niagara River. His intent was to tend to his army's wounded, replace its battlefield losses, and replenish its supplies before going back onto the offensive. Unfortunately, despite needing every available man for service in the field, General Drummond was now forced to dismiss the bulk of his Embodied Militia troops (who had been called up when the Americans had invaded) so that the men could return to their homes and bring in the approaching harvest of ground crops — most of which would then be commandeered for the use of the army. Fortunately, a thousand regular troops from the De Watteville Regiment arrived on July 29, bringing Drummond's command back to a serviceable level. In addition, Drummond received a new second-in command, Major General Henry Conran, in replacement for Major General Riall, who had been wounded and captured by the Americans at Lundy's Lane. Finally, on July 31, movement orders were given for the restructured "Right Division" to advance and link up with its scouting parties, which had been watching as the Americans were digging in around Fort Erie.

CHAPTER 3

The Siege of Fort Erie: Encirclement

As the British forces marched toward Fort Erie, Lieutenant General Drummond received intelligence reports from his scouts of the massive efforts being undertaken by the Americans to strengthen their defences at the fort. Without any proper siege artillery or a corps of engineers to undertake a formal siege, he recognized that any delay would only make the army's job of evicting the Americans that much harder to achieve. Furthermore, the threat that Commodore Chauncey's fleet could arrive off Fort Niagara, Burlington Heights, or York had forced him to leave behind large detachments of troops to protect these locations, further depleting his available force in the field.

At the same time, the advance units that had been maintaining a watch on the Americans had already taken the initiative by driving in the American pickets and capturing the ferry-dock guard connecting Fort Erie with Black Rock — an engagement later recorded by an American officer who had faced this incursion:

> Soon after our arrival at the fort it fell to my lot ... to be stationed in the edge of ... [a] ... wood near the river ... [when] ... two small detachments of the enemy were seen by several of our men to enter the wood of two different points at a distance from our station and suspecting that their intention was to cut off the guard, I sent a message to the officer of the day stationed in the fort and requesting reinforcement. He came down and told me to assemble the sentries and if

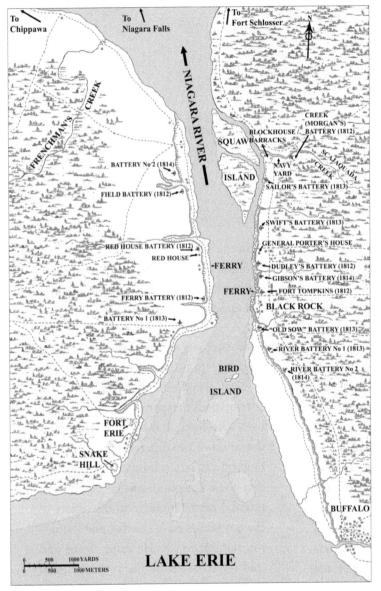

To Chippawa

To Niagara Falls

To Fort Schlosser

N

NIAGARA RIVER

FRENCHMAN'S CREEK

BATTERY No 2 (1814)

FIELD BATTERY (1812)

CREEK (MORGAN'S) BATTERY (1812)

BLOCKHOUSE

SQUAW BARRACKS

SCAJAQUADA CREEK

NAVY YARD

ISLAND

SAILOR'S BATTERY (1813)

SWIFT'S BATTERY (1813)

GENERAL PORTER'S HOUSE

RED HOUSE BATTERY (1812)

RED HOUSE

FERRY

DUDLEY'S BATTERY (1812)

GIBSON'S BATTERY (1814)

FERRY

FERRY BATTERY (1812)

FERRY

FORT TOMPKINS (1812)

BATTERY No 1 (1813)

BLACK ROCK

"OLD SOW" BATTERY (1813)

RIVER BATTERY No 1 (1813)

BIRD

ISLAND

RIVER BATTERY No 2 (1814)

FORT ERIE

SNAKE HILL

BUFFALO

0 500 1000 YARDS
0 500 1000 METERS

LAKE ERIE

The "gauntlet" of firepower lining the banks of the Niagara River by 1814. *NB* The British battery positions were abandoned when the British retreated after the capture of Fort Erie in July, but were partially recommissioned upon their return in August.

they [the enemy] proved too strong, we must retreat under the cover of the fort.

Shortly after, several shots from the sentries put us on our guard, when a sudden rush was made upon us by a party of the enemy in front, upon which we fired and received a volley in return, which struck down several of the guard and just at the same moment discovering that the other party was nearly in our rear and being outnumbered at least three to one, our escape depended upon a hasty retreat to the river and up the shore which we effected with the loss of half the guard …[1]

However, cutting off the fort from the main ferry dock did not prevent the garrison from maintaining contact with the other side of the river, as the Americans continued to obtain supplies and reinforcements directly from Buffalo under the protective artillery cover provided by three vessels of their Lake Erie squadron and the shore batteries at Black Rock. It was therefore obvious to Drummond that if he could cut the Americans' supply line, he might be able to force them to abandon the fort and thus avoid a formal siege and assault. To this end, upon arriving at Fort Erie on August 2, he issued orders for an immediate cross-river sortie by a force of around six hundred men:

The force will … land as near the lower end of Squaw Island as possible … the column … is to proceed with all possible silence and secrecy … to gain the road leading below the 12 Mile Creek from Buffalo — which place is to be the first attacked and destroyed … this effected, the troops are to march on Black Rock, attack whatever force the enemy may have there and get possession of their guns, should he have any…. The destruction of the enemy's Depot of Provisions & Stores at Buffalo is the first object — the capture of the guns, dispersion or capture of his troops at Black Rock … the second — and scarcely less important. By this blow and particularly if his stores and vessels fall into our hands, the enemy's force on this side will not only be reduced to the necessity of fighting under desperate circumstances, or surrendering unconditionally, but it may immediately lead to the re-establishment of our Naval ascendancy on Lake Erie …[2]

— Lieutenant Colonel Harvey to Major General Conran

As in the attacks of the previous year in July and December, the British intent was to land below the Scajaquada Creek and then move south upon Black Rock and Buffalo. However, the commander of this assault was Lieutenant Colonel John Tucker (41st Regiment) who was definitely not a dynamic leader in the earlier styles of General Isaac Brock and Lieutenant Colonel Cecil Bisshopp. Tucker also carried the nickname of Brigadier "Shindy" (a disparaging colloquial term for an individual who was short-tempered and ready to angrily erupt or cause a commotion if he became dissatisfied or was contradicted). Furthermore, despite the importance of the mission, indications are that Tucker failed to make any effort to conceal his intentions or preparations, which allowed an alert American commander, Major Lodowick Morgan (First Rifle Regiment), to fathom the British plan and move his force of 240 men of the First and Fourth Rifle Regiments into positions covering the main road to Buffalo and to also prepare a trap.[*3] Tearing up the roadbed of the bridge over the Scajaquada Creek, Morgan then deliberately marched his men away from their prepared positions and along the open riverbank to Buffalo, making enough noise and distraction to ensure his retreat was fully noticed by the British on the other side of the river. Once at Buffalo, he halted long enough for his men to eat a meal before silently marching them back through an inland pathway back to their former positions on the south side of the creek.

UNITS ENGAGED AT THE SCAJAQUADA BRIDGE, AUGUST 2, 1814[*3]

BRITISH (Lieutenant Colonel Tucker)
41st Regiment (Lieutenant Colonel Thomas Evans): 380 Other Ranks

Detachments (Lieutenant Colonel William Drummond)
89th Regiment, Light Company: 63 Other Ranks
100th Regiment, Light Company: 52 Other Ranks
104th Regiment, Flank Companies: 95 Other Ranks
Royal Artillery: 1 Officer, 12 Gunners
Royal Marine Artillery: 1 Rocketeer (with 8 rockets)

AMERICAN
First/Fourth U.S. Rifle Regiment (Major Lodowick Morgan): 240 Other Ranks

Unaware of what awaited them, the initial British landings took place shortly after midnight on August 3. However, instead of ordering an immediate advance or making any sort of reconnaissance, Tucker held his force at the landing ground for almost four hours, giving the Americans additional time to prepare their defences. Eventually, the British column marched south but without putting out any advance guard. Approaching the partially dismantled bridge, the column was then simply halted, completely exposed and in the open, while a detachment advanced to repair the roadbed. At Morgan's signal, the Americans opened fire, causing heavy casualties amongst the closest segment of the column. Recoiling, the British nevertheless soon rallied and returned fire before retiring to the nearby woods, there to re-form their column. Advancing again, the British troops attempted to charge the bridge en masse, only to suffer more casualties from the accurate American rifle fire. Several additional attempts were made by detachments of British troops to rush the bridge and construct some kind of walkway across the river, but each time the Americans either killed the men or drove them off.

According to some accounts, the British then attempted a flanking movement to their left, which Morgan countered by repositioning part of his force, thus preventing any advantage being gained by the attackers. After over two hours of often intense firing, the majority of the British force made a disciplined withdrawal to its waiting boats, covered by a fighting rearguard that effectively prevented the Americans from capitalising on their success by harassing the British retreat.[*4] In submitting his subsequent report on the action, Lieutenant Colonel Tucker took no responsibility for the debacle and instead laid the entire blame for the failure of the expedition on the shoulders of his troops, who he claimed "displayed an unpardonable degree of unsteadiness, without possessing one solitary excuse to justify this want of discipline …"[5] However, one of his subordinate officers who had been involved in the assault, Lieutenant John Le Couteur, saw things somewhat differently:

> About a little before daylight we moved on, left in front, without an advance guard or any apparent precaution. When I mentioned it to Col. Drummond, he said it was no business of his — the Brigadier might please himself … [once the Americans opened fire] … the men of another corps began firing in a shameful style and ran past us…. Col. Drummond sent me on with a Sergeant … and a file of men to see cautiously, what was in our front…. [after further firing] Day had now dawned and we advanced extended but the surprise was at an end thro' the misconduct of our

OFFICIAL CASUALTIES, SCAJAQUADA BRIDGE, AUGUST 2, 1814[*4]

BRITISH
Killed: 12 Other Ranks
Wounded: 17 Other Ranks
Missing/Prisoner: 5 Other Ranks

AMERICAN
Killed: 1 Officer, 5 Other Ranks
Wounded: 2 Officers, 6 Other Ranks

commander ... after keeping us in check till 7, we had the vexation to retire with the loss of twenty men, when we crossed unmolested. The failure was owing to Col. Tucker's total want of command ....[6]

To reinforce this latter opinion, Tucker's opponent, Major Morgan, also credited the British troops by stating:

At a quarter past 4 they advanced upon us and commenced the attack, sending a party before to repair the bridge under cover of their fire. When they had got at good rifle distance I opened a heavy fire on them ... and compelled them to retire ... they then formed in the skirt of the woods and commenced a fire ... and then attempted to flank us by sending a large body up the creek to ford it ... where they were again repulsed with considerable loss and retreated by throwing six boat loads of troops on Squaw Island, which enfiladed the Creek and prevented me from harassing their rear.... The action continued about two hours and a half ...[7]

It has therefore been suggested that the "unsteadyness" referred to in Tucker's report was not entirely on the part of the troops but rather partly in the mind of their commander, seeking to explain away his total failure to successfully conclude a vital strike against the enemy.

Whatever the reality of the matter, the consequences were grim for Drummond's plans to quickly finish off the campaign, as he knew that from then on, the American forces on the east bank would be fully alert to any further incursions. In the circumstances, his only recourse was to initiate a formal siege of the fort. Despite his anger at this failure, Drummond was forced to accept Tucker's version of events and officially censured the troops involved in the night's attack, withdrawing the bulk of the 41st Regiment to Fort George and keeping only the two flank companies at Erie, while bringing up in its stead the newly arrived De Watteville Regiment, as well as additional artillery that would be required for the assault batteries, which he now ordered constructed opposite to the fort.

Placing his main encampment amongst a dense wood, almost two miles (3.2 kilometers) away from the fort, Drummond's small detachment of military engineers, assisted by officers and men from other regiments who had knowledge of engineering, began the construction of the first line of entrenchments near to the riverbank. However, as these were located at a distance

Encampment of the Royal Regiment at London, Upper Canada, F.H. Ainslie, artist, circa 1842. Although a postwar image, it clearly shows how British troops in Upper Canada had to encamp as best they could amidst the over-sized stumps of the ever-present trees.

of around one thousand yards (914 meters) from the American positions, it was well beyond the best effective range for the field artillery that was immediately available. In front of these works, the Canadian-raised Glengarry Light Infantry and Incorporated Militia Regiments were assigned the task of pushing back the American pickets and then maintaining a round-the-clock picket in defence of the lengthening siege lines. According to Lieutenant John Le Couteur:

> August 4th … Appointed as an acting Engineer till some Engineer sub. comes up. Constructed a battery on our left, facing that of the enemy. Col. Harvey gave me carte blanche as to the numbers

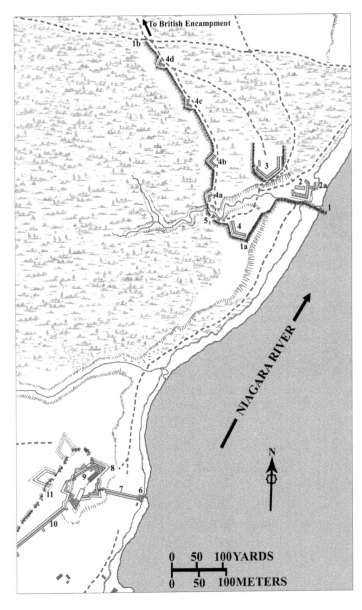

THE SIEGE OF FORT ERIE: SIEGE LINES, AUGUST 2–12, 1814

British Lines

1-1a–1b. Forward line of abattis
2. Initial battery position (later Battery No. 1)
2a. Supplementary earthworks and single battery position to cover the river frontage
3. Reserve earthworks and redoubt
4. Main advance guard post earthwork redoubt
4a–4d. Flanking guard post earthwork redoubts
5. Sally-port exit from British lines

American Lines

6. Douglass battery earthwork
7. "Epaulement" earthwork
8. Northeast demi-bastion of Fort Erie
9. Interior earthwork curtain wall, under construction (Fort Erie)
10. Line of earthworks leading from Snake Hill, under construction and incomplete
11. Line of abattis from Snake Hill, under construction and incomplete

of men — thus I had a Gun mounted in the day behind a half-moon battery ...

August 6th ... Constructed the front of a two-gun battery within one thousand yards of Fort Erie last night as the first breaching battery.... [We] ... had a sharp skirmish with the enemy's riflemen in our right advance.... Their object was to turn our right, but our pickets were well placed — they were driven off soon. Our loss about twenty killed and wounded. The enemy [artillery] got our range and the shot came plunking into our battery pretty hotly ...[8]

According to a letter by General Gaines to General Brown dated August 7, the respective losses for this engagement were: eleven British killed (including five Native warriors) and four wounded; five Americans killed and four wounded.[9] The Native war leader Captain John Norton later wrote:

The position chosen for this work [the battery] was joined by a ravine which extended to the right, inclining towards the out posts of the enemy, and following the course of a Morbid Run that issued from an adjacent swamp in heavy rains.... It was required that we should take post on the right of the advance, which covered the working party. Here we found ourselves at the extremity of the ravine, and within sight of a considerable party of the enemy. They fired at some of our men, which we returned with more effect, but we made no attempt to close, — because they were under the protection of the fort.... The next day [August 6] ... in the afternoon, we heard a firing commence on our left, near the water side: — Desirous to assist our friends, I proposed moving in that direction, and while my men hastened on under cover of the ravine ... I perceived through the foliage of the woods a number of men in light-coloured frocks [lightweight

British field artillery, placed in a modern reconstruction of the initial siege-work battery at Fort Erie.

smocks/jackets frequently worn by both American riflemen and Canadian militias]. At first sight I supposed them to be our men from the camp, moving on to our assistance — and only discovered my mistake when the foremost of them pointed their rifles to me ... [and] ... fired.... Many of our warriors came running to our assistance & we compelled them to retire with some loss; on our side we had a few killed and wounded ...[10]

Watching as the Americans continued their intensive efforts to expand their defences, Drummond was also frustrated that his own forces were working on their own field fortifications with a woefully inadequate supply of shovels, picks, and other essential tools.

This situation was their own fault, as most of the stocks of these tools had been destroyed or left behind by the British when they had retreated from Queenston on July 9. Nor could Drummond simply order up additional stocks of these items from York or Kingston, as Chauncey's fleet had finally arrived off the mouth of the Niagara River on August 4. This unwelcome arrival had the immediate consequence of the loss of the schooner *Magnet*, which had simultaneously arrived at the Niagara River, laden with vitally needed artillery ammunition and powder. Chased west by Chauncey's ships, the *Magnet's* commander had finally resorted to the desperate measure of deliberately wrecking his vessel onshore and blowing it up to prevent it being captured. In addition, the British supply vessels *Star*, *Charwell*, and *Netley* now found themselves trapped in the river, prevented from bringing over any more supplies to the army on the Niagara. Nor did matters improve once Chauncey sailed off, taking most of his fleet to Sackets Harbor on August 7, as he left behind three of his smaller warships anchored off the river mouth to maintain the blockade.

Forced to detach additional troops to protect the three forts at the mouth of the river, Drummond continued to prepare his first line of entrenchments. However, the riverbank position chosen for the bombardment battery left it exposed to flanking gunfire from the American batteries at Black Rock, as well as the three American vessels patrolling unopposed offshore from Buffalo. In response, Lieutenant John Le Couteur ordered a suspension of construction upon the main battery in order to build additional flanking earthworks.

August 8th ... The schooners fired at us the whole day long. Threw up an epaulement to guard the men from flank fire without orders from the Engineer, though with

40

Colonel [Hercules] Scott's entire approbation and aid. It secured the men's lives, but when Lieutenant Ph[illpotts] came down at night and saw what had been done, he got into a violent passion and wanted me to take it down again, which I declared I would not certainly do as he chose to be absent all day ... we had such high words that I said I would no longer serve under his orders and the next day I rejoined the company ...[11]

Hearing of this event, General Drummond privately reprimanded Le Couteur for his injudicious words, but censured Phillpotts for being willing to demolish a completed defensive work that could save lives, in order to prove a point of authority. In fact, by now Drummond was so frustrated at the obvious signs of delays and incompetence being shown by his engineers, and in particular his senior engineer, Captain Samuel Romilly, that he removed the captain from front-line command and sent him down to supervise work at Fort George. Unfortunately, Drummond was then forced to endure further delays as he now had to rely on the limited expertise of the remaining two junior officers to complete the fortifications. General Drummond's spate of bad luck also continued when his newly appointed second-in-command,

Major General Conran, was thrown from his horse and injured severely enough to necessitate his relinquishing his position, only days after having taken up his duties — leaving a still-wounded General Drummond to continue as the sole senior commander for the forces on the Niagara frontier.

It was therefore not until August 12 that the British battery of three 24-pounder guns, a 24-pounder carronade, and an 8-inch mortar finally began their bombardment of the American defences with some ranging shots, only to quickly confirm the previous suspicion that at around one thousand yards (914 meters), any firing served only to compact the fort's earthen defences into a denser mass, while the masonry of the original fort simply caused solid shot to bounce off. Furthermore, throughout this period, the Americans not only made increasingly aggressive sorties to disrupt construction, but seemingly also to execute a commando-like raid aimed at capturing General Drummond in his own headquarters.

Drummond has not yet opened his batteries upon us. I have been looking out for an opportunity to carry his principal work and had provided parties for the purpose night before last [August 8] in conjunction with an enterprise by Major Wood to take Drummond himself with

his guard at Miller's in the rear of his army, but the plan was wholly frustrated. 1st for want of light boats & 2nd on account of rain. On further reflection … finding them in strength near their batteries and moreover considering the scarcity of officers here and the injury that might result from a failure of the enterprise, I am disposed for the present to suspend it …[12]
— General Gaines to General Brown

Once the British battery opened fire, Gaines was forced to reconsider his decision and mount a larger operation, which resulted in a particularly fierce confrontation within the dense forest on August 12.

It was about 1 o'clock in the day [afternoon] when … we heard the drums beat to arms … in Fort Erie — an ominous sound of preparation for an attack. [Captain] Shore desired us to return to our picquets and place our men in readiness. the picquet in my charge was placed behind a stout breastwork with a heavy abbatis in its front about thirty yards [twenty-seven meters] off, it would be a difficult matter to pull it aside, or cut it down under the fire of forty or fifty men…. Some time about three I heard … [firing off to the

FORT ERIE DEVELOPMENT, JULY 27–AUGUST 5, 1814

During this period, principal American construction efforts consist of:

1–1a. Erecting an abattis line, developed from south to north
2.–2a. Excavating a ditch from south to north
3.–3a. Building a breastwork earthwork, developed from south to north
3b. Excavating a ditch and the initial construction of earthworks for a northwest bastion
4. Constructing an artillery platform and protective earthworks in the southeast demi-bastion
5–6. Building an earth embankment for a firing step at the back of the western wall wooden picket line on either side of the central blockhouse
7. Constructing an artillery platform and protective earthworks in the northeast demi-bastion
8. Deepening the original ditch in front of the northeast demi-bastion and the mounding of the earth on top of the position and along the outer rim of the ditch
9. Erecting an abattis line across the gap between the ravelin and epaulement earthwork
10–11. Building an epaulement earthwork and the excavation of a ditch connecting the fort to the Douglass battery
12. Building the Douglass battery artillery position

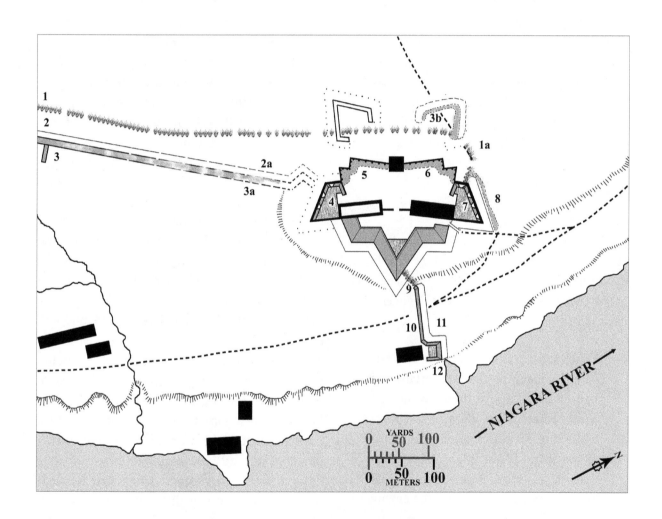

right] … I instantly placed my men under cover all along the breastwork…. The fire was ragged and closing on me fast…. The enemy made a desperate attempt to turn our flank but after an hours hard fighting they were driven back with serious loss, leaving many of their dead and rifles along our front. I did not lose a man….We lost several men in the other two picquets — my having concealed my men saved them all while our own fire was deadly …[13]

— Lieutenant John Le Couteur

While on the American side, General Gaines's report for the engagement included the fact that the commander of the Scajaquada Creek engagement, Major Lodowick Morgan (First Rifle Regiment), had been killed:

He fell at the head of his corps in an affair with the enemy on the 12th instant…. I had desired him to send a detachment of from 80 to 100 men to cut off a working party, supported by a guard of the enemy's light troops, engaged in opening an avenue for a battery…. This detachment … drove [back] the enemy, but when about to return to camp he discovered a large force approaching.

The firing having continued longer than the major expected, he moved up the moment the enemy's reinforcements made their appearance. A warm conflict ensued, in which they [the enemy] were forced back, but discovering additional reinforcements and receiving my order to fall back on the appearance of a large force, the major gave the signal with his bugle to retire; at this moment he received a ball in his head …[14]

With the American harassment driven off and the bombardment begun, General Drummond decided that the ongoing threat posed by the offshore American vessels required eliminating. Recognizing that any attempt to sortie from the direction of the Niagara River would undoubtedly alert the enemy at the fort as well as the nearby vessels, Drummond decided to mount the attack from the Lake Erie shore. This would now require moving the attack boats from their base at Frenchman's Creek in the Niagara River overland to the lake. Consequently, shortly after noon on August 12, the required six bateaux were dragged from the water and mounted on sleds, then hauled across eight miles (thirteen kilometers) of dense forest and swampland before finally being launched into Lake Erie around

British forces capture the USS *Ohio* and *Somers*, while the *Porcupine* (far left) escapes into the darkness.

midnight, whereupon the sailors and marines climbed aboard to undertake their mission.

Hidden by the darkness, the boats were quietly rowed down the lake and approached the three American vessels.*15

Tricking the American sentries into believing that they were supply boats for the Fort Erie garrison, the attackers swarmed aboard the *Somers* and *Ohio* and quickly overpowered their crews; while the *Porcupine*, alerted by the noise of the fighting,

---

FORCES ENGAGED, CAPTURE OF THE *SOMERS* AND *OHIO*, AUGUST 12/13, 1814*15

BRITISH
Royal Navy and Marines (Captain Dobbs, R.N.): 70 Sailors and Other Ranks

AMERICAN
Somers and *Ohio*: 70 Crew (Composed of Sailors and Infantry detached for duty on board the vessels)

OFFICIAL CASUALTIES, CAPTURE OF THE *SOMERS* AND *OHIO*, AUGUST 12/13, 1814*16

BRITISH
Killed: 1 Officer, 1 Sailor
Wounded: 2 Sailors, 2 Other Rank (Royal Marines)

AMERICAN
Killed: 1 Sailor
Wounded: 3 Officers, 4 Other Ranks (Eleventh/ Twenty-First Infantry Regiments)
Missing/Prisoner: 62 All Ranks

cut her anchoring cables and fled. Towing the two seized vessels into the Niagara River, the prize crews sailed the *Somers* and *Ohio* past the American batteries at Fort Erie and Black Rock without incident and reached the Chippawa River, where they were moored under the guns of the British depot.[*16]

Encouraged by this display of daring, General Drummond looked for a similar effort from his ground troops and ordered a night assault on the fort as soon as the artillery had done sufficient damage to the American defences. Unfortunately, he badly underestimated what level of damage would be required to ensure a successful assault and how long it would take to achieve this effect with the guns at his disposal. Consequently, after only two days of firing, he ignored the cautionary advice of his more experienced subordinates for a longer preparatory fire and scheduled the assault for the night of August 14/15.

Why he made this decision to attack in the face of the obvious ineffectiveness of the artillery bombardment is debatable, but one reason may be attributed to the continued difficulty of maintaining his supply lines and feeding his men, while the Americans continued to control Lake Ontario. This left General Drummond in the contradictory position of having the dominating control of the entire Niagara Peninsula — with his enemy's army firmly on the defensive and bottled up in a narrow enclave, while

his army was suffering from the American naval blockade to such a degree that he had to seriously consider retreating and abandoning the siege. He was already commandeering as much grain and cattle as the surrounding region could supply, leaving scarcely enough for the civilian population to feed itself, while his Native allies continued to demand their full quotas of food and in July had complained in no uncertain terms about seeing their rations partially reduced, at the same time as the dependants of the army had seen their rations cut in half.

Even his superior, Sir George Prevost, who had previously brushed off the difficulties and needs of Upper Canada for supplies and reinforcements, had seemingly finally gotten the message, if one is to believe the statement he made in his letter to Lord Bathurst (Henry Bathurst, Third Earl Bathurst, British Secretary of State for War and the Colonies), dated August 14:

> The naval ascendancy possessed by the enemy on Lake Ontario enables him to perform in two days what our troops going from Kingston to reinforce the Right Division require from sixteen to twenty of severe marching to accomplish. Their men arrive fresh, whilst ours are fatigued and with an exhausted equipment. The route from Kingston to

the Niagara frontier exceeds two hundred and fifty miles [402 kilometers] and passes in several places through a tract of country impracticable for the conveyance of extensive supplies …[17]

Meanwhile, the Fort Erie garrison had undergone a significant transformation, as General Ripley had, by now, been replaced as the commander of the Fort Erie position by General Gaines, who had arrived on August 5. According to the openly biased reports of General Brown, this replacement came because:

General Ripley continued to despond and although in command was in the habit of saying the army could not maintain its position…. This arrival [of General Gaines] relieved General Ripley from the responsibility he so much dreaded, gave hope to the army and reassured the Commander in Chief that it would be in his power to close the campaign with glory …[18]

Under Gaines, the garrison had worked around the clock to improve their defences and stockpile supplies of food and ammunition. By August 14, the defences had been significantly improved but

were still incomplete, the development of which was later recorded by Lieutenant Douglass, one of the principal architects of these works.

Fort Erie … was originally designed for a mere trading post…. Its form was quadrangular, nearly square, with four bastions; only two of them, however, forming the southeast or water front, had been wrought upon to any extent, at the time the garrison capitulated to general Brown. They were secured on the land side by a line of pickets, extending from gorge to gorge…. [On the lake side were] two large block-houses. The gateway of the fort was in the intermediate curtain, covered by a sort of ravelin of earth…. It was on the 27th of July that general Ripley … took up this position; his right flank being supported by the fort, and his left resting on a hillock seven hundred yards [640 meters] distant, upon which a battery was immediately commenced for its protection … other batteries were also commenced in the various exposed parts of our line … [so that]… on the 14th [August] we stood as follows: our line in front and on the left, including Towson's and the other batteries nearly completed and secured by abbatis in the most exposed parts; on the right, however, we were less secure, the space between the Douglass battery and the fort being little more than half closed up, except by a slight abbatis; no abbatis in front, and the fort itself yet in a very feeble state of resistance.... On the evening of the 14th, General Gaines ... having observed some signs of an approaching visit from the enemy, put his force in the best situation for a proper reception ...[19]

On the other hand, across the river at Buffalo, the earlier call for a wholesale turnout of the state militias to reinforce the troops in Fort Erie had failed dismally. As a result, General Porter was persuaded to supervise a new recruiting campaign for the support of the Erie defences; although how these troops would be supplied with clothing, weapons, food, and shelter was anyone's guess, as military supplies were scarce in the extreme, leaving Porter with no alternative but to subsequently order those militiamen turning out for service to bring their own weapons, accoutrements, and clothing.

Every soldier must furnish himself with a musket or rifle, knapsack, canteen, cartridge box, three flints, a watchcoat, and clothing for three months. Those who are unable to equip themselves with muskets and rifles or cartridge boxes will be supplied from the public deposit, but it is required ... that all who can supply themselves do so ...[20]

At the same time, the arrival of additional British regular regiments at Quebec persuaded the American secretary of war, John Armstrong, that Prevost would not waste these veteran troops on the relatively minor positions at Plattsburgh (New York) and Burlington (Vermont), but would forward these resources up to Drummond — first for use against the American army on the Niagara, and then secondly to strike at the American control of the Detroit River and Michigan Territory. He therefore ordered Major General George Izard to relocate a large number of his regular and militia troops from the Lake Champlain area to defend Sackets Harbor. What Armstrong failed to recognize was that instead of forwarding these men and associated supplies directly to Upper Canada, Prevost had indeed chosen to keep most of them for use in an attack out of Lower Canada, directly down the Lake Champlain corridor, which coincidently began almost as soon as Izard and his troops had left.

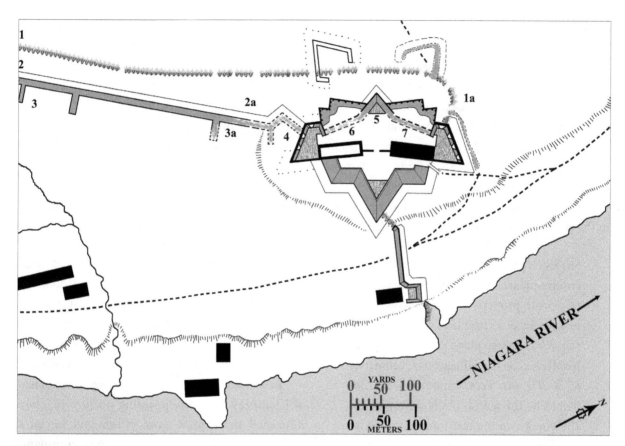

FORT ERIE DEVELOPMENT, AUGUST 6–12, 1814

Principal and continued work takes place upon:

1–1a. An abattis line, from south to north

2–2a. Ditch excavation, from south to north

3–3a. Breastwork earthworks with perpendicular traverses, from south to north

4. Filling in the line of the trace line of the original ditch and the initial laying out of the Fontaine battery artillery position

5. An earthwork redan artillery position with an exterior ditch, built over the blockhouse position and piercing the picket wall line

6. The initial embankment of an interior earthwork curtain wall from the southeast demi-bastion to the new redan

7. The initial embankment of an interior earthwork curtain wall from the northeast demi-bastion to the new redan

In a similar manner, because the end of the war in Europe had released the powerful British navy from blockading Napoleon's ports, it was already in the process of transporting convoys of British troops to directly attack the U.S. East Coast. Furthermore, the troops' commander, Vice Admiral Sir Alexander Cochrane, carried with him an extraordinarily strong endorsement from Sir George Prevost for exacting retaliation for the actions of the American troops on the settlements of Upper Canada earlier in the year. (For details see *The Tide of War*)

> Sir, Since writing to you on the 20th June, communicating the wanton destruction of private property on the north shore of Lake Erie, a repetition of similar outrages has taken place on the Niagara frontier ... as the villages of Queenston & St. Davids were committed to the flames by them and totally destroyed.... The enemy on the last moment of retiring [after the battle of Lundy's Lane] added another act of outrage to those before committed, by the destruction of Messr's Clarke & Street's Mills [at Bridgewater, just above the Great Falls, on July 26] the most useful and valuable in the country and the loss of which will be long & severely felt by the peaceful and unoffending inhabitants.... These events, so dishonourable to the American character and so little merited by the forbearance I have preached ... I deem it my duty to bring to your consideration as affording ample grounds of justification for any conflagrations which may have taken place on the coast and as calling loudly for a severe retribution, which I trust when opportunities offer, you will not fail to inflict ...[21]

Consequently, Washington was to find itself fully occupied with problems right on its doorstep and therefore had little time to pay attention to the needs of the Northern frontier. Thus, Brown and Gaines were effectively told to fend for themselves or get help from Chauncey and Izard at Sackets Harbor.

Regrettably, Brown's previous open criticism of Chauncey (for not appearing on July 10), had infuriated that proud naval officer and forced a wedge of animosity between the two commanders that would effectively cripple the American war effort on the Lake Ontario front for the remainder of the war. Responding in vitriolic kind, Chauncey publicly condemned Brown's management of the land campaign. He also claimed that he and his fleet had something better to do than to simply fetch and carry for the army.

From the tenor of your [July 13] letter, it would appear that you had calculated much upon the co-operation of the fleet. You cannot surely have forgotten the conversation we held on this subject at Sacketts Harbour previous to your departure for Niagara — I then professed to feel it my duty as well as inclination to afford every assistance in my power to the army, and to co-operate with it, whenever it could be done without loosing sight of the great object for which this fleet had been created — to wit, the capture or destruction of the enemy's fleet…. That you might find the fleet somewhat of a convenience in the transportation of provisions and stores for the use of the army, and an agreeable appendage to attend its marches and counter-marches, I am ready to believe, but, Sir, the Secretary of the Navy has honoured us with a higher destiny — we are intended to seek and to fight the enemy's fleet. This is the great purpose of … this fleet and I shall not be diverted in my efforts to achieve it by any sinister attempts to render us subordinate to, or an appendage of, the Army …[22]

— Commodore Chauncey to General Brown, August 10, 1814

To further prove this point, Chauncey had already sailed from the Niagara River on August 7, leaving only three of his smaller warships to maintain the blockade, while the rest of the fleet proceeded to circle Lake Ontario by way of Burlington Heights, York, and Kingston in an unsuccessful attempt to entice Yeo out to fight. Nevertheless, because of the American vessels maintaining the blockade, Drummond's ships were unable to sail to obtain the by-now vitally needed supplies of food, ammunition, assault equipment, and reinforcements that would be required to continue the siege. Despite these shortages and difficulties, General Drummond was determined not to await a possible favourable change in circumstances but to pursue his course of making a full-scale assault on the American positions as soon as possible.

CHAPTER 4

Assault and Disaster: August 14/15, 1814

In ordering an assault on Fort Erie, General Drummond hoped to repeat his previous success at the taking of Fort Niagara the previous December, by again attacking at night. However, he failed to take into account the fact that conditions for this attack were far different from those at Fort Niagara.

First, the attack was fully expected by the American garrison. The defences were well manned,

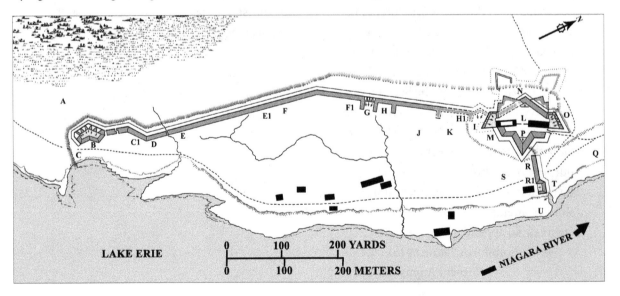

THE FORT ERIE ENCAMPMENT DEFENCES AND THE AMERICAN TROOP DISPOSITIONS, AUGUST 15, 1814

Left Flank (Brigadier General Ripley)

A. Picket Guard: Detachment from the Twenty-Third Regiment (Lieutenant Belknap). Est. 20 Other Ranks

B. "Towson's," or "Snake Hill," battery (6 x 6-pounders). U.S. Artillery Regiment (Captain Towson). Est. 100 Other Ranks

C–C1. Waterfront and abattis line below Towson's battery and the curtain earthworks to the north: Twenty-First Regiment (Captain Marston). Est. 475 Other Ranks

D. Curtain earthworks: Detachment from Seventeenth/Nineteenth Regiments (Captain Chunn). Est. 64 Other Ranks

E–E1. Curtain earthworks: Twenty-Third Regiment (Major Brooke). Est. 350 Other Ranks

Centre (Brigadier General Porter)

F–F1. Curtain earthworks: First/Fourth Rifle Regiment (Captain Birdsall/ Captain Armistead). Est. 350 Other Ranks

G. "Biddle's" battery: 2 x 12-pounders, 1 x howitzer. U.S. Artillery Regiment (Captain Biddle). Est. 40 Other Ranks. The main American ammunition magazine position.

H–H1. Curtain earthworks: New York Militia (Lieutenant Colonel Dobbins), Pennsylvania Militia (Major Wood). Est. 500 Other Ranks

I. "Fontaine's" battery: 2 x 6-pounders. U.S. Artillery Regiment (Captain Fontaine/Captain Fanning) Est. 30 Other Ranks

Centre Reserve (Lieutenant Colonel Aspinwall)

J. Eleventh Regiment (Major Merrill). Est. 250 Other Ranks

K. Twenty-Second Regiment (Major Martin). Est. 275 Other Ranks

Fort Erie (Major Trimble)

L. Nineteenth Regiment (Major Trimble). Est. 120 Other Ranks

M. Southeast demi-bastion: 1 x 12-pounder, 1 x 18-pounder, (possible 1 x 6-pounder), U.S. Artillery Regiment. Est. 25 Other Ranks

N. West redan battery: 1 x 18-pounder (*en-barbette*). U.S. Artillery Regiment. Est. 10 Other Ranks

O. Northeast demi-bastion: 1 x 12-pounder, 1 x 6-pounder, 1 x 12-pounder, and 1 x 24-pounder. U.S. Artillery Regiment, (Captain Williams/ Captain Gookin). Est. 30 Other Ranks

P. East ravelin earthworks and battery: 1 x 12-pounder(*en-barbette*). U.S. Artillery Regiment. Est. 10 Other Ranks and a small detachment of the Nineteenth Regiment

Right Flank (Lieutenant Colonel MacRee)

Q. Picket Guard: Detachment from New York and Pennsylvania Militias. Est. 20 Other Ranks

R–R1. Epaulement earthwork: Ninth Regiment (Captain Foster). Est. 175 Other Ranks

S. North Reserve: Detachment of New York and Pennsylvania Militias (Captain Harding). Est. 120 Other Ranks

T. "Douglass" battery: 1 x 18-pounder, plus 1 x 6-pounder (to the right-rear of the battery at ground level). U.S. Artillery Regiment (Captain Douglass). Est. 50 Other Ranks

U. Waterfront: New York Militia Cavalry (Captain Boughton). Est. 80 Other Ranks

with pickets on the alert during a warm summer's night, instead of huddling indoors during the bitter cold of a December winter.

AMERICAN FORCES, ASSAULT ON FORT ERIE, AUGUST 14/15, 1814[2]

Command Staff and Support: 23 Officers
Dragoons: 1 Officer, 38 Other Ranks
Corps of Bombardiers: 47 Other Ranks (plus 8 Other Ranks sick/wounded)
Artillery: 12 Officers, 231 Other Ranks (1 Officer, 30 Other Ranks sick/wounded)
First Brigade: 29 Officers, 608 Other Ranks (5 Officers, 143 Other Ranks sick/wounded)
Second Brigade: 41 Officers, 854 Other Ranks (4 Officers, 238 Other Ranks sick/wounded)
Third Brigade: 37 Officers, 417 Other Ranks (6 Officers, 89 Other Ranks sick/wounded)
Plus: 1 Officer, 26 Other Ranks (under arrest)
Total: 161 Officers, 2,525 Other Ranks (fit); 16 Officers, 551 Other Ranks (sick/wounded)

> The expectation was, of course ... that we should have a desperate attack, from them, without much further delay. In anticipation of this attack, the men were distributed for night-service, in three watches: one to be on duty under arms; and the other two to lie down in their accoutrements, with arms at hand, so as to be ready for action at a moment's notice. In the batteries, the guns were carefully charged afresh, every evening. In my own battery, in addition to other missiles, bags of musket-balls had been quilted up, in the fragments of an old tent.... The cannon were loaded, habitually, for short quarters. They were filled with roundshot, grape and canister, and bags of musket balls, at discretion, till I could touch the last wad, with my hand, in the muzzle of the piece ...
> —Lieutenant Douglass[1]

Second, Drummond's plan required three separate columns to successfully make a coordinated set of attacks — from three completely different directions, separated by more than a mile of dense forest, in the middle of the night — with no communication between the columns and without any artillery support or covering fire.[2,3]

The general order issued for the direction of each column stated:

> The Right Column [Lieutenant Colonel Fischer] ... is to attack the left of the enemy's position ... the Centre Column [Lieutenant Colonel Drummond] ... is to attack the fort.... The Left Column [Colonel Hercules Scott] ... will attack

the right of the enemy's position towards the lake, and endeavour to penetrate by the opening between the fort and the entrenchment, using the short ladders at the same time to pass the entrenchment…. The infantry picquets on Buck's road to be pushed on with the Indians to attack the enemy's picquets on that road. [The reserve regiments] … under Lieut. Col. Tucker are to be posted on the ground at present occupied by our picquets and covering parties. Squadron of 19th Dragoons in rear of the battery nearest to the advance ready to receive charge of prisoners and conduct them to the rear …[4]

In addition, Drummond issued more detailed orders to Lieutenant Colonel Fischer for the conduct of his column:

You are to advance to the attack precisely at two o'clock. You are to enter the enemy's position between Snake Hill and the lake, which is presented as sufficiently open, but this is not to prevent your making your arrangements for assaulting any other point of the position by means of the short ladders or hay bags with which you will be furnished…. Turning to the left after entering the position, the whole of the enemy's diminished and dispirited

BRITISH FORCES, ASSAULT ON FORT ERIE, AUGUST 14/15, 1814[*3]

RIGHT COLUMN (Lieutenant Colonel Fischer)

Targeting the defences between Snake Hill and Lake Erie
Advance/Forlorn Hope
8th [King's] Regiment, Volunteers from the Light Company
De Watteville Regiment, Volunteers from the Light Company

Est.: 100–150 men

Targeting Snake Hill
8th [King's] Regiment, Remainder of Regimental Companies
89th Regiment, Light Company
100th Regiment, Light Company
DeWatteville Regiment, Remainder of Regimental Companies
Royal Artillery, Detachment (1 Officer, 12 Gunners)
Royal Marine Artillery (1 Rocketeer with 12-pounder rockets)

Est. 1,100–1,200 men

CENTRE COLUMN (Lieutenant Colonel Drummond)

Targeting the defences at the fort
41st Regiment, Flank Companies
104th Regiment, Flank Companies
Royal Marines, Detachment (50 Volunteers, All Ranks)
Royal Navy, Detachment (90 Volunteers, All Ranks)
Royal Artillery, Detachment (1 Officer, 12 Gunners)

Est. 700–750 men

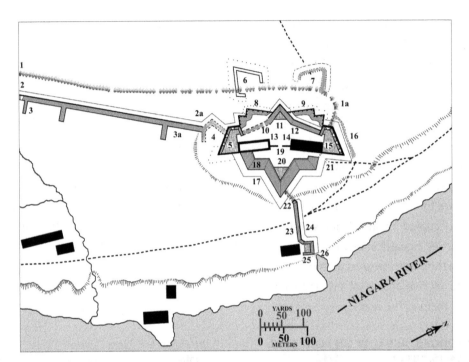

FORT ERIE, AS IT APPEARED ON THE NIGHT OF AUGUST 15/16, 1814

1–1a. Line of abattis from Snake Hill: Incomplete and undergoing strengthening from south to north.

2–2a. Line of ditch from Snake Hill: Incomplete and undergoing expansion from south to north. Varying from 6–10 feet (1.8–3 meters) wide and 3–4 feet (.9–1.2 meters) deep.

3–3a. Line of breastwork curtain earthworks from Snake Hill: Incomplete and under construction from south to north. Standing 6–7 feet (1.8–2.1 meters) high above ground level and varying between 5–16 feet (1.5–5 meters) thick, backed by intermittent perpendicular traverses.

4. Fontaine battery: Incomplete and under construction, with an intermittent low raised line of earthworks and a shallow exterior ditch. Containing 2 x 6-pounder guns.

5. Southeast demi-bastion: Exterior stone face, 76 feet (23 meters) long, 10 feet (3 meters) high (above ground level), and 3 feet (.9 meters) thick. Extensively altered internally by the construction of a wooden deck 5 feet (1.5 meters) above the interior ground level and augmented by 3–4 feet (.9–1.2 meters) high earthwork merlons across the top. Containing 1 x 12-pounder, 1 x 18-pounder, and 1 x 6-pounder (unconfirmed) guns. Possibly with a ready-use ammunition magazine underneath the platform.

6. Southwest bastion (foundation trace): Incomplete, consisting of a stone-faced foundation built to ground level, a shallow exterior ditch excavation, and scattered uneven piles of spoil.

7. Northwest bastion (foundation trace): Incomplete and under construction, with the exterior ditch partially excavated and the spoil piled up to create a low earthwork mound foundation for a breastwork.

8. Southwest picket wall of fort: An 11-foot (3.5-meter) high wooden stockade "picket" line backed internally by a low earth embankment (to act as a firing step) and partially covered externally by a shallow ditch.

9. Northwest picket wall of fort: An 11-foot (3.5-meter) high wooden picket line, partially damaged by British artillery fire. Backed internally by a low earth embankment (to act as a firing step) and only the trace of an external ditch.

10. Southwest earthwork curtain wall: Incomplete and under construction, standing only 3–4 feet (.9–1.2 meters) high above the fort's courtyard and with no appreciable external ditch.

11. Redan battery earthwork: Built over the partially dismantled wooden blockhouse. Standing 12 feet (3.7 meters) square and 12 feet (3.7 meters) high (above ground level), with an external ditch 8 feet (2.4 meters) wide and 3–4 feet (.9–1.2 meters) deep. Containing 1 x 18-pounder gun en-barbette.

12. Northwest earthwork curtain wall: Complete to approximately 12 feet (3.7 meters) above ground level with an internal firing step and external ditch 8 feet (2.4 meters) wide and 3–4 feet (.9–1.2 meters) deep.

13. South mess house: Two storeys, stone, 90 feet by 30 feet (27.5 by 9.1meters). Fire gutted and derelict.

14. North mess house: Two storeys, stone, 90 feet by 30 feet (27.5 by 9.1 meters). Reconstructed and repaired on both floors, with a completed roof. Some minor damage in the north gable end from British artillery fire.

15. Northeast demi-bastion: Exterior stone face, 76 feet (23 meters) long and 10 feet (3 meters) high, topped by an earthwork revetment of 8–10 feet (2.4–3 meters) high (including 3–4 foot [.9–1.2 meter] merlons). Extensively altered internally by the construction of a wooden deck 5 feet (1.5 meters) above the interior ground level, with a ready-use ammunition magazine underneath. Containing (L to R) 1 x 12-pounder, 1 x 6-pounder, 1 x 12-pounder, and 1 x 24-pounder.

16. Northeast ditch: In the process of being deepened, with the spoil mounded on top of the demi-bastion and along the outer bank "counterscarp," 15–17 feet (4.6–5 meters) wide and 6–8 feet (1.8–2.4 meters) deep.

17. Eastern ravelin ditch: 14 feet (4.2 meters) wide and 4–5 feet (1.2–1.5 meters) deep.

18. Eastern ravelin earthwork: 16 feet (5 meters) thick at the parapet and 6–7 feet (1.8–2.1 meters) high above ground level.

19. Main entrance to the fort and curtain wall: 83 feet long by 15 feet high by 3 feet thick (25.3 by 4.5 by .9 meters). Pierced by a central closable wooden gate.

20. Eastern ravelin artillery platform: Containing 1 x 12-pounder gun en-barbette.

21. Outer fort entrance (no gate, but possibly at least partially blocked with an abattis). NB The ditch was spanned with a temporary bridge that was removed prior to the attack.

22. Main northern access to the American positions: A gap of 30 feet (9.1 meters) plus 14 feet (4.2 meters) for the ditch, blockaded by an abattis

23. Northern epaulement earthwork: Running 123 feet (37.4 meters) from the northern "gap" to the Douglass battery. Constructed with almost perpendicular sides 6–7 feet (1.8–2.1 meters) high.

24. Northern epaulement earthwork ditch: Excavation line with the spoil piled on the interior slope to produce the breastwork, 6–10 feet (1.8–3 meters) wide and 3–5 feet (.9–1.5 meters) deep.

25. Douglass battery: Artillery platform earthwork built up around a ruined limestone kiln, 8–9 feet (2.4–2.7 meters) high with steep sloped sides. A 16-square-foot (1.49-square-meter) platform with a thick earthwork frontal parapet. Containing 1 x 18-pounder gun *en-barbette*.

26. Eastern gap to water's edge: 22 feet (6.7 meters) wide, covered at the right rear of the Douglass battery by 1 x 6-pounder gun and a detachment of troops.

troops will be found either in the trench extending from Snake Hill to the fort or in rear of the White House near the lake shore, and in either case will, as well as the batteries, be completely taken in reverse and exposed to your attack.... Two other columns will advance from this side as soon as it is ascertained that that [force] under your command has entered it — one to attack the fort ... the other to assault the line of entrenchments extending from the fort down to the lake. A demonstration will be made a few minutes before two o'clock by an attack upon the enemy's picquet opposite to the centre if his entrenchment.... A detachment of Royal Artillery will accompany the column for the purpose of either spiking or turning the enemy's guns against himself ...[5]

Third, while his troops had advanced upon Fort Niagara with unloaded muskets, this time General Drummond ordered the complete removal of the igniting flints from the muskets, making them impossible to fire until those flints were replaced.

In order to *ensure secrecy* the Lieut-General most strongly recommends that

the flints are taken out of the firelocks, with the exception of a reserve of select and steady men who may be permitted to retain their flints ...[6]

The advantages which will arise from taking out the flints are obvious. Combined with the darkness and silence, it will effectually conceal the situation and number of our troops and those of the enemy being exposed by his fire and his white trousers ... it will enable them [the British troops] to use the bayonet with effect ...[7]

However, while a subsequent objection from several senior officers persuaded Drummond to rescind the order for the removal of the flints for the two columns approaching the fort from the north, it was kept in place for the column attacking Snake Hill, a decision that had fatal consequences once the attack began. Drummond also seems to have imposed additional conditions upon Lieutenant Fischer's column, perhaps indicating that he had less than a complete trust in their commitment to the enterprise:

You will march immediately in order to pass through the woods before dark. On reaching Baxter's, you will halt ... using every precaution ... to prevent desertion

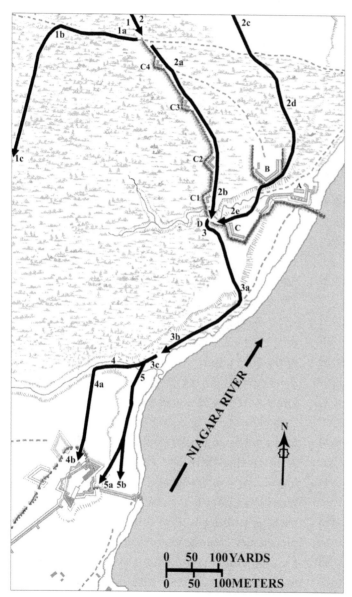

BRITISH TROOP MOVEMENTS IN THE ADVANCE ON FORT ERIE, AUGUST 15/16, 1814

British Positions
A. Principal battery (No. 1)
B. Reserve earthwork and redoubt
C–C4. Advance line of guard redoubts and main line of abattis
D. Sally-port gap in the abattis line

1. Before sunset, Lieutenant Colonel Fischer's column advances from the British encampment (1) and bypassing the British lines (1a), takes a circuitous line-of-march (1b–1c) to get to its initial assault position beyond Snake Hill.
2. Later that night, the double columns of Lieutenant Colonel Drummond (2) and Colonel Hercules Scott (2c) march from the British encampment and pass through the British lines (2a–2b, 2d–2e) before exiting at the sally port (D).
3. Marching to the riverbank road (3–3a), the two columns advance toward the fort (3b) before separating (3c) to advance on the fort according to their battle orders.
4. Lieutenant Colonel Drummond's column moves up the ravine (4) and advances across the open ground (4a) to attack the picket wall on the northwest side of the fort (4b).
5. Colonel Hercules Scott's column advances along the riverbank road (5) in order to make its assault on the gap at the north end of the epaulement earthwork (5a) and the adjacent earthwork (5b).

and the consequent discovery of your situation and intentions to the enemy.... No fires must be lighted, nor any ... chatter by your sentries or patroles permitted. Frequent (hourly) roll calls must take place and no officer to be allowed to quit his company, section, or subdivision for a single moment ...[8]

In hindsight, the cumulative effect of these difficulties and handicaps have been claimed to have doomed the assault, even before it was begun. Nevertheless, the determined efforts of the troops undertaking the assault were such that despite horrendous losses, they nearly carried it off.

Throughout August 14, the British artillery bombardment of the fort continued, but seemingly only resulted in a few casualties and the detonation of a small cache of ammunition, which did little damage, and only served to initiate a contest of cheering between the two armies.[9] With the farthest distance to go in order to reach its point of assault, Fischer's Snake Hill column marched out in the late afternoon, only to be delayed by rain, the dense undergrowth of the forest, and a detour around an impassable bog. In addition, the heavy assault ladders and cumbersome bags of hay (designed to be thrown into the fort's ditches) proved to be additional burdens and impediments, leaving the men practically exhausted before they even began the attack. In addition, while most of the troops in the northern assaults were from British regiments, the principal unit assigned to the Snake Hill column was the De Watteville Regiment, a foreign corps composed of a polyglot mixture of nationalities, many of whom had no particular enthusiasm for the British cause. As a result, General Drummond's instructions to remove the flints and hold roll calls while on the march (ostensibly to prevent desertions) was perceived as showing a lack of confidence in this regiment in particular, which, in turn, caused an erosion of the men's morale before the firing had even begun.

As soon as the British artillery was heard to have ceased firing on the far (north) side of the fort, Fischer's column marched out from the cover of the forest, heading toward the line of American defences that ran between Snake Hill and Lake Erie. Due to the low cloud and humidity, the night was unusually dark, and contemporary sources state that a body of troops could not be distinguished at more than fifty feet (15.24 meters), while an individual could approach within eight feet (2.4 meters) without being seen.[10] Nonetheless, the element of surprise was quickly lost as the American pickets detected the enemy's approach and opened fire on the advancing column. Withdrawing to their lines, the pickets alerted the defenders at Snake Hill and the adjacent line of abattis, allowing them to open fire upon the approaching British troops at a range of only ten feet (three meters).[11] According to Brigadier General Ripley:

> The enemy advanced with fixed bayonets and attempted to enter our works between the fort [Towson's battery] and the water. They brought ladders for the purpose of scaling … on the enemy's approach, [the defenders] opened their musketry in a manner most powerful. Fort Williams [Towson's battery] and this little band emitted one broad uninterrupted sheet of light. The enemy were repulsed. They rallied, came on a second time to the charge, and a party waded round our lines by the lake and came in on the flank, but a reserve of two companies, posted … to support this point … fired upon the party, who were all killed or taken. Five times in this manner did the enemy advance to the charge; five times were their columns beaten back …[12]

In all, the repeated attacks were estimated to have lasted up to thirty minutes, but eventually, finding they were unable to breach the solid line of entrenchments and barricades — all backed by the continuous fire of untouched infantry and artillery — coupled with the cumulative casualties and loss of discipline in several of the leading British units, proved too much for the attacking troops and they routed, as later documented by Lieutenant Colonel Fischer.

> In compliance with the orders I received, the brigade under my command … attacked this morning at two o'clock the enemy's position at Snake Hill and to my great concern failed in the attempt. The flank companies of the brigade who were formed … for the purpose of turning the position between Snake Hill and the lake … found [it] impenetrable and was prevented from supporting Major DeVilatte of De Watteville's and Captain Powell … who actually with a few men had turned the enemy's battery [by wading into the water]. The column of support, consisting of the remainder of De Watteville's and the King's [8th] regiment forming the reserve, in marching too near the lake, found themselves entangled between the rocks and the water, and by the retreat of the flank companies were thrown into such confusion as to render it impossible

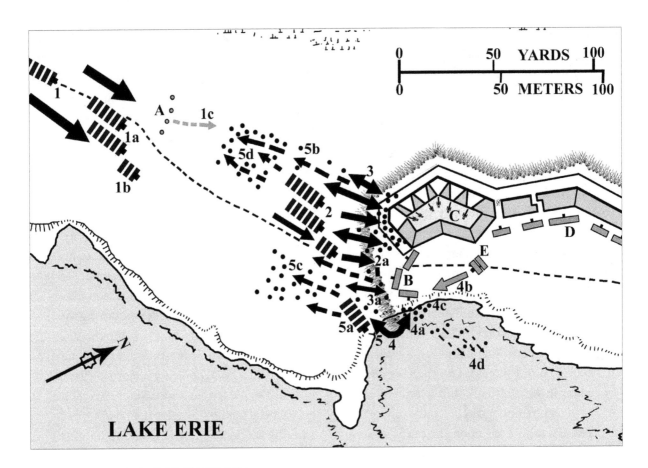

THE BRITISH ASSAULT ON SNAKE HILL

American Positions

A. Twenty-Third Regiment, detachment (American pickets)

B. Twenty-First Regiment (manning the abattis line below Snake Hill and the lakefront)

C. "Towson's," or Snake Hill, battery (6 x 6-pounders) plus artillery crews

D. Twenty-First Regiment and detachments of the Seventeenth/Nineteenth Regiments (manning the northern curtain line of earthworks)

E. Twenty-First Regiment (reserve companies)

1. Despite being detected by the American picket guards (A), the British column (1–1a) and "Forlorn Hope" (1b) advance upon the Snake Hill position as the American pickets make a fighting retreat (1c).
2. Approaching the American lines with weapons that are both unloaded and without flints, the British troops nonetheless attempt to storm (2) both the battery (C) and the adjacent line of abattis leading to the lake (2a), only to find that their assault ladders are too short and the abattis is far denser than anticipated. Opening fire at point-blank range, the American defenders (B–C) are eventually able to repel the initial British assault.
3. Regrouping, the British forces make repeated attempts to breach the American line (3–3a), but are just as repeatedly repulsed and with increasingly heavy losses.
4. Unable to break through the American lines, detachments of British troops attempt to outflank the defences by wading into the lake and around the end of the abattis line (4–4a). However, American units stationed on the shore (B), plus reserve detachments (E) (4b), open fire and inflict heavy casualties on the troops floundering chest-deep in the water, with casualties either being captured (4c) or swept down toward the Niagara River by the swift current (4d).
5. Survivors of the flanking attack make their way back to shore (5) and retreat in confusion, impacting on the column moving up in support (5a), while similar retreats from the abattis lines impact on the already disorganized columns behind. A cascade rout ensues (5b–5c) and the entire British attack on this flank collapses (5d).

to give them any kind of formation during the darkness of the night, at which time they were exposed to a most galling fire of the enemy's battery and the numerous parties in the abbattis ...[13]

Retreating in confusion, the wounded survivors blundered through the rear of the column, precipitating a cascade retreat. Only the men of the 89th Regiment are credited with having stood firm, until they too were forced to make a fighting withdrawal in the face of an American advance out from their lines. The entire attack on the British right flank had now collapsed, while the assaults by the other two columns had not even begun.

Meanwhile, on the opposite (north) side of the American position, the alerted defenders stood by their guns, expecting an attack at any moment. However, apart from the sounds of distant fighting at Snake Hill and some sporadic firing from the approximate location of Fanning's battery (where troops were firing into the darkness in response to some sniping from a party of Natives and British picket detachments), no enemy appeared. For some, the tension of the moment was intolerable and a portion of the men from the advance picket on this flank abandoned their posts and retreated to the fort walls, only to be met with a torrent of abuse from the men in the defences. Shamed into returning to their

The British Assault on Fort Erie and the Northern Flank

American Positions

A. New York and Pennsylvania Militia Regiments (manning the curtain earthworks leading to Snake Hill)

B. Eleventh and Twenty-Second Regiments (in reserve)

C. Fontaine battery (2 x 6-pounder guns) plus artillery crews

D. Southeast demi-bastion (1 x 12-pounder, 1 x 18-pounder, possible 1 x 6-pounder) plus artillery crews

E–E1. Nineteenth Regiment detachment (manning the central yard)

E2. Nineteenth Regiment detachment (manning the firing step of the northeast curtain wall)

F. West redan artillery battery (1 x 18-pounder) plus artillery crew

G. Northeast demi-bastion (2 x 12-pounders, 1 x 6-pounder, 1 x 24-pounder) plus artillery crews

H. Detachment of Nineteenth Regiment (manning the north flank of the east ravelin earthworks)

I. East ravelin (1 x 12-pounder) plus artillery crew

J. Detachment of New York and Pennsylvania Militias (in reserve)

K. Detachment of Ninth Regiment (manning the abattis line gap)

L. Ninth Regiment (manning the epaulement earthworks)

M. Douglass battery (1 x 18-pounder) plus artillery crew

N. 1 x 6-pounder gun, plus artillery crew

O. New York Militia cavalry (in reserve)

1. The "centre column" (Lieutenant Colonel Drummond) (1) advances across the open ground north of the fort, pierces the partially completed line of abattis, and assaults the northwest line of picketing (1a) in order to break into the fort.

2. Breaking through the picketing (2), the British find they are trapped between two lines of defences in a virtual "killing zone" by the American troops lining the inner earth curtain wall (E2). Multiple attempts to scale the embankment are made (2a–2b) but without success and at an increasingly heavy cost in casualties.

3. Breaking off the assault on this position, the British troops withdraw (3) and regroup (3a) before moving to the east and linking up with elements of the left column (3b).

4. Simultaneously, the left column (Colonel Hercules Scott) (4) brushes aside the American picket line and advances down the riverbank road (4a) before moving across the rising ground of the knoll (4b) in order to reach its attack target at the gap (K) between the fort's east ravelin earthworks (I) and the epaulement earthwork (L) (4c).

5. Alerted by the detachment at the gap (K), the Ninth Regiment (L) and Douglass battery (M) pour in a heavy oblique fire on the British, driving them back (5). Regrouping, the column makes repeated attempts (5a–5b) to storm the gap and adjacent earthworks but without success.

6. Withdrawing north (6), part of the column establishes a loose formation (6a–6b) that engages the Americans, while other sections withdraw and regroup (6c) before moving to the west (6d) and linking up with elements of the centre column (6e).

7. Combined elements of both columns (7–7a) advance to attack and storm the fort (7b), forcing a passage into the northeast demi-bastion (G).

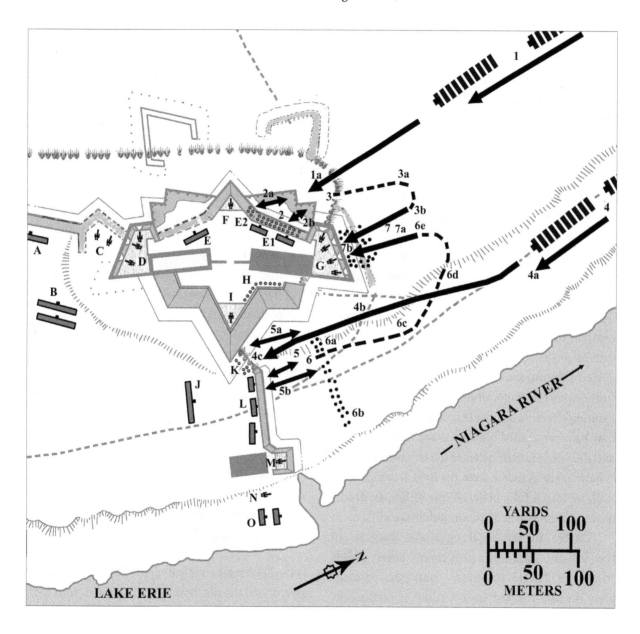

NIAGARA RIVER

LAKE ERIE

YARDS
0   50   100

0   50   100
METERS

duty, the delinquent men had hardly moved when firing began farther out as the remaining pickets encountered the two approaching British columns.

According to the original orders drafted by General Drummond, the two columns had been expected to attack the fort "as soon as it is ascertained that that [Fischer's column] has entered it...."[14] In theory, this timing was designed to use the confusion generated by Fischer's surprise attack and breaching of the American line as a cover for the double-column second assault, while a British advance through the American camp would have supposedly forced Gaines to withdraw troops from the fort and adjacent lines to counter this threat, leaving the northern flank more susceptible to assault. Unfortunately, the sounds of extended firing from Snake Hill possibly convinced Drummond to wait until firing was heard from inside the camp, while the returning fire from Fanning's battery against the unseen Native troops may have persuaded him the attack had succeeded and thus he belatedly ordered the columns forward. Whatever the actual reason, the British troops were walking into a fully manned line of fire, as deadly as that which had echoed around Snake Hill.

Unable to see anything useful because of the intense darkness, Lieutenant Eben Childs from the Ninth Regiment, stationed immediately outside the fort in a section of earthworks (referred to in many documents as an "epaulement") that led down to the Douglass battery and the lake, decided upon a novel means of assessing the approaching enemy's movements:

My particular station was upon the left of our [regiment's] line at a passage which was left for a road between the left of our parapet & the ravelin of the fort.... The enemy could not be discovered as he advanced until he came very near. Being confident that the enemy must attempt to pass the opening on our left ... I detached a Corp'l & twelve men and placed them at this point. The corporal ... I directed to lay down with his head on the ground a little back from the abbatis, which brought the top of the knoll [raised ground in front of the position] between his view & the stars, the only manner in which an object coming over the knoll could be discovered [because it would block the starlight] ... whereupon the corporal would give me the information and we made an oblique fire [to our left] over the knoll ...[15]

As the lieutenant anticipated, the British left column approached the northern line of defences with the

A modern reconstruction of a wooden "picket wall" and blockhouse (at Fort George) clearly show the kind of obstacle such a structure would have presented to the attackers at Fort Erie on the night of the assault.

obvious goal of breaking through at the perceived weak spot at the gap lying between the walls of the fort and the earthwork. With the warning provided by the recumbent corporal, however, the American troops opened fire, blasting the British column with both artillery and musket fire. Stopped short, the column recoiled and then again pressed forward, receiving a similar deadly portion of fire for its efforts and cumulatively losing over a quarter of its men in casualties in this and its subsequent charges.

The enemy appeared to be thrown into confusion by our fire, as he evidently seemed to retire and advanced three or four times. The only method of judging was [from the warnings called] ... by the corporal.... I think our fire continued something more than a half an hour, from the time it commenced until it ceased at the knoll ...[16]

— Lieutenant Eben Childs

Unable to breach the American line, some of the British troops spread out and commenced a firefight with the Americans, while others moved inland, where they advanced on the fort's northeast demi-bastion and met up with the centre column.

This column too had suffered setbacks; for in their initial briefings, the British reconnaissance reports had indicated that while the Americans had replaced the original small wooden block-house (located at the centre of the wooden stockade on this flank of the fort) with a new earthwork redan artillery position, the two flanking lines of wooden stockades or "pickets" remained apparently unchanged and had additionally been damaged by the British barrage. As such, it would only seemingly require the attackers to hack their way through or scale this single wooden obstacle in order to penetrate to the very centre of the American position. What the British did not know, however, was that behind the stockade "picket wall" the Americans had constructed a secondary defensive line of ditch and earthwork that would connect the two demi-bastions to the artillery platform. While the line of the earthwork on the left (southern) side of the new redan was still only a stump of an obstacle and remained unfinished, the ditch and earthwork on the right (the one facing the anticipated attack) was fully erected. It also had a protected firing step from which the defenders

MODERN VIEWS AT THE FORT ERIE HISTORIC SITE
Rebuilt as a make-work project during the Depression of the 1930s, Fort Erie today is administered by the Niagara Parks Commission.

1. Looking south from the main entrance into the outer ravelin earthwork courtyard, showing the south mess house/barracks and inner gate.
2. The same location, showing the north mess house/barrack.
3. A view of the inner courtyard, looking north from the line of earthwork curtain:

   A. Southwest earthwork curtain wall
   B. Redan battery artillery platform
   C. Northwest earthwork curtain wall
   D. The memorial monument outside the fort
   E. The northeast demi-bastion
   F. The north mess house/barracks
   G. Main entrance to the fort and curtain wall

4. The view of the northeast demi-bastion and north mess house from the enlarged and deepened ditch alongside the northwest bastion position. The American flag flying in the bastion is part of the annual re-enactment that takes place in early August. The two north British columns entered the fort through this position.
5. The American viewpoint of the narrow gorge into the northeast demi-bastion. It was through this bottleneck that all of the British attacks had to pass while under an intense fire from the front and the upper windows (right) of the north mess house/barracks.

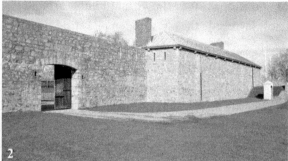

could shoot down into the virtual killing ground that now lay inside the old wooden picketing.

Despite coming across this unwelcome and lethal surprise, the British forces, led by a party of sailors and Royal Marines, pressed forward and in a series of costly assaults almost succeeded in scrambling up the wet and muddy steep slope of the inner bank, only to be repeatedly driven back by the heavy American firepower from above. Eventually, having suffered serious casualties and unable to break through, the troops from this column broke off this attack and then moved back and then east, meeting up with elements of the left column. Together, this combined force pressed forward once again and succeeded in reaching the walls of the northeast demi-bastion. Clambering up their scaling ladders to the shouts of their officers calling, "No quarter," the British fell upon the small detachment of American artillerymen manning the four guns in that position, resulting in a desperate melee of fierce hand-to-hand combat within a very confined space. Although greatly outnumbered, the American gunners nevertheless put up a spirited opposition but were soon either killed or forced to abandon their positions and retreat through the narrow gap at the inner face of the demi-bastion (known militarily as the "gorge") that led into the fort's inner courtyard.

Reacting to this breach of their lines, part of the Nineteenth Regiment (Captain Alexander Hill) previously stationed behind the earthen wall raced across the fort's interior courtyard and blockaded itself in the upper floor of the northern "mess house," while the remaining troops of the Nineteenth Regiment redeployed into an arc reaching from the main gate, across the courtyard, to the earthen embankment wall. In addition, the single 18-pounder gun on the newly built emplacement at the ravelin was turned around and fired point-blank into the confined space of the gorge. Despite the devastating weight of fire now being directed onto them, the attackers surged out into the courtyard and attempted to advance upon the Americans and also break into the mess house, desperately seeking to eliminate the fire pouring down on them from the windows above. Unfortunately, the constricted space of the body-strewn gorge made progress almost impossible and despite numerous attempts, the attackers were unable to push enough men out into the open to maintain a secure foothold in the main fort. They did succeed in turning at least one of the guns in the demi-bastion and fired it down toward the Douglass battery, forcing the troops at that station to seek cover and cease firing toward the remaining troops of the stalled left column.

Meanwhile, the collapse of the British attack at Snake Hill allowed General Ripley to detach men from the Twenty-Second Regiment (Lieutenant John Brady) and the Eleventh Regiment (Captain

William Foster) to reinforce the fort's garrison, while a detachment from the Ninth Regiment (under Captain Birdsall of the Fourth Rifles), was ordered from the northern flank and pushed into the fort to reinforce the effort to evict the British. After reinforcing the American line blocking the courtyard (from the redan to the main gate), the Americans fired a couple of volleys at the northeast demi-bastion and charged with the bayonet. However, the restricted space of the courtyard now served in turn to hinder their efforts, resulting in a contest of firing where neither side could gain the advantage and cause the opposition to cede ground, while continuous, but indiscriminate, firing from the American troops inside the stone mess house added to the casualties of both sides. According to at least one report, this stalemate of attack and counter-attack, across a space of only twenty yards [eighteen meters], lasted for up to an hour, until a final catastrophe sealed the fate of the attackers when a massive detonation and fireball erupted from the centre of the demi-bastion, sending rock, planking, cannons, and bodies into the air, as well as blasting off their feet most of those within the fort and outside in the ditches. Deafened by the explosion and with heads reeling from the concussion, the surviving British attackers in the ditch were also bombarded with the airborne debris, inflicting even more casualties and sealing the fate of the attack.

Suddenly, every sound was hushed by the sense of an unnatural tremor, beneath our feet, like the first heave of an earthquake; and, almost at the same instant, the centre of the bastion burst up, with a terrific explosion; and a jet of flame, mingled with fragments of timber, earth, stone, and bodies of men, rose, to the height of one or two hundred feet, in the air, and fell, in a shower of ruins, to a great distance all around ..."[17]
— Lieutenant Douglass

Few eyewitnesses from inside the bastion survived to write about the actual explosion, however one lucky individual later wrote:

I had mounted the ladder, got over one palisade into an embrasure and was in the act of jumping into the place, when I saw it full of combatants ... when, just then, I remember seeing a black volume rise from the earth and I lost my senses. After I had recovered them, I was lying in the ditch fifteen or twenty feet down where I had been thrown by a tremendous explosion of gunpowder which had cleared the Fort of three hundred men in an Instant.... But what a horrid sight

presented itself. Some three hundred men lay roasted, mangled, burned, wounded, black, hideous to view. On getting upon my legs, I trod on poor Lieutenant Horrens broke leg ... which made me shudder to my marrow. In placing my hand on Captain Shore's back to steady myself ... I found my hand in a mass of blood and brains — it was sickening ..."[18]
— Lieutenant Le Couteur

Because of this relative lack of certainty, several contradictory theories on the cause of the detonation appeared in later accounts of the battle. These ranged from a suicide bombing by a British turncoat deserter, to the deliberate mining of the bastion in case it was overrun. More likely, and the most frequent explanation given, however, is that the detonation was entirely accidental and can be narrowed down to two main possible causes. What is known is that a five-foot (1.5-meter) high elevated platform of planking had been constructed within the bastion for the emplacement of the four artillery pieces. To the rear of the guns, a wooden ladder led down to the parade square, while under the cover of the planking of the platform, a cache of artillery ammunition was stored for easy access and to maintain a rapid fire from the pieces.

During the initial assault, it would therefore have been entirely possible for at least one cartridge to have spilled its flammable black powder onto the ground, while during the subsequent hand-to-hand combat, more could have been dropped or lain exposed — only awaiting a stray spark to detonate it. According to this interpretation of events, as long as the guns were directed to fire out from the fort, this danger was minimal, but once the attackers reputedly turned a cannon around and attempted to fire it through the narrow opening at the Americans in the courtyard, the muzzle blast would have showered the ground in front of the cannon with a stream of sparks, thereby igniting the magazine. On the other hand, Major Trimble of the Nineteenth Regiment claimed that after a number of unsuccessful attempts to break out of the bastion area, several British soldiers were seen firing from underneath the platform, thus causing the detonation. Whatever the cause, the resulting explosion was catastrophic and effectively ended the British assault.

Without any form of surviving command structure, the dazed, battered, burned, and bloodied British survivors around the base of the fort's northern flank ran, staggered, or crawled away, pelted by a renewed firing from the American lines alongside the fort. Estimates are that in the instant of detonation, over four hundred casualties were inflicted on the exposed British troops — while the very structure of the fort protected most of the Americans from the deadly blast. In fact, only one American soldier is officially recorded as having been directly killed by debris from the explosion. How many in the confined space of the courtyard and mess house suffered blast concussions, sonic damage to their hearing, or other invisible injuries was never recorded. Fearing an immediate sortie and counterattack from the Americans, General Drummond, watching from his command position in front of the British siege lines, immediately ordered forward his reserves to cover the inevitable retreat. Returning surviving officers, if not seriously wounded, were corralled and ordered to re-form any rank and file survivors into ad hoc units, without regard to any regimental affiliation.

At daybreak, under a pall of drizzle and intermittent rain, the carnage of the night was exposed for view, revealing not only the usual dead and injured of a battlefield, but in addition, the smouldering remains of those who had been partially dismembered and cremated by the fireball of the explosion. Nevertheless, the Americans immediately began undertaking repairs to the destroyed defences to counter the possibility of a follow-up attack by the British.

The battle is over; the day had now fully broke; but oh God! What a scene! At every point where the battle had raged, were strewed the melancholy vestiges of the recent terrible conflict ... the ruined bastion, the scene of such desperate strife, smoking with the recent explosion, and all around it, the ground covered with the bodies of the dead and wounded — the former in every stage and state of mutilation.... In front of our fires, between the bastion and the water, the ground was literally piled with dead.... Several hours were employed in carefully disengaging the wounded and burnt from the ruins: those who were yet alive were sent to the care of the Army Surgeons; while the dead bodies were passed over the embankment. While the repairs were in progress, the parties detailed for the purpose excavated large graves a little distance without the fortification and gathered the dead, who were buried, forty and fifty together, side by side, with the honors of War ...[19]

— Lieutenant Douglass

The platform of the battery was replaced, as well as the darkness would permit, a twelve pounder restored to its embrasure and preparations made for defence … about two hundred and fifty dead bodies were thrown over the walls and parapets into the ditch and outside the walls…. Day soon after dawned and an appalling scene presented itself — some dying, others groaning under their wounds and dead bodies heaped upon them, others burnt and blind, many crying for water to slake their burning thirst, in short every form of human suffering and misery …"[20]

— Lieutenant Jonathan Kearsley, Fourth Rifle Regiment

OFFICIAL ESTIMATE OF CASUALTIES, ASSAULT ON FORT ERIE, AUGUST 14/15, 1814[21]

British
Killed: 4 Officers, 53 Other Ranks
Wounded: 1 Staff, 22 Officers, 285 Other Ranks; Navy, 1 Master, 12 Seamen
Missing: 2 Staff, 6 Officers, 530 Other Ranks; Navy, 1 Midshipman, 7 Seamen
Total: 924 All Ranks

NB According to an American body count, the British losses included (killed and wounded left on the field):
Killed: 222 All Ranks
Wounded: 174 All Ranks
Prisoners: 186 All Ranks
Confirmed Total: 582 All Ranks

Plus an unconfirmed number, estimated at up to two hundred, who were killed in the water at Snake Hill and whose bodies floated away.

For their own part, the British were in no state to make any kind of offensive and were fully occupied in simply recovering as many of their scattered troops as possible, while General Drummond sent off urgent calls for reinforcements from Fort George. He also had to face the unpleasant duty of reporting his failure and high numbers of casualties to his superior, General Prevost.[21]

Unwilling to admit his plan was overambitious in scope, flawed in application, and crippled by having its main column deprived of its musket flints, General Drummond sought to lay the bulk of the blame on the "failure" of the De Watteville Regiment to fulfill its objectives, and he completely ignored the bravery of that regiment's leading elements in repeatedly attacking an entrenched enemy without the benefit of being able to fire back.

For his part, Brigadier General Gaines was justifiably ecstatic over his success and made particular reference in his official report of the huge imbalance of casualties suffered between the two armies.[22]

OFFICIAL ESTIMATE OF CASUALTIES, ASSAULT ON FORT ERIE, AUGUST 13–15, 1814[*22]

American
During the preliminary bombardment:
Killed: 10 Other Ranks
Wounded: 4 Officers, 31 Other Ranks

During the assault:
Killed: 2 Officers, 15 Other Ranks
Wounded: 7 Officers, 55 Other Ranks
Missing: 1 Officer, 10 Other Ranks

Interestingly, not being influenced by any prior bias toward Brigadier General Ripley, as was the case with Major General Brown, Gaines made particular references to the efforts of General Ripley, stating the general deserved "… much credit for the judicious disposition of the left wing, previous to the action and for steady disciplined courage manifested by him and his immediate command and for the promptness with which he complied with my orders for reinforcements during the action…."[23]

On the other hand, Gaines did seemingly have some apparent personal issues with Major Trimble (Nineteenth Regiment), which caused him to omit mentioning virtually all of the contributions of the major and his regiment whilst acting as the garrison of the fort on the night of the attack. This omission so incensed Major Trimble that he later pressed a litany of official charges against Gaines, resulting in an official court martial in 1816. However, following the pattern set by the similar inquiry over Brown's reports on Chippawa and Lundy's Lane, postwar political necessities overrode military and personal grievances and, although the issue was officially heard (thus becoming one of the best sources of eyewitness testimonies to the circumstances and events of that night), the verdict of not guilty was never in doubt. Meanwhile, having made his report, Gaines found that his accomplishment went almost unnoticed, as the American administration was far more concerned with a more immediate threat that was literally on its own doorstep, for the British had just attacked and captured Washington.

This turn of events was a direct result of the British Royal Navy's blockade of the northeast coast of the United States, which had already resulted in parts of Maine coming under British military occupation. Pressing the navy's maritime advantage of being able to land troops wherever it wished, Vice Admiral Sir Alexander Cochrane landed Major General Robert Ross and a force of over four thousand troops near Washington on August 19. Despite the substantial warnings provided by previous British activities and raids around the coastline and outer Chesapeake Bay region, the relatively inland location of the capital, and a general sense of self-delusion in the populace and administration, the defences around Washington had been relatively ignored compared to those erected in other eastern seaboard communities — a weakness that was compounded by Secretary of War Armstrong's preoccupation with the events taking place on the Northern frontier. As a result, the imminent arrival of a British army within marching distance of Washington threw the city into a panic, while the administration quickly descended into chaos, leaving no effective command structure or system of defence in place to oppose the advancing enemy. Belatedly placed in charge of the city's defences only a month before, Brigadier General Winder had attempted to cobble together a force of regulars and militia to defend Washington but had found himself repeatedly overruled by a series of politically motivated and contradictory instructions simultaneously emanating from the offices of President Madison, Secretary of State Monroe, and Secretary of War Armstrong. So bad did this command situation become, that Armstrong openly criticized Madison and Monroe for interfering in the jurisdiction of the army and abdicated all further responsibility for the disaster he foresaw coming.

The final showdown in the "Battle for Washington" came near Bladensburg, Maryland, on August 24, 1814, when an apparently formidable triple line of over seven thousand American infantry (principally composed of militia regiments), backed by detachments of cavalry and eighteen pieces of artillery, all sited in strong defensive positions, found themselves shuffled around the battlefield during the day prior to the actual engagement by a series of contradictory orders emanating from a set of politicians that were each claiming to be the "commanding officer." Consequently, the final American lines were disconnected and overextended when the British redcoated juggernaut eventually arrived and made its attack.

Initially putting up a show of resistance, the American positions began to crumble when the militiamen came under bombardment from the British Congreve rocket detachments accompanying the attacking infantry. Starting with a series of withdrawals by sections, companies, and then entire regiments comprising the first two lines of troops, the retreat rapidly degenerated into a wholesale rout as the later-named "Bladensburg Races" began — so called as the British unsuccessfully sought to catch up to the fleeing American troops.

By nightfall, the city of Washington had fallen and senior British officers were enjoying their evening meal inside the President's mansion. With the city in British hands, the commandant of the Washington navy yard quite properly followed the order of the secretary of the navy, William Jones, to deprive the British of his yard's military supplies and vessels by setting fire to his depot. Unfortunately, this fire soon spread to nearby civilian buildings, causing much destruction. Once begun, this already existing conflagration was then added to by the British, with the later official explanation that it was in retribution for the destruction wrought by the Americans on the Lake Erie and Niagara frontiers earlier in the summer. In this manner, the Capitol building, several other government buildings, and after dinner was concluded, the president's mansion, were all consigned to the flames.

The following day, the British withdrew to their fleet and moved north, capturing the port of Alexandria, along with all of that city's warehouses and vessels, before heading toward their next target, Baltimore.

Forced to flee and abandon Washington, and with many of their principal buildings gutted, the American government, and Secretary of War Armstrong in particular, came under intense criticism. Consequently, the political ramifications of the incompetent defence of the nation's capital were not long in coming to a head. Although General Winder was militarily the officer delegated with the responsibility for the defence of Washington, he successfully avoided most of the blame and officially retained his post. Instead, with public and political opinion riding high against Armstrong, President Madison took advantage of the moment to make Armstrong the scapegoat and simultaneously unburden himself of a staunch critic within his cabinet. Replacing him, James Monroe now became secretary of war, as well as retaining his post as secretary of state.

The burnt-out shell of the president's mansion in Washington after the British had finished with it.

Benson Lossing, *Pictorial Field Book of the War of 1812.* New York: Harper and Brothers, 1868.

CHAPTER 5

Stalemate: August 17–September 16, 1814

Despite inflicting a grievous failure upon the British, the Americans in Fort Erie made no offensive counterattack but remained entirely on the defensive.

It became my duty, as an Engineer, to overhaul and repair the ruins … the whole bastion and its immediate neighbourhood were heaped with dead and desperately wounded; while bodies and fragments of bodies were scattered on the ground, in every direction.… The losses of the enemy … were so severe, that we were permitted to enjoy a few days of comparative rest from the fires of his artillery; and the interval was diligently improved by us, after repairing the bastion in completing the residue of the defences, along the line of our intrenchment.… The attack had made us aware of our weak points; and we lost no time in improving our defences.… On many parts of the line, where there was any exposure to attack, pikes of a rude construction were prepared by fitting rejected bayonets on poles of sufficient length to reach over the parapet …[1]
— Lieutenant Douglass

For his part, in the aftermath of the failed attack General Drummond's immediate reaction was to give serious thought to abandoning the entire siege, for as he notified Sir George Prevost on August 16, "… I am now reduced to a most unpleasant

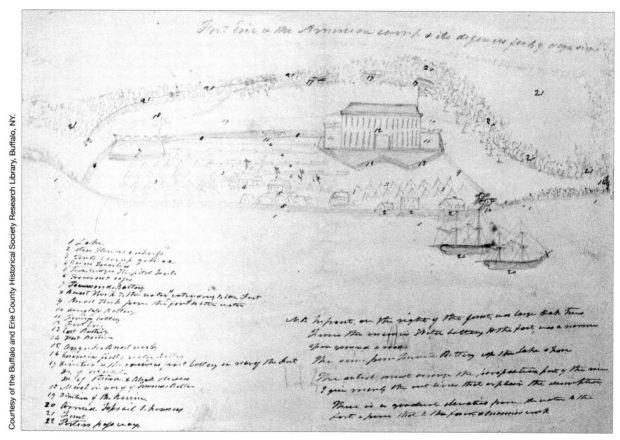

Fort Erie, as sketched at the time of the siege. From the A. Conger Goodyear Manuscript Collection, Vol. 9.

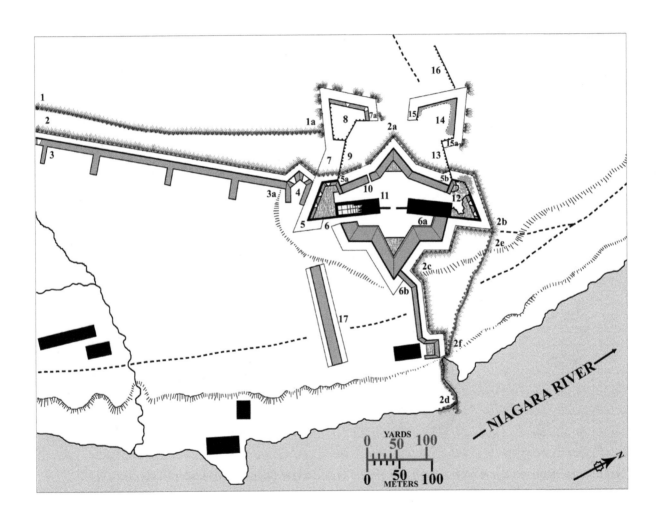

FORT ERIE DEVELOPMENT, AUGUST 16–25, 1814

Principal and enlargement work takes place upon:

1–1a. The original line of abattis, now connecting Snake Hill to the southeast bastion ditch, becomes an outer abattis line.

2–2a–2b–2c–2d. A new line of abattis, constructed directly along the outer line of the ditches around the original fort and adjacent earthworks to the line of the river. 2e–2f. A new line of additional abattis on the northern flank.

3–3a. Completion of the line of earthworks from Snake Hill and construction of additional perpendicular traverses.

4. Reduction of the Fontaine battery to half its size (due to the work referenced in 5).

5. Re-excavation of the ditch below the southeast demi-bastion. 5a–5b. Widening and deepening of the ditch outside the curtain wall alongside the redan battery.

6. Infilling of the ditch and excavation of an internal access route through the eastern ravelin earthwork. 6a. Closure and filling of the original fort entrance through the eastern ravelin earthwork. 6b. Closure and filling of the gap between the epaulement earthwork and the eastern ravelin.

7–7a. Excavation of the ditch around southwest bastion.

8. Construction of the southwest bastion with a combination of earthworks on the northern flank and a picket line on the south.

9. Construction of a picket wall connecting the southwest bastion to the southeast demi-bastion.

10. Construction of the south flank curtain wall between the redan battery and southeast demi-bastion, with a sally-port access to the outer works.

11. Reconstruction and re-roofing of the south mess house.

12. Reconstruction and repair of the northeast demi-bastion.

13. Construction of a picket wall connecting the northwest bastion and the northeast demi-bastion.

14. Construction of earthworks behind a picket wall to create the northwest bastion.

15–15a. Excavation of ditch for the northwest bastion.

16. Construction of a protective picket wall to shield the troops working on the new exterior defences.

17. Construction of a large earthwork traverse to shield the main American encampment from British artillery fire.

predicament with regard to force as the Royals, the King's [8th], 41st, 89th, 100th, and now the 103rd are so much weakened as certainly not to be fit to keep the field ..."[2]

Fortunately, Drummond soon learned that additional forces were on their way in the form of the 82nd and 6th Regiments. Consequently, despite having suffered such heavy casualties, coupled with the difficulties of obtaining reinforcements and supplies from York and Kingston (due to the continued American naval blockade), the general not only decided to maintain the siege (by expanding Battery No. 1 to include additional guns and the Royal Marine's Congreve rocket battery) but also ordered the construction of a second battery of guns, closer to the fort, in order to inflict greater damage on the defences prior to making another attack. Work on these entrenchments now began in earnest, while the already poor summer weather deteriorated into an unseasonably cold, rain-soaked autumn.

Seeking to disrupt the American repairs and improvements, Battery No. 1 began firing beyond the fort and into its adjacent encampment, causing significant damage within the unprotected American tent lines and making life highly dangerous for its occupants. In response, the Americans constructed a series of traverses (earthen embankments built perpendicular to the main line of defences) across the camp to shelter their men.

Modern reproductions of the Congreve rocket ladder as displayed in the "British siege lines" at the Fort Erie historic site.

From this time, the cannonade became severe and unremitting ... and, as the shot of the enemy passed lengthwise, through our camp, it became necessary to dispose the tents in small groups, along the line of the embankments ... for their protection. The most secluded places were selected for the horses and spare carriages of the [Artillery] Park, for the tents of the Hospital department, and for the parade and inspection of the guards. Yet, notwithstanding all these precautions, scarcely a day passed without considerable loss; and the annoyances were incessant. Shots ... were made to fall into the areas between the traverses,

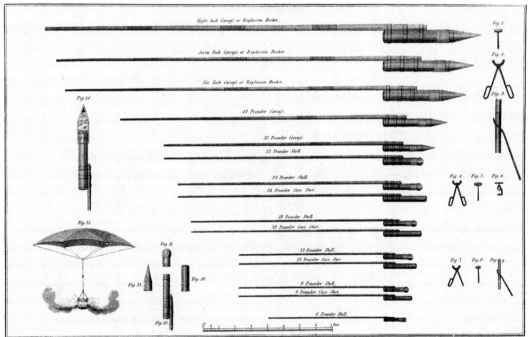

Illustrations taken from an instruction manual for the Congreve rocket system. (Above) Firing in the field from launching ramps constructed of a ladder with supporting poles and brackets. (Below) The range of rockets that was available in the Congreve arsenal of projectiles.

and sometimes, to knock over a whole range of tents, at a single stroke. Others, glancing against accidental objects, were thrown off into oblique … directions, producing the same effect. No spot was entirely safe…. A column, or a guard of no more than two or three files, sometimes a single person … drew one or more shots from the British batteries. The smallest gleam of light, in a dark night, produced the same effect; so that it became necessary to prohibit, in Orders, all lights, after dark…. In a very short time the more exposed parts of the camp were thus completely ploughed up. Many of the tents were pierced with shot-holes; and some of them … were literally shot to rags …[3]

— Lieutenant Douglass

In retaliation, the Americans sought to slow down the construction of the new battery by recommencing their sorties. By August 19, elements of the British 82nd and 89th Regiments had arrived, replacing at least some the losses suffered in the assault and allowing Drummond to send the badly depleted 103rd Regiment down to Fort George. He also chose to relocate his main encampment farther inland from the river, for by now the American battery positions at Black Rock had accurately ranged their guns onto the previously unseen British encampment position and were steadily lobbing shells and roundshot over the intervening Niagara River and a wide belt of trees. The following day, a strong American probe of the British lines was beaten off by a picket of the Glengarry Light Infantry, Incorporated Militia, and Norton's Native warriors, who were reported to have inflicted more than sixty-five casualties on the attackers for their own loss of two wounded — an encounter recorded by witnesses from both sides of the engagement.

The Expansion of the British Siege Lines During the Building of Battery No. 2, August 1731, 1814

1–1a–1b. Line of original abattis
2. Battery No. 1
2a. Riverside flanking battery
2b. Congreve rocket battery
3. Original reserve earthwork and redoubt
4. Centre earthwork and redoubt
4a–4b–4c–4d. Original guard post flanking earthwork redoubts (not occupied)
5. Original sally-port gateway
6–6a. New line of flanking abattis
7. Battery No. 2 (under construction)
8–8a–8b–8c–8d. New line of flanking guard post earthwork redoubt
9–9a. New flanking reserve earthwork and redoubt

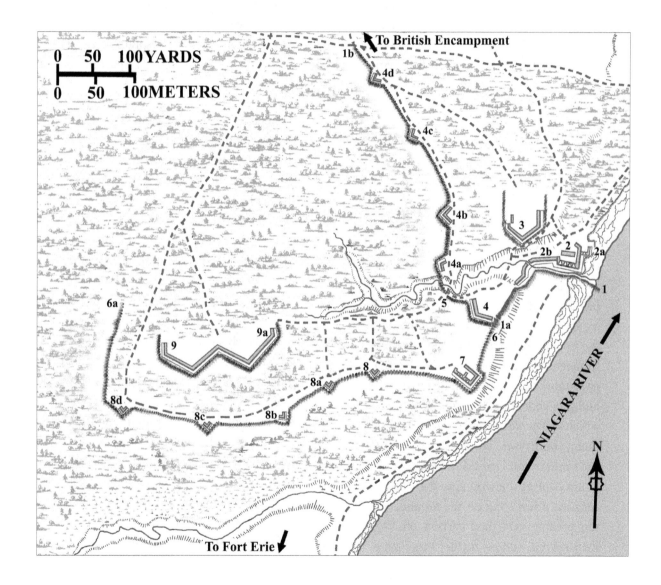

0 50 100 YARDS

0 50 100 METERS

To British Encampment

1b
4d
4c
4b
3
4a
2b 2 2a
5 4 1
1a
9a 6
6a 7
9 8
8a
8d
8c 8b

NIAGARA RIVER

N

To Fort Erie

In the morning ... [of the twentieth] ... the alarm began by a few scattered shots on our left, apparently from the sentries of our picquet. we advanced, directed by the report of the firing in such a manner as to take the enemy in the flank, should he advance from that quarter, but it happened otherwise — we met a considerable detachment of riflemen & others, which had taken a circuit to pass the flank of the picquet while the smaller party amused the left of our line in front....We gave them a well directed fire ... which brought some to the ground. At this time ... we discovered a party moving obliquely, so as to envelop us — to baffle this attempt, we divided — leaving a part of our warriors to amuse those of the enemy in front, while we hastened to meet the other Division. On the first encounter, the enemy seemed to hesitate, and in a short time began to retrograde, which move we hastened by closing on them, both our Divisions answering each other with vigourous shouts — we at last drove the enemy into their fort — they left a few lying on the ground, but the greater part they carried off. We then retired without further loss than a few men wounded.... We learned from deserters that the enemy lost 68 men in killed & wounded ...[4]

— John Norton (Captain, Indian Department)

A General sortie was planned by Genl. Gaines upon the batteries of the enemy ... the riflemen were placed in front one hundred paces and the infantry, marching by the flanks of platoons were to follow. The egress of the troops was near Towson's battery, on the extreme left and the riflemen, being fully acquainted with the ground, proceeded in the direction of a principal battery of the enemy without difficulty. The infantry ... attempted to follow, but immediately on entering the dense forest and encountering wet ground and much old fallen timber, they were thrown into confusion and the obstacles and impediments were very soon found to be insuperable. The infantry were accordingly recalled and reentered [the fort] where they had marched out. In the mean time, the riflemen, <u>uninformed</u> of this countermarch, advanced steadily toward the batteries and pickets of the enemy and commenced the engagement, expecting to be supported by the whole body of infantry. After being thus engaged for some time and the infantry not appearing, Maj. Kearsley was suddenly surprised at hearing the discharge of musketry in his rear and within the American breastworks.... An officer was despatched ... who returned with the information that the infantry had moved within the breastworks and were discharging their pieces, which had been loaded prior to their movement, and that Genl. Gaines requested Maj. Kearsley with his command to return ...[5]

— Major Kearsey

Further harassing raids were made by the Americans during the following ten days, thereby mounting the casualty lists suffered by both sides. This was particularly the case for the new arrivals at the British camp, for these troops, used to the European style of fighting, only learned the value of the readily available ground cover the hard way — through suffering losses, as documented by Lieutenant John Le Couteur of the 104th Regiment.

24 August — The left wing of the 82nd arrived this morning — a very nice corps. We have cautioned them against exposing themselves rashly to the rifleman's fire. It is not like open warfare as they have been used to against the French. If their men expose themselves in bush or forest fighting, the Americans will punish them. They laugh at the idea ...

26 August — Friday, the enemy attacked our picquets last night by way of trying what the Duke's [Lord Wellington] old soldiers are made of and what we are at. The 82nd lost two killed and thirteen wounded. The Yankees lost a Captain and left several killed behind them. The 82nd not yet aware of the value of treeing. In our last heavy skirmish, the old hands, the Glengarry's killed and wounded fifty of the Americans and only lost <u>one</u> man ...[6]

Fortunately, detachments of men from the Glengarry Light Infantry Regiment and the Incorporated Militia of Upper Canada, both by now veteran Canadian units, were attached to the 82nd, and other regiments as they arrived, to teach the new arrivals the singular survival methods that were required as part of this campaign and probably to advise them on not repeating the making of a bayonet charge against American riflemen across broken and tree-covered ground, as the 82nd had seemingly done in the above-mentioned engagement.

A reproduction of an 18-pounder artillery piece displayed as part of the "British siege lines" at the Fort Erie historic site.

Finally, on August 30, Battery No. 2 was scheduled to commence firing with two 18-pounder guns, one 24-pounder carronade, and one 8-inch howitzer. However, a thick belt of trees, which had previously provided frontal protection for the workers, now required felling to open the firing lines. Inevitably, the assigned working parties came under heavy fire from the fort's artillery, losing eight men killed and eighty-eight wounded in the process. Once the trees were cleared, though, the lack of experienced engineers on the campaign proved itself at its most embarrassing, as it was realized that the new battery had been constructed behind a low rise in the ground that was not noticeable while the trees were still standing. As a result, the higher ground in front of the battery blocked any direct firing on the defences by the cannons, leaving only the single howitzer, which could lob its shells in a high arc over the obstructing terrain, to fire on the fort.

Unfortunately, this ineptitude and total waste of manpower was only one of several additional issues plaguing General Drummond at this time.

First was the shocking news from the commissariat department that unless Commodore Yeo made an immediate effort to bring supplies up from Kingston, the entire stockpile of food in the Niagara would be totally exhausted by the middle of the following month. Obtaining supplies locally was virtually impossible, as most of the crops were not yet ripe, while those which had been prematurely gathered were not yet threshed and were showing significant signs of being infected with a crop rot due to the prevailing ground dampness and constant rains.

Despite this urgent situation, Drummond continued to be frustrated by the continued intransigence of Sir James Yeo, who had made his position clear that in view of the current ascendancy of the American program rate of ship construction, his own squadron was threatened with destruction until he could reply in kind with the launching and completion of his new mega-warship, the *St. Lawrence*. At that time he would consider emerging — but only to directly contest the control of Lake Ontario with Chauncey. Left with no alternative, Drummond made a direct plea for support from Sir James Yeo:

> 18 August 1814 … I trust your Excellency will impress on the Comm'r's [Commodore's] mind that the Right Division, after its misfortune on the 15th inst. depends almost entirely on his prompt & vigorous exertions for its relief, nay perhaps even for its safety …
>
> I have directed … at all risques to forward to York some flour in batteaux … [and] … that all the other small craft at Kingston be freighted with cargoes & kept in instant readiness to seize the first opportunity of running for the Head of the Lake either on our squadron leaving port or on the enemy's fleet betaking themselves … to their own harbour …[7]

A position that was further endorsed by the commissariat department:

> 27 August 1814 … [The commissariat department] has endeavoured by every means to forward supplies to the head of Lake Ontario and several small vessels were dispatched while the enemy's squadron was unable to leave Sackett's Harbour, but as the exertions of the enemy have been more successful than ours in building ships sufficient to command the navigation of the lake, that resource is, for the moment cut off and only batteaux can be employed … but this feeble means of transport will never effect the forming of a sufficient depot at York, Burlington Heights and Niagara and unless the commissariat can be aided to a great extent by the Royal Navy, the most disastrous consequences must ensue; which no efforts nor arrangements of mine can avert…. Your Excellency is well aware that the road between Kingston and Niagara is not practicable for loaded waggons; therefore land carriage is out of the question and the most ample assistance from the Royal Navy will be imperiously demanded as the only means of supporting the Right Division of the Army …[8]
>
> — Commissary General W.H. Robinson to Sir George Prevost

Also frustrated at this overt lack of co-operation by Yeo, Prevost, in turn, dispatched a strongly worded letter to Lord Bathurst in England:

The most pressing and important service to be performed by the Commodore as soon as his squadron shall have acquired the ascendance is the conveyance of fresh troops, with a large proportion of provisions and supplies of every description to York and the Niagara frontier before the navigation closes, and to bring from those places to Kingston the exhausted corps, the disabled and the sick who can endure transport…. The resources of the Upper Province being exhausted, a large supply of provisions of every nature must be thrown into it before the navigation of the St. Lawrence and Lake Ontario becomes impracticable…. In fact, my Lord, two-thirds of the army in Canada are at this moment eating beef provided by American contractors, drawn principally from the states of Vermont and New York …[9]

The reality was that, despite the fact that Drummond was trying to conduct a military campaign, his army was on the verge of starving. Attempting to eke out what remained of his food supplies, Drummond was forced, once again, to reduce his troops' rations. More drastically and potentially dangerously for the maintenance of good relationships and support, he was also forced to suspend most of the Native allied tribes from their daily issuances of flour and other foodstuffs. This, in turn, created massive discontent and hardship amongst those who were denied rations and left most of the few Native warriors that still remained with the troops in the field with little option but to return to their homes to ensure their families' survival in the upcoming winter — as opposed to fighting in the white man's war. General Drummond also had to resort to the draconian measure of turning on his own civilian populace in a desperate attempt to squeeze additional resources from their already meagre personal supplies of food in order to feed his men.

> Militia General Order, 25 August 1814
> … The Commanding Officers of regiments of Lincoln Militia are particularly enjoined to instruct the officers commanding companies to enforce, if required, from five to twelve bushels of wheat from each inhabitant belonging thereto, who is known to have such a quantity to spare independent of a supply for his own family…. It is hoped that the voluntary compliance of every individual will render coercion unnecessary …[10]

Beyond his food crisis, there was also the "inconvenient" fact that despite being in the middle of trying to fight a war, due to the cost-cutting attitude of the region's assistant commissary (Mr. Gordon) at the end of the previous year's campaign, the allocation of ammunition scheduled to be issued for the artillery within the entire Niagara region for 1814 had been reduced to a mere two hundred rounds per gun. Inevitably, once the fighting had begun in earnest and with the naturally heavy expenditures of shot and shell in the battles of the previous two months, this limited supply was now almost exhausted — with no ready supply of replacement rounds closer than York or Kingston. Infuriated at this bureaucratic parsimony, General Drummond demanded the man's dismissal, but was still left with no choice but to order a rationing of fire from each gun in the batteries — at a time when every shot was increasing the difficulties of the Americans.

In addition, General Drummond also had to deal with reports of American troop movements at Fort Schlosser that suggested a cross-river sortie might be made on his supply base at Chippawa, simultaneously cutting the British army's supply line and main line of retreat. It also threatened the recapture of the *Somers* and *Ohio*. In response, General Drummond was forced to order the scuttling of the vessels and the allocation of yet more of his limited resources to the task of constructing additional defences and safeguarding this location from attack.

Finally, and literally "above-all," the unusually cold temperatures and incessant rainstorms that had swept the region during the past month had turned the ground into a quagmire of semi-frozen mud. Under these conditions, the British encampment had deteriorated into a virtual lake, dotted with islands of sodden tents and leaky brushwood huts. Fires were almost impossible to keep going, which prevented the troops from warming themselves, drying out their clothes and bedding, or properly cooking what little food was being issued. Inevitably, the incidence of sickness amongst the British troops increased dramatically as the bad weather continued.

For their part, the Americans were having their own difficulties as the rain undermined their rapidly thrown up earthworks, causing slippages that required constant repair, while the expectation that the British would mount another attack forced them also to maintain a constant vigil.

> This I consider the commencement of a period by far the most trying of any during the siege. Our men, daily subjected to the most laborious fatigue-duties, were often called out during the night to perform those services which the fire of the enemy would not permit them to do

during the course of the day; while even with this precaution, we had the mortification to see them constantly falling around us ... [as] ... among the working parties, particularly those in the face of the enemy, I know it to have been severe. But that is not all, the frequent alarms, and constant expectation of another attack, rendered it necessary to put at least one third of our men under arms every night, while the remaining two-thirds lay down with their accoutrements on, their boxes stored with ammunition, their muskets in their hands, and their bayonets fixed ... as an additional precaution ... every evening, a great number of pikes, constructed of the British bayonets, which were taken on the 15th, were laid at two feet distance from each other, along the whole length of our line. These being of a length equal to the thickness of the parapet, would have been used with great effect in the event of an escalade ...[11]

— Lieutenant Douglass

In addition, the ongoing British bombardment tore up the ground, demolished tents and huts, and inflicted a steady stream of casualties of between twenty to forty men per day. Individually, these daily American casualty rates were minor; but cumulatively, and added to those suffered in making the almost-daily raids on the British entrenchments and similar increased levels of sickness within the American ranks, they represented an alarming drain on the manpower of the besieged garrison. Included in this list of injured was General Gaines, who was badly wounded on August 28 when a British shell landed on his headquarters building. Consequently, despite his personal distrust of General Ripley, Brown was left with no alternative but to reinstate him as the garrison's commander. However, once he was informed by several officers of the garrison that they had no confidence in Ripley, Brown wasted no time in transferring command to a newly promoted Brigadier General James Miller. That is, until Brown resumed command himself on September 2. After inspecting his army, the slow destruction of his once impressive army was a cause of deep concern to General Brown, as no significant reinforcements of regular troops were available and the logistical support he expected to receive from his superiors in Washington was conspicuous by its absence. To a degree, this mystery was made clearer when Brown received a letter from the then still secretary of war, Armstrong, dated August 16, 1814.

Unless the fleet of the enemy can be beaten, or Kingston taken, or Forts George and

Niagara reduced before ... the 20th of Sept ... all your prospects of doing more than illustrating your own skill and courage and those of your Division are lost. This state of things would be deplorable as regards the public interest and it becomes the duty of all and particularly of myself to secure the campaign, if possible, and to embark his [Izard's] two or three thousand men at Sackets harbour and transport them to Burlington, debark there and with the heights secured, effect a junction with your division when the whole force will be employed in beating Drummond and reducing Forts George and Niagara.... There is nothing on the cards better for us. The only objection to the game is the evils which may befall the shores of Lake Champlain in the absence of the Army.... I believe too that if you are not in condition to cut your way directly to Montreal, the better policy for us will be to carry the war westward ...[12]

To this disheartening letter, Brown was quick to reply.

I can but be very anxious for the ultimate fate of this army. If the enemy deems it an object of the first importance to destroy this force that has given them so much trouble and cost them so much, the reinforcements arriving from Europe will, I fear, give them the means. I doubt very much if a parallel can be found for the state of things existing up on the frontier. A gallant little army, struggling with the enemies of their country and devoting themselves for its Honor and its safety, left by that Country to struggle alone within sight and within hearing.... How long are the people of this country to be amused and disgraced by such a state of things? ... cannot this nation make an effort to secure the safety of this army! Retreat, I believe, it cannot, even granting that we had the boats necessary in the face of the force that will most probably be kept opposed to it ...[13]

Unable to rely on Washington for support, Brown again looked to his local militias to supply his desperately needed manpower. Despite the fact that an earlier call for militia volunteers had proved an embarrassing failure, new promises were made to provide back pay, supplies, and arms. With the prospect of actually receiving money and food, the militia began to turn out in greater numbers.

But the men were soon disappointed, as it proved impossible to clothe them all in proper uniforms, and the arriving volunteers were reduced to wearing red bandanas to distinguish themselves as troops in their civilian clothing. In addition, previously declared "unserviceable" (broken) belting and cartridge boxes were dragged out of storage and issued to carry the soldiers' ammunition. Even here, further difficulties arose, as the necessity of issuing a mixture of captured British muskets, repaired American muskets, privately owned muskets, and rifles — all of different calibres — made the supplying of standardized ammunition impossible. General Brown knew there were large stockpiles of new arms, equipment, and clothing at Sackets Harbor, but in view of Chauncey's attitude about using "his" vessels for shipping supplies, Brown recognized these may as well have been on the moon. Certain Chauncey would not co-operate and insulted by the fact that the Commodore's arrogant communication of August 10 had been deliberately made public, Brown now offered his own salvo of rebuttal on the issue of the role of the Lake Ontario fleet, driving a final and irrevocable wedge between the two commanders for the remainder of the war and beyond.

4 September 1814 ... Sir, Your letter of the 10th ultimo, after going the rounds, was delivered to me a few days since....

The exception you take at my letter to the Secretary would be very reasonable and proper, provided the fleet of Lake Ontario was your private property, over which the Government had no control. But as I have been induced to believe that it was the property of the nation, subject to the orders of the Government, and as the Government led me to believe that the fleet under your command would be on Lake Ontario to cooperate with my Division of the Army the 1st week in July; I have deemed it fit and proper to let the nation know that the support I had a right to expect was not afforded me ...[14]

Back on the other side of the siege lines, on September 1, 1814, General Drummond's new second-in-command, Major General De Watteville, finally arrived to take some of the load of command from a still-ailing Drummond's shoulders. At the same time, the American naval blockade off the mouth of the Niagara River was temporarily lifted as the vessels were driven east by a gale. This allowed the trapped British ships *Vincent* and *Charwell* to escape from the river, taking as many of the sick and wounded as possible across to York and reducing the number of mouths to feed on the Niagara frontier. The vessels then began a round-the-clock shuttle service, carrying up as much food and ammunition as possible, but were never able to keep up with the rate of consumption by the army and its associated dependants.

On September 2, an exhausted 6th Regiment finally arrived at the encampment after marching over 250 miles (402 kilometers) from Kingston, while work began on a third battery position, farther to the right of the previous two and within five hundred yards (457 meters) of the fort. Carefully sited to ensure it could be used once completed, this new work represented a serious threat to the Americans, as it would fire directly into the main encampment at lethally close range. In response, on September 4, the Americans made a major sortie involving forty men of the Twenty-First Regiment (Ensign Thomas) and one hundred of the New York Militia, all led by the turncoat Lieutenant Colonel Willcocks.[15] During the course of heavy fighting, Willcocks was killed, a fact that raised a succession of cheers once it was known in the British camp. That night, toasts were drunk to the demise of a man considered to be a principal traitor to the British cause. Similar engagements took place during the following two days and nights, as well as one singular nocturnal incident that, although undated, appears to refer to Battery No. 3.

[Whilst engaged in a probe of the British picket positions, Major George Brooke from the Twenty-Third Regiment] … discovered a new battery at an important point, which … [the enemy] … were erecting under cover of the night. It became then an object of importance to annoy the fatigue parties employed on this new work, but very difficult to effect, from the thick woods concealing all their movements from the view of our lines … carrying in his hand a lantern covered with a watchcoat … [Major Brooke] … passed during the night their [the British] line of sentinels, ascended a tree which stood about six paces in front of the enemy's new battery and fixed it there … and returned safe to camp. The American batteries, directed by the light of the lantern in the tree, opened fire upon the unsuspecting workmen, who could not divine what secret spirit had betrayed the position of their laborers until they observed the light swinging in the air …[16]

Despite this and other intense efforts, the Americans failed to prevent the completion of the third battery, nor the two associated blockhouses that had been built to provide additional defences for the extended British lines. Once complete, one 24-pounder gun and the 8-inch mortar were transferred from Battery No. 1, while the two 18-pounder guns from Battery No. 2 were similarly relocated by September 6, but no firing began, as General Drummond's temporary good fortune had evaporated and was replaced by a succession of bad news and strategic problems that brought him, once again, to the point of abandoning the siege. These included:

- Reports that large numbers of American troops massing at Buffalo, Fort Schlosser, and Lewiston. This indicated that the enemy could soon reinforce its garrison at Erie, while increasing the threat to Drummond's supply lines at Chippawa and Queenston.
- The fact that two of Chauncey's warships had returned, once again disrupting the British supply shuttle across the lake, and especially delaying the arrival of the 97th Regiment, which was supposed to have been transported up by boat and which would now have to make the arduous trek by land, around the head of the lake.
- Despite the reception of some small-arms ammunition, the continuing shortage of artillery shot and shell left nothing for the siege-guns to fire if they used up what small stockpile remained. The last of the available ammunition had already been moved up from

Fort George, while the two heavy mortars had only eighty rounds between them.

On the other hand, abandoning the siege and retiring to Chippawa or the river-mouth forts would expose his force to attack while on the march along roads reduced to deep quagmires of mud. In addition, the movement of the heavy artillery pieces by the few draft animals that were available would be made far more arduous and difficult. Furthermore, the continual rains had saturated the soil, undermining segments of the earthen embankments and defences at Fort George, while across the river at Fort Niagara, long sections of the walls facing the lake and river had collapsed, completely exposing the fort's interior to artillery fire from Chauncey's vessels. Weighing these factors, Drummond decided to maintain his main position opposite Fort Erie for a short while longer, while sending detachments of the 104th Regiment back to supplement the Chippawa garrison and the Light Company of the 100th to assist in repairs and security at Fort George and Fort Niagara.

Without the necessary artillery ammunition to continue the bombardment of Fort Erie, Drummond sought to maintain the initiative by ordering a probe against Snake Hill for September 6. This attack was to be made by a combined force consisting of a company from the 6th Regiment, a company from the

Glengarry Light Infantry, and a detachment of dismounted 19th Light Dragoons. Making a sudden rush on the American pickets, the British troops quickly routed the guards, inflicting fifteen killed and seven wounded on the Americans, for a loss of two wounded on their own part.[17] Pressing forward, the attackers reached the American lines and had every opportunity to continue into the defences, as the Americans had been caught completely unprepared for the attack, but without additional infantry or artillery support, the probe contented itself with what it had achieved and withdrew unopposed.

Beyond this piece of bravado, little offensive activity could be made by the British, and there is some reason to believe that, apart from a few ranging shots, Battery No. 3 was never used to effectively fire on the fort. Thus, with Battery No. 1 stripped of most of its guns, Battery No. 2 placed in the wrong position, and Battery No. 3 devoid of ammunition, virtually no rounds were directed against the besieged garrison for days at a time. This pause greatly improved the Americans' morale and allowed Brown to complete the construction of his own improved battery positions. He also took advantage of the arrival of part of the Lake Erie fleet, including the brig *Lawrence* and the schooners *Lady Prevost*, *Caledonia*, and *Porcupine*, to cover the crossing of some 1,500 of Porter's militia (mostly armed with captured British muskets) from Buffalo to the garrison during the nights of September 9/10 and 10/11, without suffering any casualties. With this enhanced force, General Brown now began preparations for an all-out assault upon the British lines.

Reconnaissance reports and information divulged by British prisoners and deserters had informed Brown that Drummond was using a three-brigade system of rotation for the troops at the front line: one on duty, a second in reserve at the camp nearly two miles (3.2 kilometers) to the rear, and the remainder off duty and engaged in various duties and fatigues. As a result, the British force was effectively divided and could possibly be severely mauled — *if* Brown's troops could get close enough to the British lines without being detected, overwhelm the single brigade on duty' destroy the batteries and guns, and then withdraw *before* the British reinforcements could arrive.

Although there was a general knowledge amongst the troops that an attack was being planned, as the general preparations could not be disguised, Brown kept the details of the attack's composition and targets secret, even from his senior officers, until the eve of the assault (when he briefed General Peter B. Porter and Majors William McRee and Eleazer Wood). General Eleazer Ripley, Brown's official second-in-command, was not given the courtesy of a briefing until the following morning.

Unchanging in his lack of confidence in

Brown's plans and grossly insulted by Brown's failure to involve him in the planning, or even to have informed him first, Ripley initially predicted disaster for the sortie and refused to have any part in the day's action. Later, however, he requested and received the commission to command the reserve force that was detailed to remain near to the fort and either support the attack or cover the return of the attacking force from British countermeasures. Brown also made use of diversions to cover his intended attack by leaking information that he was planning an amphibious assault on the British camp from across the Niagara River at Black Rock. To support this illusion, he ordered that the detachments of militia still on that eastern shore of the river were to parade openly along the riverbank, where they could be seen and reported on. Increasing the rate of firing from his own batteries throughout September 15 and 16, Brown used the ongoing rainstorms and noise from the guns as cover for the work parties that were sent out into the heavy woods north of the fort to cut paths that would outflank the British positions and allow the Americans to reach their points of launching the assault undetected and in good order.

What Brown did not know was that following the advice of several of his subordinates, including Major General Louis De Watteville, Lieutenant General Drummond had already given the order

for lifting the siege and withdrawing the army to Chippawa. This meant that during the night of September 16/17, several of the British guns, including two of the brass 24-pounders and three 8-inch mortars, were withdrawn from their positions, while the remainder of the guns were scheduled for removal the following day but had not been attended to when the American attack took place.

The Extended and Expanded British Siege Lines During the Construction of Battery No. 3, September 1–17, 1814

1–1a–1b. Line of original abattis
2. Battery No. 1
2a. Riverside flanking battery
2b. Congreve rocket battery
3. Original reserve earthwork and redoubt
4. Centre earthwork and redoubt
4a–4b–4c–4d. Original guard post flanking earthwork redoubts (not occupied)
5. Original sally-port gateway
6–6a. Newly revised and extended line of flanking abattis
7. Battery No. 2 and flanking earthworks
8. Blockhouse and guard post earthwork
8a. Flanking earthwork redoubt
9–9a. Flanking curtain earthworks for Battery No. 3
10. Battery No. 3 (under construction for most of this period)
11. Flanking blockhouse
12. Flanking earthwork redoubt
13. Remnant of abattis line from Battery No. 2 construction
14–14a. Reconstructed flanking reserve earthwork and redoubt (divided into two parts)

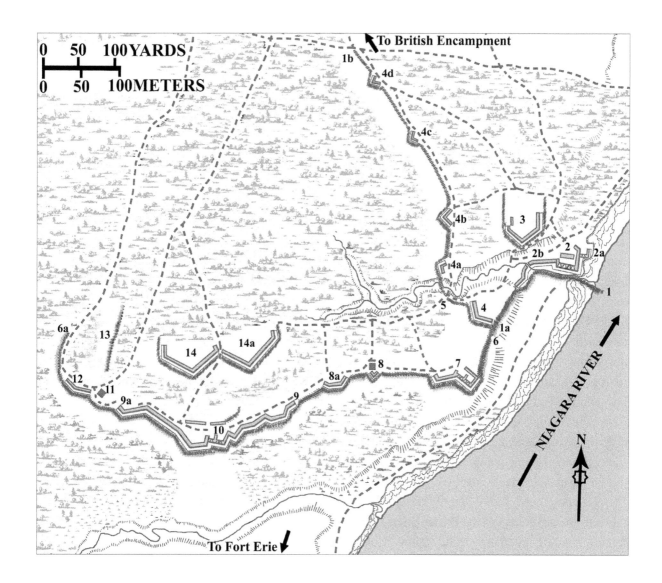

Stalemate: August 17–September 16, 1814

To British Encampment

NIAGARA RIVER

To Fort Erie

N

0   50   100 YARDS

0   50   100 METERS

CHAPTER 6

The American Sortie: September 17, 1814

For General Brown, the weather on September 17 could not have been better, with overcast conditions and intermittent rain that reduced visibility and deadened sound. The columns marched out from the new militia encampment behind the Snake Hill battery, at a point farthest from British observation. Entering the woods, the troops followed the newly cut paths until they reached the ravine that cut across the open ground, halfway between the fort and the British battery positions. Here the army divided, with General Brown accompanying General Miller's force as it marched down the ravine, out of sight of the British, to take up its assigned assault position, while General Porter's troops continued down the trail leading to the extreme right flank of the British lines. Porter's force was made up of three subdivisions: Colonel James Gibson's advance party of two-hundred riflemen and a party of Natives; Brigadier General Daniel Davis's left column of five-hundred militia volunteers; and Major Eleazer Wood's right column, made up of four-hundred regulars and five-hundred militia volunteers.

The plan was for Porter's units to breach or pass around the right flank of the British line. That done, the left column would block the road coming from the British camp and intercept any arriving British reinforcements, while the right and advance subdivisions would overrun Battery No. 3 and then clear the adjacent line of entrenchments from the rear. Meanwhile, at the ravine, General Miller's units would use the sounds of firing from Battery No. 3 and adjacent lines as their cue to breach the line of entrenchments between the two batteries and mop

AMERICAN FORCE, SORTIE, SEPTEMBER 17, 1814[*1]

Flanking Force (Brigadier General Peter B. Porter)
Advance (Colonel James Gibson)
First/Fourth Rifle Regiments (Colonel James Gibson): 200 Other Ranks
Native Warriors (Captain Fleming): Detachment

Right Column (Major Eleazer Wood)
First/Twenty-Third Regiments (Major George Brooke): 400 Other Ranks
Second Light Dragoons (Captain Harris): Dismounted Detachment
Militia Volunteers (Detachments from Lieutenant Colonel Dobbin's, Lieutenant Colonel McBurney's, and Lieutenant Colonel Fleming's Corps): 500 Other Ranks

Left Column (Brigadier General Daniel Davis)
Detachments from Lieutenant Colonel Hopkins's, Lieutenant Colonel Churchill's, and Lieutenant Colonel Crosby's Corps: 500 Other Ranks

Frontal or Ravine Force (Brigadier General James Miller)
Ninth/Nineteenth Regiments (Lieutenant Colonel Aspinwall): 350 Other Ranks
Eleventh Regiment (Colonel Bedel): 300 Other Ranks

Reserve (Brigadier General Eleazer Ripley)
Twenty-First Regiment (Lieutenant Colonel Upham): 500 Other Ranks
Seventeenth Regiment (Captain Chunn): Detachment

up any lingering opposition before uniting with Porter's troops in an advance on Batteries No. 2 and No. 1. Supporting these assaults was Ripley's reserve of regulars and militia, stationed in the ditch directly between the two newly built bastions of the fort.[*1]

Facing this attack, the British 2nd Brigade, consisting of the De Watteville and part of the 8th [King's] Regiments, was not only on picket duty in the lines but was also providing work parties preparing for the evacuation of those guns which had not already been withdrawn. Attacking at around 2:30 p.m. the Americans cut their way through the outer line of British abattis defences, and in a series of parallel files, swept down upon the British positions. According to General Brown's later official account, the initial attack was portrayed as being a total surprise, overwhelming, and virtually without loss on the part of the Americans. On the other hand, Brigadier General Porter's subsequent report indicated that the initial assault was far from being an instant success, as the British pickets not only put up a defence, but slowed the American advance long enough for the troops on work details to take up their posts. Similarly, Brigadier General Miller later recounted that his column was forced to attack an already alerted enemy that was still in possession of its defences.

> 19 September 1814 … I had taken post about fifty rods [275 yards or 251.5

THE AMERICAN SORTIE AND BRITISH RESPONSE, SEPTEMBER 17, 1814

A. Battery No. 1
B. Original reserve earthwork and redoubt
C. Centre earthwork and redoubt
D. Battery No. 2
E. Blockhouse
F. Battery No. 3
G. Flanking blockhouse
H–H1. Flanking reserve earthwork and redoubt

1. Using a pathway cut through the forest (off map), the American columns approach the western flank of the British entrenchments, where the force divides. The flanking column (Brigadier General Porter) moves north (1) to reach its assault position (1a), while the (frontal) column (Brigadier General Miller) moves down into the ravine (1b) running parallel to the British positions and takes up a holding position (1c) opposite to the British line, between Batteries No. 2 (D) and No. 3 (F).

2. Attacking in a series of parallel files (2) the Americans breach the British lines. While the left sub-column moves north on the trackway (2a) to cut off communications with the British encampment, the right column and "advance" (2b–2c) press forward, overrunning the flanking blockhouse (G), the reserve earthworks (H–H1) (2d), and Battery No. 3 (F) (2e). However, increasing British resistance slows their advance, preventing them from clearing the lines through which Miller's column is intending to attack.

3. Miller's column (3) advances from the ravine to attack the British line (3a), meeting heavy opposition. Breaching and overrunning the line (3b), the American force divides, with part turning left (3c) to assist in clearing the British defences around Battery No. 3 (F), while the bulk move right (3d) to attack the blockhouse (E) and Battery No. 2 (D) from the rear.

4. With the two batteries overrun, combined American units (4–4a) advance through the British lines (4b–4c) against stiff opposition in order to attack Battery No. 1 (A).

5. Because of the continued fighting, the American reserve (General Ripley) (5) is advanced from its position between the two new bastions to the ravine (5a).

6. Alerted to the American attack, the British command at the encampment (off map) advances with strong counterforces. The column under Lieutenant General Drummond (6) advances down the "new road" and then divides (6a), with the main force continuing down the road (6b) toward the blockhouse (G), while the Glengarry Light Infantry (6c) moves off toward the reserve entrenchments. Upon their arrival, both elements immediately begin a counterattack that eventually drives the Americans out from Battery No. 3 (F).

7. The column under Major General De Watteville (7) passes through the British lines (7a) toward Battery No. 1 (A). Upon arriving, part of the British force reoccupies (7b) the higher ground occupied by the reserve earthwork and redoubt (B) while the remainder makes a direct charge (7c) upon the Americans at Battery No. 1 (A).

8. With the sounds of renewed fighting as the British counterattack begins, General Brown commits his reserves (General Ripley) (8) to secure the breach (3b) for an evacuation of the American force.

NB From this point, accounts and movements are too confused and contradictory to present clearly, other than to say in a series of running engagements and fierce hand-to-hand combat, the American units are driven back from Battery No. 3 (F), Battery No. 1 (A), and Battery No. 2. (D) to their assault breach (3b), where they evacuate the British lines and retreat back to the fort, having suffered heavy casualties, principally in the latter stage of the engagement.

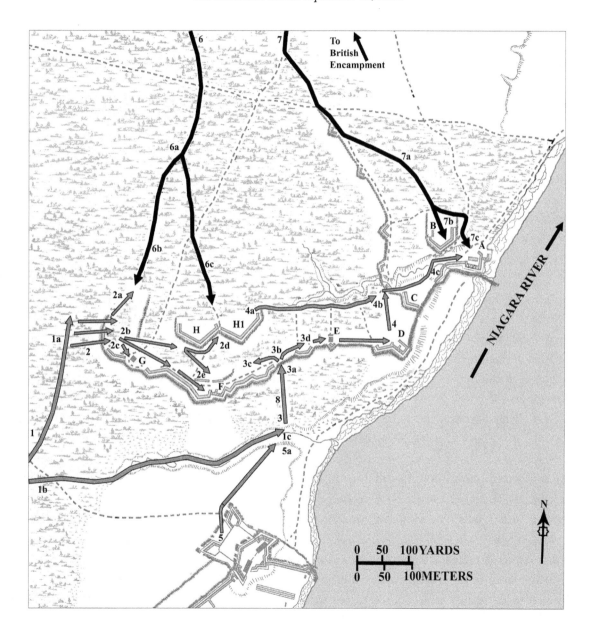

THE ASHES OF WAR

meters] in front of the enemy, in a ravine. The [flanking] columns were opposed before they arrived at either of the batteries. I was ordered [by General Brown] to advance and get into the enemies works before the column in rear had beaten the enemy sufficiently to meet us at the batteries, we had no alternative but to fall on them, beat and take them, this was a sore job for us. My command consisted of the 9th, 11th, 19th, Regt's. … [of the fourteen senior officers leading this frontal attack] … Colonel Bedel [Eleventh Regiment] was the only officer higher than a Lieutenant in my command but what were killed or wounded. I escaped again unhurt. Our loss was betwixt 4 and 500 killed wounded and prisoners …[2]

— Brigadier General Miller to his wife, Ruth Miller

As referenced above, despite suffering heavy opposition, Miller's force eventually breached the British line and spread out, with part heading to Battery No. 3 to assist in overrunning that position, while the remainder headed toward Battery No. 2. After further hand-to-hand combat, the Americans finally succeeded in capturing both batteries and

set about destroying everything that they could. The cannon that remained in the positions were spiked and the wheels smashed, while the two recently constructed wooden blockhouses were torched, as were any other nearby structures and defences. This included the ammunition magazine in Battery No. 3. Unfortunately, the officer detailed to undertake this duty (Lieutenant Riddle) underestimated the concussion such a detonation would produce and several Americans, including Riddle, were injured in the blast.

For all intents and purposes, the attack had achieved its prime objectives and could have been concluded without the attackers suffering any significant losses. Instead, the Americans pushed their luck too far by pressing on, toward Battery No. 1. According to Brown (who, it should be noted, remained outside the British lines throughout this action and therefore had absolutely no direct way of knowing what was going on), this further attack was also claimed to be a rapid and total success. However, Brown's version of events was subsequently contradicted by his own subordinates, Generals Porter, Miller, and Ripley, as well as equivalent British documents. In these, indications are that if the Americans did indeed enter Battery No. 1, it was against fierce opposition and was a momentary possession only, as their time had run out and the British reinforcements now arrived from the camp — sweeping down on the disorganized Americans with a vengeance.

On the other side of the field, although General Drummond had been expecting the Americans to make some kind of move for some days, Brown's misinformation had convinced him that the threat from Black Rock would be stronger than it was. Accordingly, additional detachments of troops were stationed along the riverbank to circumvent any assault from this direction. Drummond was simultaneously fully occupied by the combined logistical problems of establishing a new line of defence on the Chippawa while attempting to solve his continuing crisis of lack of food supplies. Fortunately, a new senior officer, Major General Stovin, had arrived only that morning and together with Brigadier General De Watteville these two capable commanders reacted promptly to the sounds of firing coming from the front lines.

Calling out the reserve 1st Brigade (1st [Royal Scots], 82nd, and part of the 6th Regiments) as well as part of the 3rd Brigade (Glengarry Light Infantry and 89th Regiments), De Watteville led his force, supported by several parties of Norton's Native warriors, forward at a run, while General Stovin remained at the camp with the remainder of the 6th Regiment and the Incorporated Militia Regiment to maintain a watch on the riverbank in case the supposed attack from Black Rock materialized.

Reaching the crossroads that connected the main road from the camp to the various battery positions, De Watteville met with General Drummond and together they decided to divide the force and counterattack on both flanks. Accordingly, General Drummond accompanied the 1st (Royal Scots) and 89th down the "new road" path leading to Battery No. 3, while De Watteville led the 6th and 82nd Regiments, plus Norton's warriors, toward Battery No. 1. Behind them, the Glengarry Light Infantry (Lieutenant Colonel Battersby and Lieutenant Colonel Pearson) initially followed Drummond's force and then branched off along the "centre road" toward Battery No. 2 and the new reserve entrenchments, with orders to prevent the Americans from mounting any kind of flanking attack on the two outer columns through the intervening gap.

Approaching the British front lines, De Watteville saw that the Americans had already overrun most of the positions and that any delay in counterattacking would be fatal. While some troops were detailed to occupy the elevated position of the reserve entrenchment and redoubt, the remainder immediately advanced in a charge with the bayonet. This attack impacted upon the already disorganized Americans, who had previously lost a number of their leaders (Colonel Gibson, Brigadier General Davis, and Major Wood) as casualties to the fire of the defenders. After some severe hand-to-hand combat, the Americans at Battery No. 1 began to give ground and retired toward Battery No. 2, coming under fire from the men in the reserve entrenchments. At the same time, General Drummond's part of the British force reached Battery No. 3 and likewise made an immediate attack under the direction of Lieutenant Colonel Gordon, throwing the Americans onto the defensive, while in the centre, Lieutenant Colonels Battersby and Pearson, with the Glengarry Light Infantry, advanced to clear the "new entrenchments."

Outside the line of entrenchments, the sounds of renewed fighting alarmed General Brown, as he realized that his attack had taken too long and that with the arrival of the British reinforcements, extracting his assault force without suffering heavy casualties would become increasingly difficult. He therefore decided to commit his reserves. Despite his already openly expressed lack of confidence in Ripley as a commander, Brown ordered Ripley to lead the reserves into the lines and secure the extraction of the other units. Accounts indicate that once inside the British lines, Ripley wisely chose to use his forces to secure Miller's breach and provide a corridor for an orderly retreat. However, only moments later, new orders arrived from General Brown (who was still at the ravine) stripping away the Twenty-First Regiment from Ripley's command and directing it to join the fight at Battery No. 2, leaving Ripley with only a detachment from

the Seventeenth Regiment to maintain the breach.

Elsewhere within the lines, the onslaught of the British pushed many of the Americans back into Battery No. 2, where they were crammed within the confines of that enclosure. After firing several volleys into the disorganized enemy, Captain Pattison (82nd Regiment) stepped forward and demanded the surrender of the Americans. Initially it seemed that the trapped troops were surrendering, as some laid down their arms. Tragically, one American decided to continue the fight and fired, killing Captain Pattison. Shocked at seeing this seeming betrayal of the codes of war, Pattison's men as well as other companies of the 82nd and 6th avenged Pattison by charging into the disorganized mass of Americans with the bayonet, resulting in numerous casualties, as no quarter was asked for or given by either side.

Meanwhile, over at the far side of the British lines, the 1st (Royal Scots), 89th, and Glengarry Light Infantry Regiments had pushed back the American left column, cleared Battery No. 3 and the reserve entrenchments, and began firing upon the Americans milling about in the area between the two batteries. Caught between multiple sets of fire, the American assault now became a retreat that got more hectic and disorganized as time passed. Certain officers, such as Brigadier General Miller, made strong efforts to carry out a disciplined withdrawal, while General Ripley left his remnant of the reserve column to consult with Major Brooke (Twenty-Third Regiment) about establishing a secure line of defence to allow the other units to escape. Unfortunately, while consulting with the major, Ripley suffered a severe wound in the throat, which immediately placed him hors de combat, leaving only General Brown to make the command decisions, although he continued to remain steadfastly remote from the fighting, outside the British lines.

As the American bridgehead collapsed and they began to evacuate the British lines, the Glengarry Light Infantry and Native warriors seized the initiative and charged forward, attacking those who attempted to stand and fight, capturing numerous stragglers, and harassing the Americans right up to the ditches of the fort — until they, in turn, were halted by covering fire from the fort's uncommitted garrison.

At the end of the day, the British had regained possession of the entire line of the entrenchments, but the casualties resulting from the action were extremely heavy, especially in terms of those captured by the initial American assault. Officially recognizing the loss of 314 (all ranks) as missing, Drummond's assessment was almost certainly deliberately underestimated, since the American report counted 385 confirmed as prisoners in the fort.[*3] In addition, the damage wrought by the Americans had rendered Batteries No. 2 and No. 3 unusable and the cannon within inoperative, but these points were glossed over in Drummond's subsequent report to Prevost in favour of emphasizing the poor living conditions and supply situation of the army.

21 September ... Within these last few days, the sickness of the troops has increased to such an alarming degree, and their situation has really become one of such extreme wretchedness from the torrents of rain which have continued to fall for the last 13 days, and from the circumstances of the division being entirely destitute of camp equipage, that I feel it to be my duty no longer to persevere in a vain attempt to maintain a blockade of so vastly a superior and increasing force of the enemy.... Their present camp literally resembles a lake in the midst of a thick wood.... These untoward circumstances, together with the want of ammunition and my increasing difficulties with respect to provisions, added to the protracted period to which we have to look for supplies and reinforcements by the squadron from Kingston, and the rapidly increasing force of the enemy, altogether render my situation and that of the whole of this frontier extremely critical ...[4]

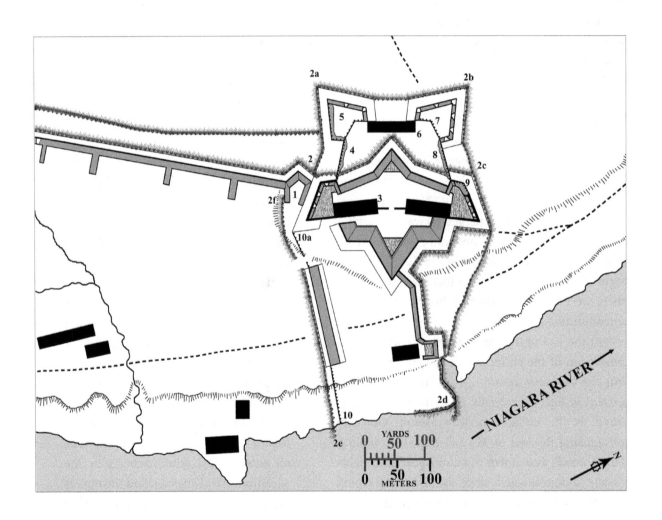

FORT ERIE DEVELOPMENT, SEPTEMBER 18–NOVEMBER 5, 1814

Principal and enlargement work takes place upon:
1. Conversion of Fontaine's battery into a redoubt
2–2a–2b–2c. Erection of a new line of abattis directly along the outer line of ditches surrounding the outer bastions
2d. Enlargement of the waterfront abattis
2e–2f. Erection of a new line of abattis (facing into the camp) between the waterfront and the former Fontaine battery position
3. Completion of repairs to the south mess house
4. Construction of an earth embankment firing step behind the picket wall connecting the southeast demi-bastion and southwest bastion
5. Construction of an earth embankment firing step behind the picket wall on the south side of the southwest bastion
6. Construction of a single-storey log blockhouse/barracks between the two outer bastions
7. Completion and enclosure of the northwest bastion
8. Building of an earth embankment firing step behind the picket wall connecting the northeast demi-bastion and northwest bastion
9. Completion of repairs to the northeast demi-bastion
10–10a. Construction of a wooden "picket" wall joining the waterfront to the main earthwork traverse and then above to the western ditch of the fort, creating an inner defence perimeter and last-resort escape route between the fort and the waterfront

Having already decided to retire his force to Chippawa, General Drummond was now, ironically, forced to remain at Erie until sufficient repairs had been made to the artillery carriages to allow some of them to be removed, along with the small remaining stocks of ammunition and food. This was completed by September 20, and the following day Drummond issued orders for the evacuation of the camp, but without destroying the encampment or otherwise alerting the Americans.

> General Order … The troops will change ground and take a position near Frenchman's Creek, the left of which is at present held by the 97th Regiment…. They will move this evening immediately after the tattoo has sounded. All fires to be left burning and huts standing, no huts to be set fire to on any account…. The pickets are at the same time to fall back to the open ground on the left of the Concession road, where the old reserve used to be posted, from whence they will be further retired after the troops have taken up their new position …[5]

Not knowing of Drummond's previous decision to raise the siege and evacuate the position, nor the fact that if he had waited only twenty-four

OFFICIAL ESTIMATES OF CASUALTIES, SORTIE FROM FORT ERIE, SEPTEMBER 17, 1814[3,6]

British
Killed: 3 Officers, 112 Other Ranks
Wounded: 17 Officers, 161 Other Ranks
Missing/Prisoners: 12 Officers, 1 Assistant Surgeon, 303 Other Ranks

NB American accounts claim a prisoner roll call for the sortie as 13 Officers and 374 Other Ranks.

American
Killed: 79 All Ranks
Wounded: 216 All Ranks
Missing: 216 All Ranks

NB British records for prisoners of war at Quebec list 9 Officers, 1 Drum Major, and 185 Other Ranks for this action.

In writing his official report, Brown made the self-justification that "In such a business we could not but expect to lose many valuable lives ..."[7], directly contradicting his earlier avowed goal "to storm the batteries, destroy the cannon, and roughly handle the brigade upon duty, before those in reserve could be brought into action ..."[8]

He also claimed that in addition to sending in the reserve, he delegated the command of the troops inside the line to Ripley, a curious thing to do if he had no trust in the man. However, in examining the exact wording of the instructions he later claimed to have provided to Ripley:

> As he [Ripley] would be the senior in advance, to ascertain as near as possible the situation of the troops in general, and to have a care that not more was hazarded than the occasion required; that the object of the sortie effected, the troops would retire in good order.... Soon after I became alarmed for General Miller and sent an order for the 21st [the main unit with Ripley] to hasten to his support ...[9]

And recognizing that he would be required to account for the heavy casualties that were subsequently suffered in the withdrawal, it is equally likely that Brown was seeking to deflect criticism

hours, his troops could have occupied the British line without firing a shot or losing a man, General Brown was genuinely happy over the results of the sortie. Nevertheless, he was still faced with the fact that although he had achieved the stated goals of the assault without suffering significant losses, the failure to withdraw early enough had resulted in heavy casualties during the British counterattacks and the final retreat to the fort, including 216 missing and presumed captured.[6]

of the day's losses onto the severely injured Ripley's shoulders.

Whatever his motives, Brown's report categorized the day as a major victory for the American cause and he was particularly generous in his praise of virtually every senior officer and made mention of many of the officers who suffered wounds. That is, of course, except for Ripley, who was effectively excluded from the credits and ignored, despite his serious, life-threatening wound. Unfortunately for Brown, his self-proclaimed declaration of victory were overshadowed by events elsewhere.

At Kingston, the construction of Sir James Yeo's pet naval megaproject, the *St. Lawrence* (a virtual black hole of a demand for resources and materials that could have outfitted half a dozen smaller warships, plus a virtual fleet of gunboats and supply vessels), was finally coming to fruition with its launch on September 10. Weighing in at a massive prospective 2,305 tons (2,342 tonnes), the *St. Lawrence* would carry a devastating official broadside armament of two 68-pounder carronades, thirty-two 32-pounder carronades, thirty-four 32-pounder long guns, and thirty-four 24-pounder long guns.

Although this vessel had yet to be fitted out and crewed, it nonetheless represented such a threat to Chauncey and his fleet (even then patrolling immediately off the Kingston headland and

The memorial monument to the fallen during the siege of Fort Erie. Located outside the fort's northeast demi-bastion.

including the 58-gun *Superior* and 42-gun *Mohawk*), that Chauncey was making plans that unless circumstances shifted dramatically in his favour, he would abandon his blockade of Kingston and withdraw his entire fleet into the protective enclave at Sackets Harbor. That is, at least until his own new supersized warships, later to be assigned the names *New Orleans*, *Chippawa*, and *Plattsburgh*, could be brought into commission and take on the *St. Lawrence* and the rest of the British Lake Ontario squadron on more favourable terms.

In addition, and farther afield, the saltwater British fleet on the Atlantic and its accompanying landing force had arrived at Baltimore on September 12, 1814. Having received ample warning of the British approach, the city had created a series of defences, with vessels deliberately sunk in the shipping channel to prevent the close approach of the British fleet, while entrenchments and shore batteries added to the existing string of fortifications, including Fort McHenry, guarding the approaches to the city. Seeing these defences, Major General Ross and Admiral Cochrane decided to make "a demonstration upon the City of Baltimore, which might be converted into a real attack should circumstances appear to justify it …"[10]

This time the defenders, consisting of over 3,500 American militia and regulars, made a valiant stand, losing 24 killed, 139 wounded, and 50 pris-oners, before retreating. In comparison, the veteran British regulars suffered 46 killed and 273 wounded, among whom was their commander, Major General Ross. Advancing toward the city, the second line of American defences persuaded Ross's replacement, Colonel Brooke, that without the supporting bombardment of the fleet, any frontal assault would be costly in casualties. Instead, the fleet contented itself by bombarding Fort McHenry and any other defences within range throughout the following night. This cannonade, an otherwise minor incident within the wider scope of the war, was to have lasting implications, as it inspired a local American lawyer, Francis Scott Key, to pen a poem entitled "Defence of Fort McHenry" that described the bombardment and was subsequently matched to a popular bawdy British tavern song of the day, "To Anacreon in Heaven," a tune that he was well familiar with and had perhaps heard sung while he dined aboard the HMS *Tonnant* as part of an American delegation to the enemy's fleet the previous night. Today we recognize this song as the American national anthem, "The Star-Spangled Banner," beginning with *O! Say can you see by the dawn's early light …*"

With nothing more to gain without suffering inordinate casualties, Brooke and Cochrane agreed to conclude what had generally been a reasonably successful campaign and sailed for their home base

HMS *St. Lawrence*. Yeo's ultimate warship for dominating the American fleet.

Toronto Reference Library, MTL JRR 1186.

at Jamaica. By this time, almost all of Maine was in British hands; the East Coast and most of the U.S. navy was under blockade; the Americans' war treasury was empty; the nation's capital remained partially gutted; and even the president's mansion required a wholesale interior refitting and several coats of whitewash outside to cover the scorch marks of the flames (which forced President Madison to live elsewhere until his restored "White House" was fit to live in once more). The American administration was therefore desperate to raise the nation's support for the war, and so as much as possible was made of the "local" victory at Baltimore. Even so, Brown's sortie would probably have received far more publicity if the Baltimore event had not been immediately followed by the news that a British invasion from Montreal, under Sir George Prevost, had been "routed" by a greatly inferior number of American regulars and militia at Plattsburgh, New York.

On that front, the arrival of British troops from Europe had finally provided Prevost with the opportunity to take the offensive by pushing an invasion force down the Champlain Valley to eliminate that corridor as a threat for the invasion of Lower Canada. In this he was to be inadvertently helped by the American secretary of war, John Armstrong, who had issued orders for Major General Izard to transfer most of his regular troops from Plattsburgh to Sackets Harbor, leaving the Plattsburgh and Lake Champlain defences primarily in the hands of semi-trained militia and skeleton regiments of regulars and convalescents. In view of the vast superiority in number and quality of troops at his disposal, Prevost's invasion force should have had no difficulty in overcoming any opposition; instead the single largest offensive campaign of the war mounted from Canada (composed of over ten thousand experienced regular soldiers, troops of the Lower Canada militia, and a well-supplied train of artillery, all backed by a secure and overflowing commissariat of food supplies — a combined force that General Drummond could only dream of and would have given his right arm to have commanded) foundered when Prevost pressured Captain George Downie the naval commander for the proposed operation, to commit his small squadron of vessels before they were properly ready and manned.

As a result, the British fleet was beaten in a severe action on Lake Champlain on September 11, while Prevost and his troops stood and watched impotently from the shore. Shaken by this defeat, for which he was more than just a little responsible, Prevost made no attempt to redress the setback by allowing his land troops to complete their assault upon the American defences. Instead he ordered the abandonment of the invasion. This capitulation and outright humiliation was the final straw to many of Wellington's veteran troops (who had already developed a scathingly low opinion of Prevost's military command abilities) and in consequence, army discipline lapsed during the subsequent retreat into Lower Canada. For all intents and purposes, Prevost's war leadership was discredited by this debacle, especially when he was subsequently openly condemned by Commodore Yeo for ignoring the advice and requests of Downie, precipitating a battle on unfavourable terms, and failing to support Downie, as he supposedly promised. Although Prevost continued to serve for the duration of the conflict, once the war was over, he was recalled to England to face a less-than-friendly official inquiry into his command decisions during the war, and over the Lake Champlain debacle in particular.

For the Americans, their success at Lake Champlain was not a matter of having won a battle, but rather of the British throwing an entire campaign away. Nevertheless, the American administration broadcast the news of this "glorious victory" at every opportunity, while Brown's extremely costly sortie at Fort Erie became news that was better kept low-key. These successes also gave the American negotiators in Ghent, Belgium, some welcome ammunition in the ongoing negotiations for concluding a peace treaty with the British, a treaty both sides were now finally serious about concluding.

Meanwhile, back in Upper Canada, the 1814 campaign on the Niagara ground its way to a finale as Drummond withdrew his forces from their waterlogged camp to Chippawa on September 21. Brown congratulated himself on achieving a "major" victory, and vessels detached from Chauncey's fleet sailed from Sackets Harbour carrying Izard's troops toward the Niagara.

However, before continuing with the story of the events on the Niagara frontier and in the south, it would be appropriate at this point to pause long enough to tell the story of the northern campaign that was simultaneously taking place to dominate the upper Great Lakes: a contest that centred on the isolated military post of Michilimackinac (Mackinac), located at the strategic junction point of Lakes Huron, Michigan, and Superior.

CHAPTER 7

An Exercise in Futility and Frustration: The American Expedition to Recapture Michilimackinac

Since the beginning of the war, the American garrison post at Michilimackinac (Mackinac) had been in British hands, thanks to a daring pre-emptive strike made by the British garrison at nearby St. Joseph Island. Notified of the declaration of war on July 8, 1812, the British garrison's commander, Captain Charles Roberts (10th Royal Veteran Battalion) had led a small combined force of some 630 regulars, militia, and Natives to attack Michilimackinac. Totally unaware of the formal onset of war, the American garrison's commander, Lieutenant Porter Hanks (U.S. Artillery) was officially in command of around sixty men. However, even of this small number, several men were sick, while many of the remainder were relatively elderly or otherwise considered unfit for active service. Consequently, when the British suddenly appeared on the high ground behind his principal fort with troops, artillery, and a demand for the immediate and unconditional surrender of the American position, Hanks was forced to comply without firing a shot in reply. (For details see *A Call to Arms.*)

Tactically this victory was of only minor value, but strategically, it swung the balance of power in the upper Great Lakes by securing the alliance of the Western Native nations to the British war effort. It also had a subsequent decisive effect on the events that were to unfold on the Detroit frontier when Major General Isaac Brock, backed by the not inconsiderable might of the Shawnee war chief Tecumseh and his Native tribal alliance, intimidated the vacillating American military commander (and territorial governor), Brigadier General William Hull, into not only surrendering his entire

The British Supply Lines to St. Joseph and Michilimackinac.

MACKINACK, FROM ROUND ISLAND.[4]

A postwar view of the south side of Michilimackinac (Mackinac). From *Pictorial Field Book of the War of 1812*.

army and the strategic post of Detroit, but ceding the territory of Michigan to the British Crown. (For details see *A Call to Arms*.)

Following a number of failed attempts to take back this lost territory and mount invasions of Upper Canada through the Detroit corridor at the beginning of the year, these humiliating American losses were redressed by the end of October 1813. This came about by the combination of:

- The crushing defeat and complete elimination of the British fleet on Lake Erie (September 10)

- The retreat of the British army from Amherstburg (September 23)
- The routing of the retreating British forces at the Battle of the Thames/Moravianstown (October 5)
- The destruction of the united Native tribal alliance following the death of the war chief Tecumseh at the Battle of the Thames

(For details see *The Tide of War* and *The Flames of War*.)

THE BRITISH SUPPLY LINES TO ST. JOSEPH AND MICHILIMACKINAC

Locations

A. Montreal
B. Kingston
C. Sackets Harbor
D. York (Toronto)
E. Burlington Heights (Hamilton)
F. Newark (Niagara-on-the-Lake)
G. Queenston
H. Chippawa
I. Fort Erie
J. Buffalo
K. Long Point transfer point area (Port Dover, Port Rowan)
L. Presque Isle (Erie)
M. Amherstburg
N. Detroit
O. Fort Gratoit (Port Huron)
P. Fort Willow
Q. Nottawasaga River transfer point (Wasaga Beach)
R. Fort St. Joseph
S. Fort Michilimackinac (Mackinac)
T. Sault Ste. Marie.

The Various Transportation Routes to Fort St. Joseph and Fort Michilimackinac

1812–1814

- Cargo ship from Europe or Quebec City to Montreal (A)

1812–1813: Primary Supply Routes

- Boat and bateaux from Montreal (A) via the St. Lawrence River to Kingston (B)
- Boat from Kingston (B) to Burlington Heights (E), overland by portage to the Long Point region (K)
- Boat from Kingston (B) to Newark (F) or Queenston (G), overland by portage to Chippawa (H), bateaux to Fort Erie (I)
- Boat from Long Point (K) or Fort Erie (I) to Amherstburg (M)
- Boat and bateaux from Amherstburg (M) via the Detroit River, Lake St. Clair, and the St. Clair River into Lake Huron
- Boat through Lake Huron to Fort St. Joseph (R) and Fort Michilimackinac (S)

1814: "Northern" Passage Supply Routes

- Canoe from Montreal (A) via the Ottawa River to Lake Nipissing and down the French River to Georgian Bay (*NB* with multiple rapids and portages)
- Boat or canoe through the North Channel to Fort Joseph (R) and Fort Michilamackinac (S)

1814: "Southern" Passage, Alternate Supply Routes

- Boat and bateaux from Montreal (A) via the St. Lawrence River to Kingston (B)
- Boat or bateaux from Kingston (B) to York (D)
- Overland from York (D) to Lake Simcoe
- Bateaux across Lake Simcoe, overland by portage to Matchedash Bay
- Bateaux across Lake Simcoe, overland by portage to Fort Willow (P), down the Nottawasaga River (Q) to Nottawasaga Bay
- Boat, bateaux, or canoe across Georgian Bay, through the North Channel to Fort St. Joseph (R) and Fort Michimackinac (S)

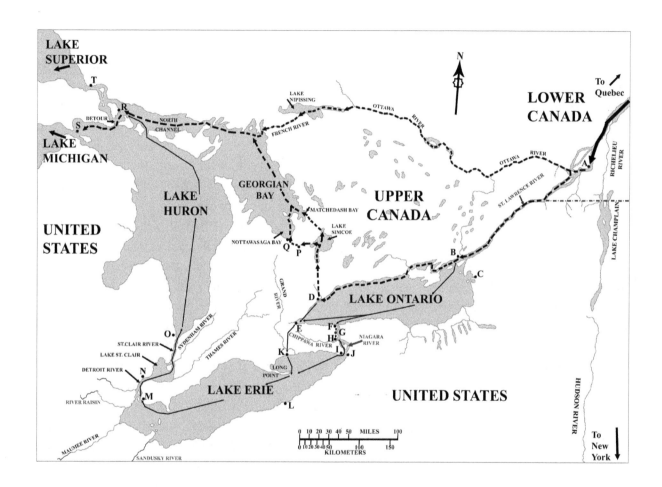

From that point onward, the Americans had dominated the southwestern corner of Upper Canada and effectively cut off Michilimackinac from its main supply route, which originated at Montreal and stretched a distance of almost one thousand miles (1,609 kilometers) by way of Kingston through Fort George, Fort Niagara, Lake Erie, Amherstburg, and along the Detroit River and Lake Huron.

Instead, the garrison was kept supplied by resorting to one of two "back door" routes. The "northern" route meant travelling upriver three hundred miles (483 kilometers) on the rough and dangerous Ottawa River to what today is called Mattawa, portaging and sailing forty miles (sixty-four kilometers) through a tortuous series of small rivers to Lake Nipissing, and, after crossing that lake, making a final, dangerous, seventy-seven-mile (125-kilometer) passage down the French River to the northern extremity of the "Great" (Georgian) Bay. From there, "normal" transportation could be resumed by canoe or aboard one of the few remaining British sailing vessels that had not been involved in the Lake Erie catastrophe on September 10. Alternately, there was the "southern" passage through Kingston and York, from where personnel and supplies destined for Michilimackinac were transported forty miles (sixty-four kilometers) overland to Lake Simcoe and then sailed across the lake. This was then followed by making one of two connections to the Great Bay. The "easy" one was a passage across a rough nine-mile (14.4-kilometer) portage to the way station of Fort Willow, followed by a journey down the barely navigable Nottawasaga River to the southern extremity of Nottawasaga Bay (at today's Wasaga Beach). The "harder" route involved an arduous thirty-mile (forty-eight-kilometer) overland trek from Lake Simcoe to Matchedash Bay (north of the modern-day community of Midland).

Although the American secretary of war, John Armstrong, had drawn up detailed plans for an expedition to eliminate the British supply route at Matchedash and recover Michilimackinac by the end of 1813, the opportunity was lost once the troops were committed to the St. Lawrence and Niagara fronts and the navigation season ended. Frustrated in his ambition to see the British evicted from Michilimackinac, Armstrong became almost fixated in his determination to finish the job as soon as possible in 1814. As a result, once Armstrong received General Brown's (April) plan to use the entire Lake Erie fleet to ferry an invasion force across the lake from Presque Isle (Erie, Pennsylvania) and Buffalo for an amphibious landing at Long Point, Armstrong's own plans to retake Michilimackinac were put at risk. Replying on June 9, Armstrong expressed support for Brown's plans

A sail-past of replica vessels of the types used during the War of 1812–1815. Part of the bicentennial celebrations in the Great Lakes during 2013.

MOVEMENTS IN THE UPPER GREAT LAKES, JUNE–AUGUST 1814

Locations (See map on page 119 for additional locations)

D. York (Toronto)
L. Presque Isle (Erie)
M. Amherstburg
N. Detroit
O. Fort Gratoit (Port Huron)
P. Fort Willow
Q. Mouth of the Nottawasaga River
R. Fort St. Joseph
S. Fort Michilimackinac (Mackinac)
T. Sault Ste. Marie

American Movements

1. June 18: The *Lawrence* and *Niagara* leave Presque Isle (L).
1a. June 22: The two vessels arrive at Detroit (N) and meet with the other vessels of the squadron. Here they load troops and supplies but are then stalled by strong headwinds and adverse river currents.
1b. July 3: The squadron leaves Detroit (N).
1c. July 4–13: Passage through Lake St. Clair and the St. Clair River.
1d. July 13: The squadron arrives at Fort Gratoit (O) and loads the remainder of the troops and supplies.
1e. July 14: The American squadron sails for Matchedash and Michilimackinac and makes good headway before encountering dense fog banks.
1f. July 15: The vessels sail west and then south in the mistaken belief that they are beyond Cabot Head and inside Georgian Bay (the grey dotted line indicates the conjectural course that they may have believed they were on). After abandoning its search for Matchedash, the squadron sails north for Michilimackinac.

1g. July 16: Sighting a sail at long range and believing it to be the *Nancy*, they give chase but lose it in the fog and return to their original course.
1h. July 18: The squadron enters the North Channel.
1i. July 19: It arrives at Fort St. Joseph (R).
1j. July 22: An expedition is sent to Sault Ste. Marie (T).
1k. July 26: The squadron arrives off Michilimackinac (S).
2-2a-2b. Lieutenant Worsley and his crew leave York (D) at the start of July and after travelling by Lake Simcoe and Fort Willow (P) arrive at the mouth of the Nottawasaga River (Q), only to have to wait a week before the *Nancy* arrives.

The Estimated Course of the *Nancy*

3. July 14: The *Nancy* passes through the North Channel en route to the Nottawasaga River.
3a. July 16: The *Nancy* is possibly sighted by the American flotilla.
3b. July 20–31: At some point, the *Nancy* arrives at the Nottawasaga River and command is transferred to Lieutenant Worsley. The new crew familiarizes itself with its new vessel and loads the supplies destined for Michilimackinac.
3c. August 1: The *Nancy* sails for Michilimackinac but is intercepted by Livingston and returns to the river.
3d. August 2–13: Work is done to erect a blockhouse on shore.
4. July 28: Robert Livingston (black dotted line) leaves Michilimackinac with dispatches for the *Nancy*.
4a. August 1: Livingston intercepts the *Nancy* and accompanies her back to the Nottawasaga River.
Q., P., -D. August 1–13: Robert Livingston makes a round-trip journey of 186 miles (300 kilometers) between the Nottawasaga River (Q) and York (D).

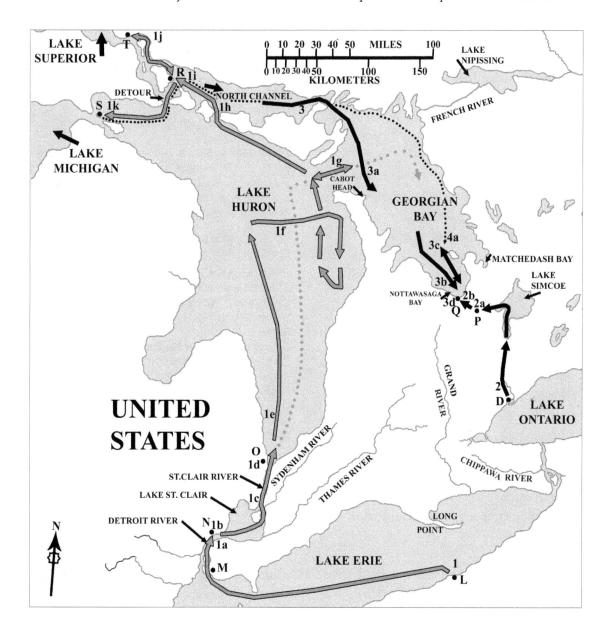

in theory, but in reality effectively vetoed this operation by providing Brown with a copy of the orders he had already issued to the Lake Erie squadron commander, Captain (brevet Commodore) Arthur Sinclair, for the mounting of an expedition against Michilimackinac.

> 1st. Capt. Sinclair will go up to Detroit with a part of the Flotilla, he will there embark Lieut. Col. [George] Croghan, and as large a number of troops as his vessels will accommodate with the necessary supplies of provisions and ammunition. He will then enter Lake Huron, and proceed to Gloucester Bay [Georgian Bay], where the troops will debark to attack, and carry, the enemy's new establishment at Matchedash ... this effected, the fleet will go up to the mouth of the St. Josephs and Mackinaw —
>
> 2nd. What remains of the flotilla in Lake Erie [only five of the smaller vessels] will be put under orders to support your Division to the Canada shore ...[1]
>
> — John Armstrong to General Brown, June 9, 1814

Consequently, left without the essential transport for his primary invasion plan, Brown was forced to resort to making his landing in Upper Canada at the more easily accessible Fort Erie. (For details see *The Tide of War*).

AMERICAN EXPEDITIONARY FORCE TO MICHILIMACKINAC, JUNE–OCTOBER 1814[2]

Lawrence (Lieutenant [acting] Captain Daniel Dexter): 20 guns
Niagara (Captain [acting] Commodore Arthur Sinclair): 20 guns
Tigress (Sailing Master Stephen Champlin): 1 gun
Scorpion (Lieutenant Daniel Turner): 2 guns
Caledonia (Lieutenant Samuel Woodhouse): 3 guns
Ohio (Mr. Augustus Conklin): 1 gun; (Supply vessel sent back down on July 17 to Detroit.)

Landing Force (Lieutenant Colonel George Croghan [Second Rifle Regiment])

Five Companies (Major Andrew H. Holmes [Thirty-Second Regiment]) drawn from detachments of: Seventeenth, Nineteenth, Twenty-Fourth, and Twenty-Eighth Infantry Regiments: Est. 500 All Ranks
Ohio State Volunteer Regiment (Colonel William Cotgreave): Est. 250 All Ranks
Artillery Corps (Lieutenant Lewis Morgan): Detachment
U.S. Marine Corps: Detachment

Total: 750–850 All Ranks

Fitting out his expeditionary squadron during April and May, Commodore Sinclair sent some of his smaller vessels (*Scorpion*, *Caledonia*, and *Ohio*) ahead to obtain intelligence and make a reconnaissance of the route into Lake Huron, while he followed some weeks later, bringing the larger *Lawrence* and *Niagara*. Arriving at Detroit on June 22, Sinclair found preparations aboard his advance vessels well underway for the expedition, and after loading the first consignment of troops and supplies on the *Lawrence* and *Niagara*, he had planned to depart upriver as soon as possible. However, once the winds shifted and blew from the northeast, he was effectively trapped for the next fourteen days. Unable to make any headway against the combined force of contrary winds and the river's strong southbound current, Sinclair was forced to wait until July 3, before the winds shifted to the southwest and the journey could recommence.*2 Fortunately, the ship's surgeon aboard the *Lawrence*, Doctor Usher Parsons, maintained a journal, which includes many fascinating details of this expedition's difficult passage to reach its target.

July 3 — Wind SW and we sailed for Mackinack, 241 soldiers on board under Major Holmes, Col. Croghan commands the expedition. The design is to retake Mackinack by storm and to destroy

shipping on the upper lakes. The fleet will return in four weeks …

July 4 — We arrived in [Lake] St. Clair early in the morning; distance from Detroit is 10 to 12 miles [16–19 kilometers] … about two thirds the way from the lower towards the upper end of the lake … we ran aground, as did the *Niagara* we remained all night … [off] the mouth of this river …

July 5 — The soldiers were sent from the mouth of the St. Clair River in order to lighten the vessel. The schooners *Scorpion* and *Tigris* [*Tigress*] came alongside p.m. and lightened us some. Soon we grounded again and remained all night…. The *Niagara* succeeded today in reaching the other bar, six miles [9.6 kilometers] ahead ….

July 6 — We got over the bar about 10 o'clock. We passed the *Niagara* at 1 o'clock on the bar where we were detained two hours. We proceeded five miles [eight kilometers] to the head of the lake and again took in our ballast iron …

July 9 — Sailed about 3 p.m., made only 3 miles [4.8 kilometers]. The river is very crooked and winding from St. Clair lake to Huron lake, a distance of nearly

4 miles [as written in the manuscript; actually it is nearer forty miles (sixty-four kilometers)]. The river … is about 20 yards [18 meters] wide and the banks very steep, so that our … sail yards touched the trees & banks …

July 11 — The soldiers debarked and walked to Fort Gratiot …

July 13 — Arrived in Lake Huron about 4 p.m. The rapids are 3/4tr of a mile in length & run at 4 to 5 knots. Fortunately, we had a six knot [wind] which carried us through into Lake Huron. There are no settlements at the head of the rapids as we enter the lake except Fort Gratiot [built in 1814 and located in present-day Port Huron]. Some cleared spots and houses on the Canada shore …

July 14 — Took all our troops aboard, amounting to 750 Rank and File. More than 300 on board the *Lawrence*. Made more than 100 miles [161 kilometers] in the direction of Cabot's Head [and Matchedash] … wither we are bound before proceeding to Mackinack …

July 15 — Hazy, unable to see vessels ½ mile off. We saw land ahead which made the comm'dr think we were within the Great Bay [Georgian Bay] …

accordingly we sailed in a southerly direction … but no entrance could be found into the bay [leading to Matchedash.] It was thought by many that we were running back to the rapids by keeping along this shore, and that the land is a cape dividing the lake from the Great Bay and that we did not ascend the lake far enough to warrant our trying to enter the bay …

July 16 — Saw … a vessel at a great distance but soon lost sight of … [it] … in a fog. The sail was probably the *Nancy*. We changed our pursuit and directed our course [back] towards Mackinack …[3]

Awaiting the Americans at Michilimackinac was the isolated and relatively weak garrison of less than two hundred British troops, many of whom were, due to age or ill-health, virtually unfit for active campaigning and drawn from a miscellany of regimental detachments. These were then supported by a miscellaneous and fluctuating cadre of fur traders, local untrained settlers/militias, and a never-constant-in-number and always-demanding body of Native allies. Effectively cut off from the rest of the war by the loss of the British Lake Erie fleet the previous year, the garrison had almost starved during the winter of 1813/14 and was only now beginning to recover its strength.

Commanding the position was Lieutenant Colonel Robert McDouall (Glengarry Light Infantry) who had arrived only on May 18, after having made the arduous journey north by the York–Lake Simcoe–Nottawasaga River–Lake Huron route, with a complement of some ninety men of the Royal Newfound Regiment, eleven Royal Artillery gunners, and four field guns. In addition, there was a detachment of twenty-one sailors, under the separate command of Lieutenant Newdigate Poyntz, who were to man the supply vessel *Nancy*, then refitting at Fort St. Joseph.[4] Officially taking command of his new post and its garrison,[*5]

GARRISON AT MICHILIMACKINAC AND DETACHMENT AT FORT ST. JOSEPH, JUNE–JULY, 1814[*5]

41st Regiment: 1 Officer
10th Royal Veterans Regiment: 3 Officers, 39 Other Ranks
Royal Artillery: 14 Other Ranks
Glengarry Light Infantry: 1 Officer
Royal Newfoundland Fencible Regiment: 6 Officers, 130 Other Ranks
Michigan Fencible Regiment: 2 Officers, 50 Other Ranks
British Native Allied Warriors: Est. 350–500 Warriors

NB Most of the 10th Royal Veterans went down-lake in late June.

Lieutenant Colonel McDouall immediately set about strengthening its defensive capabilities by repairing and strengthening the perimeter of the existing fortifications on the south side of the island and the site's natural harbour. In addition, because the British had succeeded in capturing the position by the simple expedient of taking the high ground to the north (rear) of the fort and threatening it with destruction on its exposed rear flank, McDouall had a new redoubt built on the overlooking high ground, which he named Fort George (Fort Holmes).

Unfortunately for McDouall, even those manpower resources that he had on hand were soon to be depleted, as most of the prior garrison's 10th Royal Veteran detachment were either too debilitated to undertake active duties or were ordered down-lake. Reports of American activities farther west led to the mounting of a two-hundred-man strong expedition toward Prairie du Chien at the headwaters of the Mississippi to forestall this potential threat. Left with a decidedly reduced disposable force and receiving reports of American warships being seen in the southern part of Lake Huron, McDouall decided to concentrate his resources at Michilimackinac and reduced the detachment at St. Joseph to a skeleton crew. He also established watching posts along the various channels any American approach would follow, and on July 19, the sails of American vessels were sighted in the

NIAGARA

Views of the reconstructed American flagship *Niagara* participating in the War of 1812 Bicentennial tall ships festival in 2013. In 1814, the *Niagara*, and her sister ship, the *Lawrence*, were the largest warships in the upper Great Lakes.

North Channel, apparently heading toward Fort St. Joseph. According to Usher Parsons:

July 19 — At noon made sight of land … [at] … the St. Joseph [River]. In the afternoon we entered the mouth of the said river. The shores in every direction as we passed it presented fires, supposed to be signals or telegraphs to the enemy in Mackinack. The smoke arose on the land in the straits of St. Joseph on our left side from a high bluff when we were within three miles [4.8 kilometers] of it. Soon after … we discovered Fort St. Joseph a few miles ahead…. Anchored three or four miles [4.8–6.4 kilometers] from it. A flag was sent in the evening to demand a surrender of the fort, but no person was to be found…. The houses are good and seemed to have been recently inhabited, even within 24 hours.

July 20 — The two launches were sent on shore today, containing about 200 men. The fort and public buildings were destroyed. We found cattle and three of them were bro't off and six sheep for our sick … men very sickly with pleurisy…[6]

The following day, the British supply vessel *Mink* was sighted and forced to surrender while sailing from Sault Ste. Marie to Michilimackinac with a cargo of furs and 230 barrels of flour. After questioning the *Mink*'s crew, Sinclair also gained the valuable intelligence that the British garrison consisted of: "500 regulars, 2,100 Indians & 100 volunteers …"[7]

On the twenty-second, two of the larger launches brought up with the fleet were detached with orders to sail up to the small trading station of Sault Ste. Marie, located forty miles (sixty-four kilometers) away at the strategic waterway intersection of Lake Superior and Lake Huron. According to Lieutenant Daniel Turner, who was in charge of this expedition:

I proceeded on the expedition to Lake Superior with launches … [and] … rowed night and day … but information had reached the enemy at St. Maries [Sault Ste. Marie] of our approach, about two hours before I arrived at that place…. The force under Major Holmes prevented anything like resistance at the Fort…. I then proceeded across the strait of L. Superior … and on my appearance the enemy finding they could not get off with the vessel I was in quest of, set fire to her in several places, scuttled and left her. I succeeded in boarding her and by considerable exertion extinguished the flames and secured her from sinking. I then stript her and prepared for getting her down the Falls [large rapids]…. Adverse winds prevented my attempting the falls until the 26th, when every possible effort was used, but … she [struck the rocks and] bilged, but was brought down so rapidly that we succeeded in running her on shore below the rapids before she filled and we burnt her. She was a fine new schooner, upwards of 100 tons, called the *Perseverence*…. I have however brought down four captured boats loaded with Indian goods to a considerable amount, the balance contained in four large and two small store houses, which were destroyed, together with a very superb mill amounting in value to, from 50 to 100 thousand dollars …[8]

This "victory" achieved, the American landing party sailed for Michilimackinac, there to rejoin its fleet, which had already sailed for its encounter with the British garrison.

CHAPTER 8

All For Nothing: The Battle of Michilimackinac Island, August 4, 1814

Approaching the island of Michilimackinac (Mackinac), Commodore Sinclair and Lieutenant Colonel Croghan were in no hurry to make an assault on the apparently strong British defensive position until they had made a thorough reconnaissance and weighed their options. Apart from exchanging some desultory cannon fire with the enemy's shoreline positions and realizing that none of their shipboard artillery could be elevated enough to fire on the dominating main fort overlooking the town, they spent the next few days sailing round the island's rocky shoreline, looking for options to landing directly below the untouchable British positions and acutely aware of the constant presence of British Native allied warriors, who were shadowing and reporting back on the Americans' movements from under the cover of the densely wooded shoreline.

The fortification of Fort Michilimackinac dominates the harbour in this postwar view. From *Pictorial Field Book of the War of 1812*.

Courtesy of the Mackinac State Historic Parks Collection.

A photograph taken circa 1900, looking north across the Michilimackinac battlefield from the perspective of the British defensive positions. Today the ground to the left is partially occupied by a local golf course and aircraft landing strip, while the encroaching treeline has substantially reduced the open ground to the north.

Unhappy with what they found, in the end it was decided that under the cover of a bombardment of the shore by the guns aboard the American fleet, the landing would be made on August 4, utilizing a small beach located on the far side of the island (the very same beach the British had used for their landing in 1812). The American troops would then secure a beachhead perimeter, erect defensive positions, and engage the British at an advantage if they counterattacked or advance to defeat them with the support of artillery brought over from the ships, as their own artillery had gone missing with the hopefully temporary disappearance of the *Mink* (aboard which the artillery had

been previously loaded). Of increasing concern to Sinclair was the fact that despite having captured some enemy supplies, his own stocks of food were rapidly running out, leading him to place his otherwise inactive passenger soldiers on half-rations, while his working sailors got a three-quarter ration (a fact that did not improve inter-service relations).

In the diary of Usher Parsons, watching from on board the decks of the Lawrence, the sequence of events on August 4 was as follows:

> At 9 o'clock, signal was made for armed vessels to get underway — at ½ past 9 came to anchor in line of battle on the N. West

side of the island.... At 1 the troops began to debark — At 2 a firing commenced to cover the landing of our troops — at 3 pm the troops were formed on the shore and commenced marching toward the fort. In a few moments a heavy fire was opened upon them by British and Indians with musketry — a cessation of fire followed & renewed till ½ after three. There was a constant crackling of musketry — and ringing of warwhoop — then the firing abated a little till 10 minutes after 4 when the firing recommenced with a rapidity, accompanied with yells & lasted till ¼ past 5, the musketry was very frequent and irregular. At ½ past 4 the direction of the firing indicated that our troops were retiring — at 5 o'clock the troops reached the shore to reembark. Boats were on shore ready to receive them.... The report of killed and wounded were thus; Regulars Infantry killed 12, wounded 39, & 3 missing. Marines one badly wounded others slightly. Of the artillery and militia none hurt ... we raised anchor and dropt it about one mile off ...[1]

What Parsons heard, but was unable to see, was the engagement that had taken place on the inland

farmstead of Michael Dousman. This farm consisted of little more than a clearing in the otherwise untouched demesne of dense forest and measured perhaps 1,500 yards (1,371 meters) from north to south and 1,000 yards (914 meters) east to west. Within this perimeter lay a number of impassable bogs in the lower stretches of ground and mound-shaped glacial deposits (drumlins) that together broke up the open space into an irregular patchwork of low, scrub-filled, and partially cleared fields. In addition, these areas were bordered by split-rail fences and culminated in the Dousman farm, made up of a cluster of small buildings and sheds, located close to the southern boundary of the property. Bisecting this clearing and running from north to south was the single trackway that passed for the main road connecting the north shore with the main settlement and fortifications on the south side of the island.

Upon receiving the report from his Native scouts that the Americans were definitely preparing to land on the far side of the island, Lieutenant Colonel McDouall was determined to intercept them while they were still unprepared and at a location that would give him the advantage of position on relatively open ground, so that the maximum amount of firepower could be brought to bear, but with his flanks secured by the forests. Consequently, apart from a fifty-man detachment that was left to garrison the fortifications,

McDouall marched the remainder of his available manpower to the clearing occupied by the Dousman farmstead. Here he placed his main body of men along a low ridge at the southern end of the clearing, which was further enhanced as a defensive position by a natural undulation in the ground that acted as a protective breastwork (low wall) for the defenders. At the centre of the position and astride the road were placed two artillery pieces, while the various detachments of troops formed a rough line on either side. On both flanks and secreted within the dense undergrowth of the forest perimeter were the Native warriors, thus completing three sides of a rough "box" of a defensive formation.*2

As the American leading elements emerged from

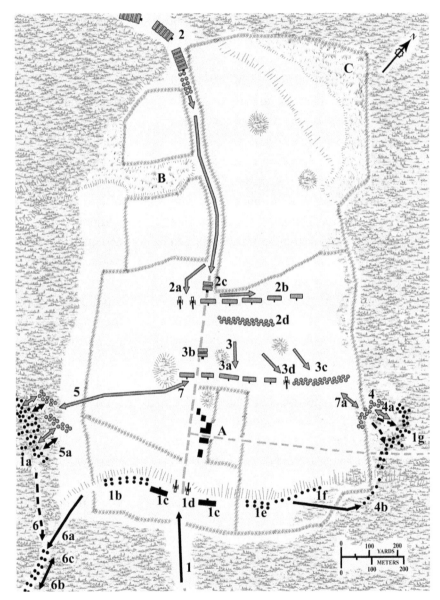

THE BATTLE FOR MICHILIMACKINAC, AUGUST 4, 1814

NB Due to a relative lack of definitive original documentation and substantive details about the deployment and manoeuvres of the troops in this engagement, the following is this author's representation of what is conjectured to have occurred, based upon the best available information.

A. Dousman farmstead

B–C.: Low-lying swampy ground

1. British forces advance (1) from Fort Michilimackinac and establish a defensive position atop a low rise of ground at the south end of the clearing: left-flank British Native allied warriors (1a), local militia detachments (1b), Royal Newfoundland Regiment (two companies) (1c), artillery (1 x 3-pounder and 1 x 6-pounder) (1d), local militia detachment (1e), Michigan Militia (1f), right-flank British Native allied warriors (1g).

2. U.S. forces advance south along the main track (2) and come under long-range fire from the British artillery (1d). Reaching open ground, the units deploy. Artillery (2 x 6-pounders) (2a). Main line: five companies of regular infantry drawn from the Seventeenth, Nineteenth, and Twenty-Fourth Regiments (2b). Reserve: detachments from the Twenty-Eighth Regiment and United States Marine Corps (2c). Advance line: Ohio State Militia (2d).

3. U.S. forces cautiously advance (while under fire) (3) to the north side of the Dousman farmstead and establish a second line, with the regular units and reserve on the American right flank (3a–3b) and militias on the left (3c). One artillery piece is moved up to the American left (3d) to support the militia. (*NB* No details are known about any movements relating to the second piece.)

4. Unable to advance through the centre, detachments from the militia on the American left (east) flank (3c) advance into the woods to make a flanking pass (4). However, upon encountering some Native warrior (1g) resistance on that flank, the militias initially stall and then press forward, forcing the Natives to retire (4a). In response, Lieutenant Colonel McDouall moves elements of the Michigan Fencibles (1f) to the British right flank (4b) to support the Native resistance and again stall the American advance.

5. Similarly, detachments from the right (west) flank of the American main (regular) line move west (5) to make a similar flanking pass. Facing only light opposition from the Natives on this flank (1a), the regulars initially push forward (5a) until Major Holmes is killed, following which the attack on this flank flounders.

6. Receiving reports the Americans have made a landing to his rear, threatening to cut off his line of retreat, McDouall leaves the field (6), taking with him some of the militias (6a), and moves south to investigate (6b). Finding the report to be false, McDouall returns post-haste with his militiamen, a reformed party of Native warriors, and (possibly) an additional detachment of militia troops from the forts (6c). Arriving as the Americans are stalled and beginning to withdraw, these relatively fresh troops are used to increase the pressure on the American right flank.

7. Unable to break through the British positions, Lieutenant Colonel Croghan orders both flanking attacks withdrawn (7–7a). He then implements a general fighting withdrawal to their boats as British Native allied warriors and militia advance and harass the Americans back to their landing ground.

the northern treeline, the British guns opened fire, doing no damage and only alerting Lieutenant Colonel Croghan to the presence of the enemy. After making a reconnaissance of the British positions, Croghan initially advanced until he reached open ground and then deployed his units in two distinct lines, with the Ohio Volunteers comprising the front line and the U.S. regular units the rear. For their own part, the Americans also had two 6-pounder guns, which opened fire at long range and with equally poor results, as the shot almost universally flew high over the British troops' heads. Using the intervening natural ground cover to advantage, the American formations approached the static British line, with the militia moving to the left and regulars to the right until they formed a single continuous line, just beyond effective musket range, of about 250 yards (228 meters). After some ineffectual exchanges of fire between the two lines, which necessitated the bringing up of one of the artillery pieces to support the militia firepower, Croghan attempted to make a pincer movement on either flank. On the American left (east), men from the militia line soon ran into the hidden British Native warriors, who appear to have made only a token resistance before beginning to retire. In response, McDouall was forced to redeploy part of the Michigan Fencible Regiment to stabilize that position, resulting in this American advance

eventually becoming bogged down and unable to proceed. On the American right (west) a similar movement by the regulars also made an initial contact with Native opposition, from which many of the warriors were reported to have either retired or begun to abandon their positions entirely.

Pushing forward, the American regulars were helped by the fact that at this moment, McDouall received word from Major Crawford at the fort that the American fleet was making a second landing of troops to McDouall's rear, threatening to cut off his line of retreat and capturing the forts.

ESTIMATE OF BRITISH FORCES, BATTLE OF MICHILIMACKINAC ISLAND, AUGUST 4, 1814[*2]

NB The numbers in parentheses indicate the recorded garrison for Michilimackinac at the beginning of August 1814 Only part of the garrison is estimated to have been engaged in this action.

Royal Newfoundland Regiment: Est. 100 All Ranks (136 All Ranks)
10th Royal Veterans Regiment: Est. 5–10 All Ranks (15–25 All Ranks)
Royal Artillery: Est. 8–10 All Ranks (12 All Ranks) with one 6-pounder and one 3-pounder gun
Michigan Fencible Regiment: Est. 20–25 All Ranks (37 All Ranks)
Local Militia: Initial Est. 50–55 All Ranks, later reinforced by 50 All Ranks (110–125 All Ranks)
British Native Allied Warriors: Est. 300–350 Warriors (350–400 Warriors)

In response, McDouall later recorded that he "therefore moved to place myself between them [the forts] and the enemy, and took up a position effectually covering them from whence collecting the greater part of the Indians who had retired and taking with me Major Crawford and about 50 militia [from the fortifications]. I again advanced ..."[3] to the field of action, whereupon these new troops were immediately pushed into action on the British left flank, bolstering the Native warriors, who had not only remained to fight, but had successfully ambushed the American regular troops, killing Major Andrew H. Holmes (Croghan's second-in-command), wounding Captain Benjamin Desha (third-in-command), and killing or wounding a sizeable number of his detachment with musket fire, before the remaining survivors were set upon by both the hidden Natives and the newly arrived troops and warriors in a melee of hand-to-hand combat. With both flanking attempts stalled, no apparent way of breaching the apparently intact central British line, his second-in-command killed, and his overall casualties mounting, Croghan called off the assault and ordered a withdrawal to their landing ground.

There he found that he had to make a fighting retreat, as the British Natives, seeing the enemy falling back and scenting blood, pressed forward with furious intent and, with the enemy now exposed and in the open, harassed the Americans back to their landing ground."[4]

Following this setback, Croghan and Sinclair effectively decided that any further attempt to attack Michilimackinac by assault would be futile. Instead, they decided to divide the flotilla, with the *Lawrence*, *Caledonia*, and *Mink* returning south to Detroit with the bulk of the troops. At the same time, the *Niagara*, *Scorpion*, and *Tigress*, with a contingent of three companies of regulars and some artillery, would take advantage of intelligence gained from the questioning of a prisoner

ESTIMATE OF LOSSES, BATTLE OF MICHILIMACKINAC ISLAND, AUGUST 4, 1814[4]

British
None recorded

British Native Allies
Wounded: 1 Warrior

American
Artillery
Wounded: 3 Other Ranks
Regular Infantry
Killed: 3 Officers, 14 Other Ranks
Wounded: 1 Officer, 43 Other Ranks
Missing: 2 Other Ranks
U.S. Marines
Wounded: 1 Other Rank
Ohio State Volunteers
Killed: 3 Other Ranks
Wounded: 5 Other Ranks

taken on board the *Mink* and go on a search and destroy mission — as they now knew of the British supply route through the Nottawasaga River, and where the *Nancy* was to be found.

I [have] ascertained … that the mechanics and others, sent across from York, during the winter, were for the purpose of building a flotilla to transport reinforcements, and supplies into Mackinac…. An attempt was made to pass them by way of Matchadash; but it was found impractical from all the portages being a morass; that they then resorted to a small river called Nautauwasaga, situated to the south of Matchadash, from which there is a portage … over a good road to Lake Simcoe … this place was never known … and … the navigation [of that river] is dangerous and difficult, and so obscured by rocks and bushes that no stranger could ever find it…. I have, however, availed myself of the means of discovering it [as] I have agreed on a reward with this man [for a success] … and the penalty of death in case of failure, who is one of a very few who have ever been there … for this place I am now on my way…. At

this place I [also] calculate on falling in with their Schooner [*Nancy*] …[5]

— Captain Arthur Sinclair to Secretary of the Navy Jones, August 9, 1814

In a final note to this minor tactical, but strategically vital, engagement at Michilimackinac, the following day, the Americans sent an emissary ashore, requesting permission to recover the body of Major Andrew H. Holmes, which had been left on the field of battle. In a gesture of military courtesy to a gallantly fallen foe, McDouall not only granted the request, but obviously having heard from the American prisoners of the American shortage of food supplies and rampant illness amongst the men, made the extraordinary offer to supply his enemy with whatever provisions, fruit, and vegetables could be spared from the British stores. Not in a position to refuse this gesture, the Americans soon learned that this generosity came at a price, as on August 6, a further note arrived from McDouall, seeking compensation for the civilian owners of the cattle and sheep appropriated by the Americans at St. Joseph.

The Americans responded by handing over $8.88 before setting sail and heading south.

CHAPTER 9

The Nancy: Loss and Retribution, June–October 1814

While the actions on the Niagara frontier were unfolding in their deadly fashion, and the American flotilla in the upper lakes were occupied at Michilimackinac, the lone British supply vessel, *Nancy*, remained elusively out of the Americans' reach.

Extensively refitted and repaired over the course of the previous winter at Sault Ste. Marie, the *Nancy*, under the command of Lieutenant Newdigate Poyntz and his detachment of sailors that had arrived in May, had spent the bulk of the shipping season making supply runs between the "Sault" (pronounced *Soo*), St. Joseph, and Michilimackinac in the north and the Nottawasaga River at the south end of Georgian Bay. She was also reported to have serviced the British position known as "Matchedash" farther to the east and located within the rocky confines of Matchedash Bay.

While this location had certainly been one of the portage routes that connected Lake Simcoe and Georgian Bay at the outset of the war, the shorter and relatively easier passage by way of Fort Willow and the Nottawasaga River effectively rendered the Matchedash route superfluous. Nonetheless, it still had a valuable role to play in the British war effort — as part of a disinformation campaign that deliberately leaked the "fact" that the British were establishing a major shipbuilding yard on Georgian Bay at Matchedash, out of reach of American interference. This was then followed by further "reports" of large amounts of supplies and shipwrights being sent to Matchedash to build a fleet of vessels that would gain control of the upper lakes, descend to

Two views of a cutaway scale model of the *Nancy*, showing the internal construction details of the hull. On display at the Nancy Island Historic Site.

attack the Detroit frontier from the north and then take on the American Lake Erie fleet. It is therefore likely that the *Nancy*'s reputed visits to Matchedash were simply part of the cover story and helped to hide the importance of the Nottawasaga route.

In July, a replacement crew for the *Nancy* was dispatched from York to Fort Willow with a substantial stock of supplies for Michilimackinac, including 157 barrels of flour, 143 barrels of salt pork, 6 barrels of salt, and 100 pairs of military boots.[1]

Upon its arrival at the mouth of the Nottawasaga River, this new crew, commanded by Lieutenant Miller Worsley, R.N., waited for about a week until the *Nancy* arrived, at which time Worsley's party took over from Lieutenant Poyntz and his crew, who were under orders to return to York. After familiarizing himself with his new command and loading the supplies, Worsley set sail on August 1. He had been underway for only a matter of hours when he was literally flagged down by a large canoe bearing dispatches from Lieutenant Colonel McDouall. The canoe's courier, Robert Livingston, of the North West Company, had already amassed a distinguished war record of acting as a courier and guide to virtually every detachment that had been sent up to garrison the northern posts. He had also twice escaped from capture by the Americans and suffered a number of battle wounds the previous year while serving on the Niagara frontier as part of the Native contingent besieging the Americans in Fort George. (For details see *The Flames of War.*) From these encounters he was now partially blinded in his right eye from a tomahawk blow, partially paralyzed in his right arm by a spear wound to the shoulder, and still carrying an un-extracted musket ball in his left thigh. Nonetheless, he had just paddled over two hundred miles (322 kilometers) across Lake Huron in only four days in search of the *Nancy* to bring those aboard the warning that the Americans were off Michilimackinac and that they needed to find an immediate sheltered location in which to hide. This message also contained instructions from Lieutenant Colonel McDouall on how they were to proceed.

> 28 July, 1814 … The American expedition destined for the attack of this island, having at length made its appearance … I hasten to apprise you of this circumstance lest the *Nancy* and valuable cargo, fall into their hands…. I would recommend you return to the Nottawasaga River, and to take the *Nancy* as high as possible — place her in a judicious position, and hastily run up a strong log house, such as were made when the boats were built, but larger, with loop holes and embrasures for your two-six pounders, which will enable you to defend her should you be attacked, which is not unlikely …[2]

Turning about, Worsley brought the *Nancy* into the Nottawasaga River, but the low water levels (inherent to that area in the late summer) prevented the vessel getting as far upriver as might have been wished. Nevertheless, Worsley anchored his vessel under the shadow of a raised part of the southern riverbank, upon which he began constructing the recommended defensive works. In addition, on the northern bank, there were a series of low, tree-covered sandbanks dividing the river from the lakefront that provided additional protective cover for the hull of the ship. At the same time, Livingstone left to report to the military command at York (Toronto). In a letter, subsequently attributed to Assistant Surgeon Thomas Samson, these events were outlined and make interesting reading:

> Nautawasauga River, 6th Aug. 1814 … It is nearly a month since I left York in company with Lieut. Worsley of the Navy…. We had waited about a week on the banks of this river before the *Nancy* arrived, during which time we suffered every misery that you can imagine from bad weather and meriads of musquettos &c.&c…. You may therefore judge

what a pleasant sight the *Nancy* was for us … [we] … got under way on Monday [August 1] with every prospect of reaching Mackinac in a short time, which is only 220 miles [354 kilometers] from hence. We had been out but for a few hours, when we met an express from Col. McDouall to say that the American squadron from Lake Erie & large forces were blockading the island, and that we could not possibly reach it, we therefore had the mortification to put back into this wretched place where we are busily employed in erecting a Block House to contain and defend the stores and schooner in case of an attack, which is an event I have no doubt of; but I hope from the strength of the fine ground Worsley has chosen, and the good [efforts] of his crew that we shall be able to beat off a very strong force — The river is too narrow to sail up, we shall therefore only have Gun boats to deal with …[3]

Despite this apparent sense of optimism, or perhaps bravado, the reality of the situation for the *Nancy* was anything but rosy, for Worsley's "garrison" consisted of a combined total of twenty seamen and men of the Royal Newfoundland Regiment, supported by nine Canadian voyageur volunteers and a handful of Natives, while his "heavy" armament amounted to two 24-pounder carronades (useful only at a short range against a large target) and a single 6-pounder gun. Matters continued unchanged for a further week, until August 13, when the sails of three major ships were sighted off to the north as the *Niagara*, *Scorpion*, and *Tigress* arrived, carrying a combined total of twenty-two shipboard cannon, two field guns, and over four hundred infantry — all determined to exact reprisal and redress for their frustrating and humiliating failure at Michilimackinac.

Without delay, the American vessels approached the river mouth, but due to the shallow summer water levels and the American vessels' size, they were unable to sail up in pursuit. Neither could they approach close in to the open shore opposite the *Nancy*, as the extremely shallow gradient of the lake at that point kept the safe-sailing channel well offshore.

Commencing with a long-range artillery bombardment, the Americans then landed a reconnaissance party, accompanied by some small-calibre 4-pounder field guns. This party soon located Worsley's position and reported back on both the enemy's strongpoint and the confirmed presence of the *Nancy*. With daylight waning, Sinclair and Croghan agreed to make their attack the following day, which was fortunate for Worsley, for that night

Robert Livingston arrived back from York, having travelled a round trip of approximately 186 miles (300 kilometers) in only six days. He brought with him twenty-three Native warriors and the mixed news that while additional reinforcements were on the way, they had no hope of arriving by the next day.

On August 14, the American offshore bombardment recommenced at around 9:00 a.m. Worsley's judicious defensive position and the covering sandbar served their purpose admirably to deflect or absorb most of the shot that came within range. In reply, the three guns of the defenders barked out their defiance — while inflicting no recorded damage on the American vessels. Nor could the American troops and small-calibre artillery that were landed onshore overwhelm the entrenched defenders, leading to a standoff by the early afternoon. Looking to break the impasse, the Americans reinforced their ground troops by landing both an 8½-inch and a 5½-inch howitzer that had been carried as cargo. These heavier-calibre guns soon tipped the balance of the battle, as their close-range plunging fire from the British flank began to take their toll on both men and defences. Vastly outnumbered and outgunned, Worsley recognized his position was now hopeless and his only option was to salvage and hide as many of the vital supplies as possible and then escape with his men in the hopes that "he who fights and runs away, lives to fight another day." Unfortunately, this inevitably meant that he would have to sacrifice his new command. According to the British version of events, determined not to see the *Nancy* fall into the hands of the Americans, Worsley ordered the detonation of pre-prepared demolition charges placed within the vessel and adjacent blockhouse, plus the spiking of the three guns. On the other hand, American accounts attribute the subsequent destruction to the howitzer fire, which struck the blockhouse and caused an unexpected ignition of material within the British position, which then communicated itself to the fuses and precipitated the resultant detonation of the charges. Either way, the British position and vessel were lost, and the new/former crew of the *Nancy* retreated up the Nottawasaga River toward Fort Willow, carrying with them as much as possible and protected from American detection by a dense cloud of smoke and the detonation of barrels of black powder within their former position.

While Sinclair had succeeded in his task of cutting off the British supply line to Michilimackinac, this success was also tinged with frustration and disappointment for the valuable vessel and its cargo had not been captured intact, thus denying the men a share of any prize money that would have accrued, as well as the actual supplies of food that would have fed the otherwise short-rationed men of the expedition. Nevertheless,

The remains of the salvaged keel and hull/ribs segments of the *Nancy* in 2014. They are preserved in a specially constructed gallery at the Wasaga Beach, Nancy Island Historic Site, located in the middle of the Nottawasaga River, exactly where the ship sank in 1814.

Commodore Sinclair subsequently characterized this incident as a major victory for the American war effort and one that would speed the capitulation of Michilimackinac by the following spring, when another expedition should be mounted to reclaim the Upper Great Lakes for America's exclusive use and control. In the interim, he instructed Lieutenant Daniel Turner, the senior officer put in charge of the *Scorpion* and *Tigress*, to maintain a close watch on the Nottawasaga to ensure no attempt was made to reopen communications with Michilimackinac, while the *Niagara* sailed south, first to Detroit and then into Lake Erie, where it would rejoin the other vessels, already en route to the Niagara frontier. He also added some words of warning that were to prove prophetic:

> Having accomplished … the destruction of the enemies whole force on this lake, I am on the eve of returning to Lake Erie; but as it is all important to cut the enemies line of communication from Michilimackinac to York, which is through the Nottawasaga River … you will remain here and keep up a rigid blockade … suffering not a boat or canoe to pass in or out of this River…. [However,] I should recommend your immediately finding out anchorage … and in a way not to be observed by the enemy, who might not only avail himself of your position to move out his boats in the night … but he might attempt surprizing you in the night by throwing a number of men on board…. Against attacks of this kind, which he might be driven to by his desperate situation, as this blockade must starve him into a surrender by the Spring …[4]

> — Captain Arthur Sinclair to Lieutenant Daniel Turner, August 15, 1814

Unfortunately, Sinclair failed to take account of the fact that in the aftermath of three severe storms that blew across the region in the following days, Turner decided that there was no value in keeping watch on an empty shore, while his vessels were in repeated danger of being driven ashore. As a result, both vessels sailed north to establish their blockade closer to Michilimackinac. Meanwhile, up the Nottawasaga River at Fort Willow, Lieutenant Worsley was determined to succeed in his assigned mission and exact revenge for the loss of the *Nancy*.

After only two days of recuperation at Fort Willow, Worsley, seventeen of his sailors, and the nine voyageurs cautiously brought two heavily loaded bateaux, carrying what had been salvaged

(Above, left) A reconstruction of the type of bateaux used by the crew of the *Nancy* to reach Michilimackinac. (Above, right; bottom) Modern-day Living History re-enactors pilot bateaux replicas of the War of 1812–1815 period during a mock engagement.

from the cargo (sixty-seven barrels of flour and three barrels of salt pork) downriver. In addition, leading this party in an equally heavily loaded long canoe and acting as advance scouts, were seven Native warriors and the seemingly inexhaustible Robert Livingston. Approaching the battle site, Livingston fully expected to see the Americans blockading the river mouth. Instead, apart from having felled some trees to augment the navigational impediment of the burnt-out wreck of the *Nancy*, which now lay almost completely submerged mid-channel, the Americans were nowhere to be seen, their sails having only just disappeared over the northern horizon.

Without the Americans to stop them, Livingston now guided Worsley and his men (all in heavily laden open small boats) in what would become a six-day marathon journey covering over 300 miles (483 kilometers) until they came to the narrow waterway known as the Detour (De Tour) that linked the North Channel to Lake Huron. Here, they had the unpleasant and unwelcome experience of seeing the *Tigress* and *Scorpion* patrolling the islands off St. Joseph Island and blocking their further passage.

Turning about to evade detection, Livingston guided the three boats into the hidden cover of a nearby inlet. Transferring the canoe's cargo into the two bateaux and mooring them securely, the entire party of thirty-five men crowded themselves into the canoe and set out shortly after dusk

in their attempt to pass the American vessels. Under the cover of darkness, the canoe crept to within one hundred yards (ninety-one meters) of the Americans before passing by undetected and gaining the open waters of Lake Huron beyond. Paddling throughout the night, the tired but exhilarated crew arrived at Michilimackinac late in the day on August 30, bearing the bad news of the loss of the *Nancy*, but the welcome promise of supplies once the bateaux were recovered.

However, far from resting on his laurels or pleading exhaustion, Worsley immediately held a conference with McDouall to propose that there was a momentary opportunity to mount an immediate strike to capture or sink the two American vessels. In his turn, McDouall fully backed this proposal and provided a detachment of volunteers from the Royal Newfoundland Regiment to supplement Worsley's crew.[*5]

Four bateaux were prepared to mount this attack, two of which were armed by the jury-rigging of a small field gun in the bow and manned by volunteers from the Royal Artillery.

Departing Michilimackinac in the late afternoon of September 1, the small flotilla arrived off the Detour near sunset the following day. With only six miles (ten kilometers) to go to reach the last known position of the enemy, it was decided to hide up for the night and make a reconnaissance

RAIDING PARTY ON THE *SCORPION* AND *TIGRESS*, AUGUST 1814[*5]

Boat 1 (Lieutenant Miller Worsley): Crew of Royal Navy sailors (1 Officer, 17 Seamen) with a 6-pounder gun
Boat 2 (Lieutenant Andrew Bulger): Crew of Royal Newfoundland Regiment and Royal Artillery detachment with a 3-pounder gun
Boat 3 (Lieutenant Armstrong): Crew of Royal Newfoundland Regiment
Boat 4 (Lieutenant Radenhurst): Crew of Royal Newfoundland Regiment

Total: Royal Newfoundland Regiment: 3 Officers, 54 Other Ranks

Royal Artillery: 6–8 Other Ranks
North West Company Canoe: Robert Livingston and volunteers
Native Allied Canoes (Mr. Dickson, Head of the Indian Department): Unspecified number of craft and warriors

in the morning. Before dawn on September 3, and leaving the bulk of the men behind, Worsley, Livingston, and a handful of experienced men moved forward in a single canoe, only to find that the *Tigress* alone was anchored in the narrows. This could not have been better for the attackers' chances of success as the entire attacking force could concentrate on the single vessel rather than having to make a simultaneous raid on two.

Wasting no time, the party returned to its advance base and made plans that would see the attack made by the four main boats, while the Native contingent would remain in support. Setting out as the sun began to set, the four boats stealthily approached the *Tigress* under the cover of darkness and then separated so that Worsley and Armstrong could board on the starboard (right) side of the vessel, while Bulger and Radenhust came from the port (left). Unaware of the approaching danger, the ship's commander, Sailing Master Champlin, and his composite crew of thirty-one sailors and troops did have at least one sentry on duty, and their 24-pounder cannon was loaded to fire at the first sign of the enemy. These precautions proved unavailing, for once the British were finally spotted they were already within ten yards (nine meters).

Challenged by the deck watch, the British made no reply but pulled hard to close the final distance as the first shots came from the *Tigress*. Fortunately, the single round (probably of canister- or grape-shot) fired from the 24-pounder cannon whistled overhead as the four boats reached their target and the men swarmed up and over the bulwarks to engage the Americans on their own deck. In the ensuing melee, surprise and swiftness proved the decisive factor, and within the hour, the captured and disarmed American crew was secured below decks, with casualties of three officers wounded, three crewmen dead, and three wounded.[6]

With one down and one to go, Worsley's interrogation of his prisoners revealed the *Scorpion* was due back at any time. Sending the American prisoners back to Michilimackinac with the Native warriors, Worsley decided to use the *Tigress* as a Trojan horse to capture the missing *Scorpion*. Sending Robert Livingston down the lake to provide an early warning, Worsley and some of his men disguised themselves as ship's crew, while the remainder hid below decks out of sight and waited. He also kept the American flag flying on the mainmast. Given ample warning by Livingston the following day, the British were primed and ready as the *Scorpion*, under Lieutenant Turner, slowly sailed to a position two miles (3.2 kilometers) off and dropped anchor, as well as giving sure signs that they saw nothing amiss aboard the *Tigress*. Allowing the night to pass uneventfully, Worsley used a light dawn breeze to quietly slip the *Tigress's* anchor cable, hoist sails on the jib and foremast, and allow the lake's current and wind to drift him down on his still-unsuspecting adversary as a duty party of five men were in the act of washing down their decks. It was therefore not until the *Tigress* opened up with her 24-pounder cannon at a paint-blistering twelve yards (eleven meters), that Turner and his thirty-two-man composite crew learned of their imminent peril. Using the cannon's fire as their signal, the British troops swarmed out of hiding, delivered a volley of musket shots across the rapidly diminishing gap between the two vessels, and as soon as the hulls scraped, clambered over the rails and onto the wet American deck. Totally unprepared, the Americans had virtually no chance to defend themselves and in a matter of minutes, with a growing casualty list of two killed and two wounded, Turner hauled down his colours. From the double attack, the British casualties were later assessed at three killed and one wounded from the sailors' detachment, one artilleryman wounded, and one officer and six men wounded from the Newfoundlanders.[7]

The battle was over and naval control of the upper Great Lakes had completely reversed itself. Michilimackinac was secure, the supply lines to the south had been restored, and two American warships were prizes of war, which promised monetary rewards for their daring captors. In addition, as the vessels were captured undamaged, they could now not only defend Britain's interests throughout the upper lakes, but under their new names, *Surprise* (formerly *Tigress*) and *Confiance* (formerly *Scorpion*), bring up substantially larger volumes of supplies on each trip. In fact, by the end of October, two large convoys of canoes and supply trips to the Nottawasaga by both vessels had restocked Michilimackinac with a staggering arsenal of weapons, food, and other supplies that included

Mackinac Island, William Dashwood, artist, circa 1820–1829. Natives watch as Fort Michilimackinac fires a gun in salute upon the arrival of the captured *Tigress* and *Scorpion*.

5,000 rounds of ammunition; 200 muskets and rifles; 3,933 pounds of black powder; 1,000 blankets; and 4,000 pounds of flour.[8]

For the remainder of the war, no further efforts were made by the Americans to recover the position of Michilimackinac, and it was not until well after the treaty of peace had been signed that this vital post was actually returned to American ownership on July 18, 1815, when the British garrison

transferred to its newly built position at Fort Collier on Drummond Island at the Detour. In a further side note, the wreck of the *Nancy*'s hull was gradually entombed within a sandbar that accumulated around its sunken timbers until it became hidden and lost to record. That is, until it was rediscovered in 1927, excavated, and put on display at what today is called Nancy Island, at Wasaga Beach.

CHAPTER 10

Finale on the Chippawa River

Back on the Niagara frontier, having retired north from Fort Erie on the evening of September 21, 1814, the British established a defence-in-depth strategy in the territory lying between Frenchman's Creek and Chippawa, so that if pressed, the advance elements could retire on successively stronger forces and slow the American advance until the main British forces at Chippawa, Lundy's Lane, Queenston, and the river mouth forts could be brought into action. This redeployment also had the advantage of placing forces at the vulnerable river-crossing points between Queenston and Lake Ontario, as there were reports that Major General George Izard was advancing on the frontier from Sackets Harbor with Chauncey's fleet in support.

Major General George Izard. From the A. Conger Goodyear Manuscript Collection Vol. 9.

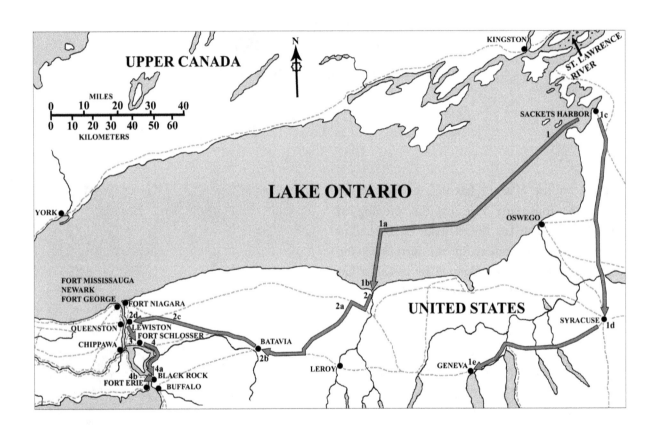

GENERAL IZARD'S ARMY'S ROUTE TO THE NIAGARA FRONTIER, SEPTEMBER–OCTOBER, 1814

1. General Izard and his troops sail (1) from Sackets Harbor on September 21, 1814. The following day, the American transport ships change course (1a) and unilaterally disembark Izard's force at the Genesee River (Rochester, NY), (1b) leaving Izard with no option but to continue the journey on foot. Simultaneously, his heavy baggage and artillery have difficulties moving overland (1c–1d–1e) along bad roads in poor weather conditions.
2. Izard's men are forced to leave most of their supplies and camp equipment behind as they start their march (2) but find that the "lower" lake road leading west is virtually impassable due to the weather and flooding. Looking for a better route, General Izard detours his force (2a) to the "higher" inland road, passing through Batavia, where he meets with General Brown on September 27 (2b). Leaving Batavia on October 1, Izard's force follows the higher "ridge" road (2c) and arrives at Lewiston (2d) on October 5.
3. Following further discussions, General Izard decides against attacking Fort Niagara or mounting a river crossing at Queenston. Instead he marches his army south (3) to Fort Schlosser on October 8, with the intent of crossing directly above the Great Falls.
4. Without sufficient boats to complete the crossing in a single wave, Izard again decides to march south (4) to Black Rock (4a) and makes his crossing there (4b) on October 10–11.

The following morning, the Americans made their regular scouting probes toward the British lines, only to find there was no one there to oppose them. Emerging from the fort, the Americans overran the deserted British encampment before moving north in a cautious and slow pursuit, until they made contact with the British rearguard at Frenchman's Creek. At this point, Brown made no further effort to press the British, as his own force was not above 2,500 regulars and a similar number of militia, a total Brown considered insufficient to deal with his (over)estimate of some four thousand British, established in strong defences, and expecting two additional regular regiments as reinforcements. On the other hand, Brown expected that General Izard would soon arrive with his force of over four thousand to attack Fort Niagara, catching the British between the two American armies. However, General Izard was having significant problems in getting his forces into the region.

This delay was once again due to the uncooperative attitude of Commodore Chauncey, who would authorize the use of only a few of his vessels for transporting troops toward the Niagara, while the rest remained at the east end of the lake to maintain the blockade of Kingston. Consequently, Izard was forced to send his artillery, cavalry, and most of his supplies overland, along roads and tracks that had deteriorated under the virtually continuous rains of the previous month. Boarding the assigned vessels, some 2,500 troops were then forced to wait on the exposed decks until the weather improved. Finally setting sail on September 21, the fleet had been underway for only a day when the flotilla commander changed course and unilaterally landed Izard's troops at the Genesee River (Rochester, New York), only halfway to the Niagara River. Without any wagons or other adequate transport, Izard was forced to abandon most of his army's tents and supplies, while the troops plodded through repeated rainstorms and the quagmire of mud that passed for roads, eventually reaching Lewiston on October 5.

While still advancing toward the frontier, Major General Izard met with Major General Brown at Batavia on September 27, and as the senior ranking officer, Izard took official command of the combined forces on the Niagara frontier. Together the two generals planned a campaign of attack that would see Izard besiege and assault Fort Niagara and then force a crossing of the Niagara River at Queenston, while Brown and his force would press north from Frenchman's Creek to the Chippawa. They also planned to deliberately leak the disinformation that a landing was to be made on the north side of Lake Erie, near to Port Dover, for an attack on Burlington Heights. Once Izard arrived at Lewiston, additional discussions with Generals Brown and Porter, supported by reconnaissance reports from his field commanders, determined that without heavy guns to batter down the walls, Fort Niagara would be a costly prize to assault. Nor were there any seaworthy boats available to ferry troops across the river below the Falls. Izard instead decided to march south to Fort Schlosser and cross there, while Brown's force would push the British back from their advance positions, uniting the American force into a single body that would greatly outnumber the British and force a passage across the Chippawa River.

On the other side of the Niagara River, although his forces were relatively well positioned, General Drummond was deeply concerned about the continued viability of maintaining his forces on the frontier. For despite having been placed under pressure from both Drummond and Prevost, Commodore Yeo had still made no effort to push the American blockade aside and bring up supplies for the army. This left Drummond with no choice but to cut the army rations once again and requisition all of the available crops and cattle within the region. He then dispatched troops to act as farm labourers in gathering and threshing what little remained of the rain-soaked crops of grain.

Through the exertions of the Incorporated Militia employed on that duty, the greatest part of the grain in the possession of the farmers in front of Chippawa has been threshed out, and the produce generally withdrawn for the use of the army. The inhabitants themselves had driven their cattle behind the Black Creek on the first movement of the troops ...[1]

— General Drummond to Sir George Prevost, October 2, 1814

Nor were matters helped by the ongoing problems caused by the rains on the forts at the mouth of the river. In fact, so weak were the defences of Fort Niagara that it was feared the remaining walls and emplacements were on the verge of collapse and could not hope to deter the Americans if they chose to attack.

I have visited the forts, and I find that of Niagara in a deplorable state as to defence against any attack by heavy cannon, the foundation of the parapet having given way, and with it the frieze; the picketing, however remains, except on the southeast bastion towards Fort George, where by an immense breach in the earthwork, the picketing has been carried off on the lake face. Almost the whole of the parapet has sunk, and in the centre demi-bastion it has been necessary to remove the gun. Nothing but piles still support any superstructure, and the difficulty attending this mode of repairs will be very great ...[2]

— Drummond to Prevost, September 28, 1814

With the arrival of Izard's force on October 5, Drummond's fear that his dispersed forces could be caught between two armies led him to order the withdrawal of most of his advance forces to the north side of the Chippawa River, leaving only a reduced screen of light troops on the south bank.

An extensive encampment was discovered opposite to Queenston (at some distance in the interior) early this morning. Lights and fires had been observed during the whole of last night, for the first time. I cannot doubt that this is General Izard's force. A number of mounted officers have been seen reconnoitring the banks of the river opposite Queenston at different times today.... Major General De Watteville ... expects to find Brown opposite to him every hour. The Major General still continues at Black Creek at my request, notwithstanding there

(Above) *Fort Niagara*, J.H. Slade, artist, circa 1814. The dilapidated and collapsed sections of picket walls are clearly seen in this view from Newark (Niagara-on-the-Lake). (Below) A similar (if better preserved) perspective in 2012.

Chippawa but the Glengarry Light Infantry, four light companies ... the Incorporated Militia and two field pieces. If pressed he is directed to fall back upon the 6th Regiment at Chippawa and to defend that post ...[3]

— Drummond to Prevost, October 6, 1814

By the morning of October 9, 1814, the bulk of the contending armies of General Drummond and General Izard were facing each other across the Falls of Niagara, while General Brown's force was preparing to advance south from Frenchman's Creek. A major battle now seemed inevitable. Unfortunately for Izard's plan, there were only sufficient boats available to transport a quarter of the army in a single crossing. Unwilling to risk having his force caught and attacked while divided, Izard decided to march to Buffalo and cross in relative safety, but was then delayed by having to rebuild the bridge to cross the Tonawanda Creek. Thus it was not until October 11 that the last of his force was on the Canadian side of the river at Fort Erie.[*4]

Joining up with the Seventeenth Regiment (497, all ranks) that had arrived from the Detroit area only days before, Izard's combined force marched from Fort Erie on the thirteenth and linked up with

GENERAL IZARD'S DIVISION, NIAGARA FRONTIER, OCTOBER 6, 1814[*4]

1st Brigade (Brigadier General Daniel Bissell)
Fifth Regiment (Colonel Bowyer): 394 All Ranks
Fourteenth Regiment (Major Barnard): 438 All Ranks
Fifteenth Regiment (Colonel Brealey): 400 All Ranks
Sixteenth Regiment (Colonel Pearce): 444 All Ranks

2nd Brigade (Brigadier General Smith)
Fourth Regiment (Colonel Purdy): 555 All Ranks
Tenth Regiment (Lieutenant Colonel Clinch): 322 All Ranks
Twelfth Regiment (Colonel Coles): 532 All Ranks
Seventeenth Regiment (Colonel Miller): 616 All Ranks

Artillery (Captain Archer)
181 All Ranks

Cavalry (Lieutenant Colonel Eustis)
Number unknown

the "remains of Brown's division and the New York volunteers under General Porter ..."[5] before continuing north toward Chippawa with a reorganized force recorded as composed of the 1st Division (General Izard): 3,500 regulars, all ranks; the 2nd Division (General Brown): 2,000 regulars, all ranks; and 800 militia volunteers, all ranks.[6]

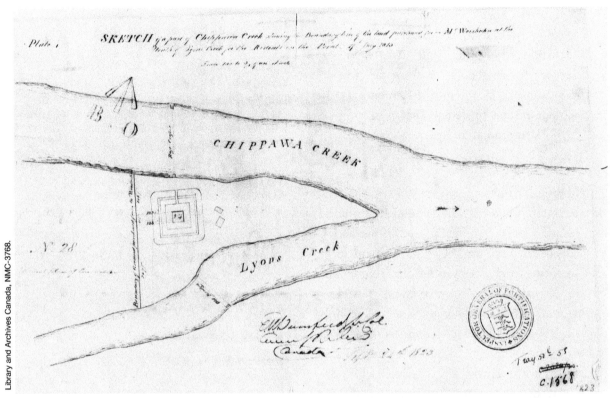

A postwar map showing the junction of the Chippawa (Welland) River and Lyon's Creek with the small redoubt and earthwork constructed on the strategic point to prevent the Americans using this location to pass over the river and outflank the British defences.

Delayed once again by the destruction of the bridges crossing the various creeks, the American army finally reached the south bank of the Chippawa River on October 15 but disconcerted at the strength of the defences thrown up by the British, made no attack. Instead, Izard initially attempted to entice the British into open battle by commencing an artillery bombardment of their defences, but without success, leaving him little alternative but to retire to Street's Creek and establish his camp on the same ground originally occupied by Brown's army at the outset of the campaign in July.

As a countermeasure to these series of movements, Drummond had maintained a close watch on both Izard's force and any potential landing point on the north shore of Lake Erie. By October 10, he undertook to redeploy his troops so as to be able to react to several possible routes of American attack. He also ordered the construction of a blockhouse at the junction of Lyon's Creek with the Chippawa River to prevent the Americans using that position to construct a bridge and outflank his defence lines, as they had nearly succeeded in doing against General Riall in July.

Notified of the advance of Izard and his army from Fort Erie by his few remaining Native scouts on October 12, Drummond maintained contact with the American advance forces and withdrew his own advance troops to an earthwork constructed at the south end of the Chippawa bridge. Here he awaited the arrival of the Americans on the fifteenth and was pleased to see them balk at the sight of his defences.

Prevented from attacking directly across the Chippawa, Izard sent scouts upstream on October 16 to locate crossing points that would allow him to cross and outflank the British positions. Drummond anticipated this probe and effectively blocked the Americans at every point. At the same time, Izard received word that with the completion of the British warship *St. Lawrence,* and the expected emergence of the entire British fleet from Kingston to contest for the mastery of Lake Ontario, Chauncey and his entire fleet had quit the lake for the season and had retired on Sackets Harbor — with no intention of emerging again that year. This finally gave Yeo control of the lake and consequently Izard fully expected Drummond to receive substantial reinforcements within days, instead of weeks.

Convinced that any further attempts to continue the campaign as originally intended would result in failure and possible disaster, Izard retired his army to Black Creek on October 17. So suddenly had this American movement taken place, that when a party of men from the Incorporated Militia Regiment reached the abandoned American camp later that day, they found large amounts of camp equipage and tents either burned or simply abandoned. In addition, they saw two boats rowing across the river from Fort Schlosser. Hiding in the undergrowth, they allowed the boats to approach the shore and succeeded in capturing one, while the other desperately rowed back out into midstream. Upon questioning the captured crew, it was revealed that they had been ordered over to Fort Schlosser only that morning, to collect food from that depot, and had no inkling of the American intention to retreat. As a result, desperately needed "fresh meat, bread, and spirits, for at least a brigade …"[7] fell into

AMERICAN FORCE, PROBE ON COOK'S MILL, OCTOBER 19, 1814[8]

Brigadier General Bissell
Fifth Regiment (Colonel Pinckney)
Fourteenth Regiment (Major Bernard)
Fifteenth Regiment (Major Grindage)
Sixteenth Regiment (Colonel Pierce/Pearce)
Fourth Rifle Regiment (Captain Irvine): 1 Company
Light Dragoons (Lieutenant Anspaugh): Detachment
Artillery (Captain Archer): Detachment

Estimated Total: 900–1,000 All Ranks

BRITISH FORCE, PROBE ON COOK'S MILL, OCTOBER 19, 1814[9]

Infantry (Lieutenant Colonel Myres, Deputy Quartermaster General)
82nd Regiment (Major Proctor)
100th Regiment (Lieutenant Colonel the Marquis of Tweeddale)
104th Regiment (Unknown Commander): Detachment
Glengarry Light Infantry (Lieutenant Colonel Battersby)

Artillery (Lieutenant Carter R.A.)
Royal Artillery: 1 x 6-pounder and Crew
Royal Marine Rocket Troop: Detachment

Estimated Total: 750 Other Ranks

the welcoming arms of the Canadian soldiers. On the eighteenth, Izard made a final attempt to outflank the Chippawa line by sending a strong force, under the command of Brigadier General Daniel Bissell, six miles (ten kilometers) inland from the Niagara to Cook's Mills on Lyon's Creek.[8]

As part of this force's mission, they were to locate crossing points along the river that could be used to move the American army around the British right flank, seize any stockpiles of grain found at the mill, and destroy the mill itself.

The Americans marched from their camp during the morning of October 18, following the line of Black Creek until they cut across country to Cook's Mills and established a camp at the mill. They then set up a strong forward picket of three companies on the north side of Lyon's Creek, while the remaining troops set about collecting the stock of grain stored at the site. While General Drummond was concerned about this American movement, and made plans to redeploy a significant number of troops west to meet this developing threat should it prove necessary, at this point he simply ordered Lieutenant Colonel Myres (Deputy Quartermaster General) to take a strong reconnaissance force and ensure the Americans did not penetrate behind the British lines. Myres was also strongly directed not to hazard his force unnecessarily.[9]

MOVEMENTS ON THE NIAGARA RIVER FRONTIER, SEPTEMBER–OCTOBER 1814

September 21: British forces abandon the siege of Fort Erie and retire to the Chippawa River, implementing a defence-in-depth strategy with advance posts as far ahead as Frenchman's Creek (1–1a).

September 22: American forces advance and occupy the British siege lines but do not initiate any pursuit beyond Frenchman's Creek (2).

October 6: With the arrival of Izard's army at Lewiston, Drummond begins a consolidation of his force, gradually withdraws his advance posts between Chippawa and Frenchman's Creek, and makes strenuous efforts to fortify the Chippawa line.

October 9: General Brown begins a cautious series of probes toward Chippawa, forcing the British outposts to gradually retire.

October 10–11: General Izard's army crosses the Niagara River at Fort Erie.

October 13: The united American forces begin an advance toward the Chippawa from Fort Erie (3–3a).

October 15: The united American forces advance to the Chippawa River but make no serious effort to test the British defences (4–4a). Instead they retire to Street's Creek (4b).

October 17: Without notice, General Izard orders a further withdrawal to Black Creek (5–5a).

October 18: An American force (Brigadier General Daniel Bissell) marches by way of Black Creek to Cook's Mills to seize any supplies and destroy the mill (6–6a).

October 18: British forces (Lieutenant Colonel Myres) are dispatched from Chippawa to counter the American movement (7–7a), leading to intermittent skirmishing late in the afternoon and throughout the night.

October 19: Following a limited engagement during the morning, heavy rain and mutual caution end the action, after which both sides retire to their original positions. The mill is not destroyed.

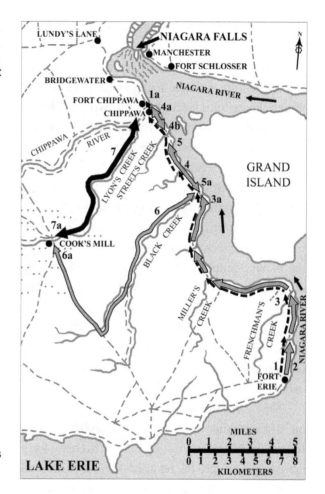

As the British advance force (Glengarry Light Infantry) made contact with the American pickets (Fifth Infantry and Fourteenth Infantry) late in the evening, sporadic firing broke out and continued throughout the night as the two small forces manoeuvred for position. The following morning, under rainy conditions, the main British force advanced and began to force the American pickets back on their camp. Retiring in good order, the pickets slowed the British progress long enough for the main American force to form along the south bank of the creek and prepare to do battle, while the pickets continued to hold onto the north side of the bridge. With the rain-swollen creek dividing the two forces and the only means of crossing held by the American pickets and covered by the fire of the main American line, the British were unable to press forward. Instead, they began a steady exchange of fire with the Americans.

Seeing that the British were not willing to hazard an attack against his strong line, Bissell decided to take the offensive. Pushing most of his main force across the bridge, he retained the Fifteenth and Sixteenth Regiments as a reserve, while advancing the Fifth Regiment to the left, in an attempt to turn the British right flank and cut off its line of retreat. At the same time, the Fourteenth Regiment was similarly moved forward and ordered to support the pickets, before charging the British guns from the front.

The modern lethargic course of Lyon's Creek at Cook's Mills, immediately adjacent to the battlefield.

Witnessing this American advance, Lieutenant Colonel Myres consulted with Lieutenant Colonel the Marquis of Tweeddale, and together they decided that maintaining their open position and engaging in close combat with a larger American force would not conform to General Drummond's specific orders not to hazard their troops. Therefore, the British force was ordered to retire, covered by a strong rearguard from the Glengarry Light Infantry.

Bissell could now have pressed his advantage, but chose instead to halt the advance and sent his pickets to shadow the British and provide warning should they return. By noon, the weather had deteriorated into a downpour of freezing rain and

The Cook's Mills battlefield memorial cairn, located on the northern bank of Lyon's Creek in the small community of Cooksmills.

there was no sign of the British making another attack. Nor could there be any advantage gained by pressing farther north through the dense bush, where his troops could be ambushed on the narrow trail. Therefore, after burying the dead from both sides,[10] he ordered his troops back across Lyon's Creek and prepared to return to the camp at the Niagara River. Removing what stores of grain were available, Bissell chose not to destroy the mill itself, perhaps recognizing that no serious advantage could be gained by this act of destruction so late in the season, and that for all intents and purposes, the year's campaign was over. Returning to camp, Bissell found that his decision to retire was matched by Izard's conclusion that with the deterioration in the weather, the lack of support from Chauncey, and the increased levels of sickness appearing among the troops, it would be in the best interests of the army to establish winter quarters back at Fort Erie and Buffalo and begin plans for next year's campaign. In addition, Izard had serious concerns about the security of Sackets Harbor and decided to detach General Brown and a sizeable part of the army back to that location to support its defences.

> I have just learned by express from Sackett's Harbor that Commodore Chauncey, with the whole of his fleet, has retired into port, and is throwing up batteries for its protection. This defeats all the objects of the operations by land in this quarter. I may turn Chippawa and should General Drummond not retire, may succeed in giving him a great deal of trouble, but if he falls back on Fort George or Burlington Heights, every step I take in pursuit exposes me to be cut off by the large reinforcements it is in the power of the enemy to throw in twenty-four hours upon my flank or rear. All the artillery and all the ordnance stores are inadequate to the siege of one of the enemy's fortresses. Three-fourths of the arms of the troops from the westward are unfit for service. The severe season is approaching.... I confess, Sir, that I am greatly embarrassed. At the head of the most efficient army the United States have possessed during this war, much must be expected from me — and yet I can discern no object which can be achieved at this point worthy of the risk which will attend its attempt.... The opinions of all the principal officers whom I have spoken with on the subject are against attempts which can result in no national advantage, and which, even if successful, would be attended by the unavoidable loss of many men now more valuable than ever. Under these circumstances, should no opening present in a few days to obtain an immediate advantage over the enemy, I shall feel it my duty to commence immediate preparations for the distribution of the troops in winter quarters at such places as will enable them to assemble with celerity round any menaced point ...[11]
>
> — General Izard to the secretary of war, October 16, 1814

Drummond soon became aware of Izard's retrograde movement and pushed forward detachments of cavalry, Incorporated Militia, and Native allies to locate and shadow the Americans. He also fully expected that with the arrival of Yeo's squadron, he would at last be receiving the vitally needed supplies and reinforcements that he had been clamouring for, for so long. Once the fleet arrived, Drummond found to his dismay that Yeo had brought up only five hundred men of the 90th Regiment, while the rest were being forced to march to the frontier along almost impassable roads. In addition, only part of the supplies designated for the army were in the ship's holds, as Yeo still considered his "mission" to be separate from the army's and was unwilling to subordinate himself and his fleet to anything less than the defeat of Chauncey's warships. To say that Drummond was infuriated by this attitude would be a gross understatement. Nor was Prevost far behind, and he made his opinion on this matter clear to Lord Bathurst in England:

> Thus instead of that zealous, prompt, and cheerful co-operation so essential to the movement and very existence of His Majesty's troops on this widely extended frontier, every demand for the transport either of men or of stores is considered as hampering the powers of the fleet and endangering its safety …[12]
>
> — Prevost to Bathurst, October 18, 1814

Without the supplies or manpower he felt were necessary to pursue the Americans back to Fort Erie, Drummond attempted to obtain the loan of a detachment of Royal Marines from Yeo's fleet to supplement his forces, but this request was immediately rebuffed by the commodore. Left without any options for resuming offensive operations, General Drummond began the process of removing as many of his sick and wounded as possible from the battle zone to Newark, where, despite Yeo's objections, they were loaded aboard the commodore's ships for the journey to York and Kingston.

Once the American army was on the march to Fort Erie, General Brown crossed over to Buffalo to begin his journey to Sackets Harbor, arriving there on October 30. Behind him, he left his troops in the hands of Brigadier General Winder, who had returned to the Niagara frontier after his poor showing at Washington and was now left with the challenge of supervising the march of Brown's once-proud and efficient army away from the Niagara frontier. In abysmal weather and along terrible roads, around two thousand veterans of the 1814 campaign began a forced march back to Sackets Harbor on October 24. From this, only 1,500 ragged and footsore individuals actually completed the journey on November 13. In a similar manner, General Porter's Militia Brigade had crossed back into the United States by the twenty-fifth and was marched to Batavia, where the men were first disarmed and then officially dismissed from service, but without receiving the back pay owed to them. After

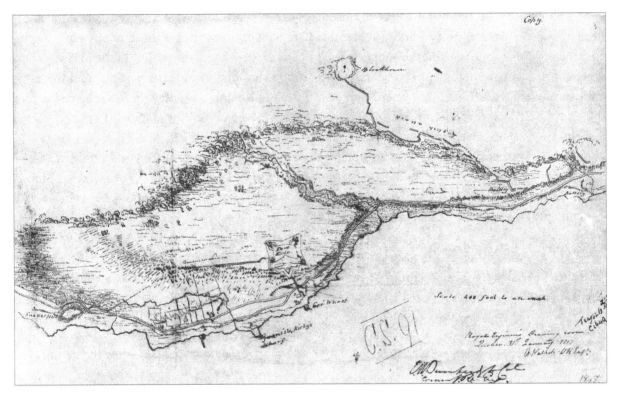

(Above) A map produced by Lieutenant A. Walpole of the Royal Engineers Regiment, Quebec, January 31, 1818, showing the abandoned 1814 British siege lines and Fort Erie after it had been "slighted" (partially demolished) by the Americans upon their departure from Canada in November 1814.

removing most of the supplies and wounded from Fort Erie, Izard was initially inclined to maintain a strong garrison at the fort, with the bulk of his force at Black Rock and Buffalo in support. However, he soon realized that the oncoming winter weather could isolate the garrison from any practical support for days at a time and leave it vulnerable to attack. He therefore made the difficult decision to abandon the Canadian side of the river entirely and destroy the encampment and fortifications of Fort Erie.

Starting on October 25, Izard's chief quartermaster, Major Camp, supervised the evacuation of Fort Erie with a round-the-clock shuttle service of boats, while Captain Archer of the artillery oversaw the demolition and destruction of the defensive works created with such effort over the previous three months. Although bad weather frequently interrupted work, the evacuation continued without interference from the nearby British pickets until the last of the American regimental forces, guns, and ammunition were removed. Finally, on November 5, 1814, the rearguard ignited the fuses on numerous demolition charges placed throughout the fort and ran for the boats waiting to ferry them to the American side of the river. To the accompaniment of repeated detonations and a swelling column of fire and smoke rising from Fort Erie, the last American troops left the Canadian shore without achieving a single one of their objectives or penetrating more than ten miles (sixteen kilometers) from the Niagara River into Upper Canada.

CHAPTER 11

Desolation and Scorched Earth: "Total War" Comes to Upper Canada, October 1814

With Izard's forces gone, the principal perceived threat to Upper Canada had seemingly ended. However, this was not to be the end of the conflict as far as the citizens of southwestern Upper Canada were concerned. For just as had occurred at the start of the year when the British command was occupied with the war on the Niagara and most of the available troops, both regular and militia, were drawn into the fighting on that front, the no man's land of the Grand River and Thames Valley were again vulnerable to American incursions. (For details see *The Tide of War*.) During August and September of 1814, a number of small American raiding parties had terrorized farmsteads throughout the area bounded by Dover Mills, the Talbot settlement, Delaware, and Oxford: burning farmhouses, barns, and crops in the fields; driving off

Although some of these images were painted some twenty or more years after the war, they still indicate the primitive frontier conditions that remained at that time and severely challenged the movement of troops in Upper Canada during the War of 1812–1815.

1. *Between York and Cobourg*, J.P. Cockburn, circa 1830.

2. *Making a Road*, J.P. Cockburn, circa 1830.

3. *Making a Clearing*, G. Whitmore, circa 1836.

4. *A First Settlement*, W.H. Bartlett, circa 1842.

5. *Corduroy Road near Guelph, Upper Canada*, H.B. Martin, artist, circa 1832. A "corduroy" road, constructed of baulks of cut timber, was designed to create a raised pathway for wagons to drive (bone-jarringly) through regions of wet or swampy ground.

or killing cattle; and engaging in wholesale looting of private property. They had also engaged in a policy of either killing or taking off men known to be officers in the local militias, while those from the ranks were forced to sign paroles. Although minor skirmishes with local militia detachments had inflicted some casualties on the marauders, these incidents of defiance seemed to have only increased the degree of wanton destruction being inflicted by subsequent raiding parties, leading to a general sense of dread amongst the communities concerned. In addition, for those regions of Upper Canada that bordered the Detroit River and were directly under U.S. occupation, the district's self-styled "Military and Civilian Commandant," Lieutenant Colonel John Miller (Seventeenth Infantry) found his command was so short of food, that he issued the following draconian proclamation:

> Whereas information has been received that the citizens of … [Upper Canada] … have on hand large quantities of surplus grain … the citizens of said district are required and positively commanded to bring and deliver … all the flour, wheat, and oats which they may have, more than is absolutely necessary for the use and consumption of their families…. [Appointed American agents will] … receive and pay for the flour and grain … [at prices unilaterally set by the agents.] … Any flour, wheat, and oats … not delivered … on or before the first day of November next, shall be immediately destroyed and the person or persons withholding such supplies … or failing to deliver within the time prescribed, shall be severely punished …[1]

At the end of October, a new level of destruction scythed its way through southwestern Upper Canada as a sizeable body of over seven hundred American militia and American Native allied troops engaged in a "scorched earth" policy during their march from Detroit, up the Sydenham River, through the Longwoods region (near present-day London, Ontario), south along the western bank of the Grand River, and then west along the Talbot Road. Ironically this incursion, led by Brigadier General Duncan McArthur (Twenty-Sixth Regiment), had actually been planned for execution in September, with the combined intent of:

- Intimidating and permanently subduing the Native tribes living along the Detroit corridor and throughout the Michigan Territory. This was considered necessary because those

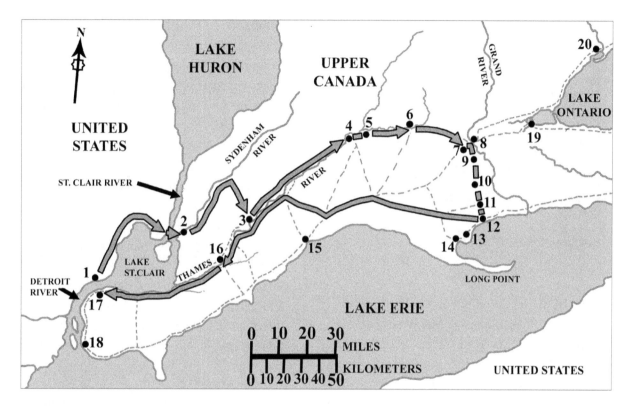

THE ROUTE FOLLOWED BY THE MCARTHUR RAID, OCTOBER–NOVEMBER 1814

1. Detroit
2. Baldroon (Wallaceburg area)
3. Moravianstown
4. Delaware
5. Westminster (London area)
6. Oxford (Ingersoll–Beachville area)
7. Burford
8. Brantford
9. Malcolm's Mills (Oakland)
10. Sovereign's and Sayle's Mills (Waterford)
11. Union Mills (Simcoe)
12. Culver's Tavern
13. Tisdale's Mills
14. Backhouse Mill (Backus Mill)
15. Port Talbot
16. Forks of the Thames (Chatham)
17. Sandwich (Windsor)
18. Amherstburg [Fort Malden]
19. Burlington Heights (Hamilton)
20. York (Toronto) [Fort York]

AMERICAN RAIDING FORCE, OCTOBER 1814[2]

Kentucky and Ohio State Volunteers: Estimated Combined Total 650 Other Ranks
U.S. Rangers (Captain W. McCormick): Est. 50 Other Ranks
Michigan Territory "Captain Audrain's" Rangers (Lieutenant Rutland) and Michigan Territory Volunteers (George McDougall): Est. 50 Other Ranks
American Native Allied Warriors: Est. 70–80 Warriors

Estimated Total: 700–800 All Ranks

Native tribes, initially cowed after the defeat of their British allies at Moravianstown and the death of their own leader, Tecumseh, had recently been showing increasing signs of vocal opposition and making threats toward U.S. authorities — especially after the failure of the American expedition to retake Michilimackinac. This led to the inevitable American conclusion that the British were once again exploiting the opportunity to incite the Native tribes to fight on their side.

- Cutting any renewed British supply corridors to the Native tribes who might become actively hostile behind the American front lines.
- Striking back against the British for the humiliations of Michilimackinac and the loss of their two warships in Lake Huron.
- Continuing the already established American policy of destroying the agricultural infrastructure of southwestern Upper Canada so as to intensify the supply crisis for the British army on the Niagara frontier.
- Striking at weakly defended posts behind the British lines or where militia forces predominated, so as to gain swift and easy victories, which would spread panic and present a significant flanking threat to Drummond's activities at the Niagara River.
- Attacking and occupying Burlington Heights and then linking up with Izard and Brown's forces on the Niagara, should the opportunity present itself.

Had McArthur's force moved off a month or so earlier, it could have precipitated a crisis for the British and forced Drummond to split his forces, giving the Americans a very significant advantage of position and numbers at a decisive moment of the campaign. However, due to McArthur's determination to fully provide his force with an adequate transport of boats and horses, plus his excessive security measures (to prevent any warning reaching the British), the preparations took far longer than anticipated.

Consequently their departure from Detroit was delayed until October 24, 1814.

Once on the move, McArthur led his troops,[*2] all of whom were mounted, north from Detroit, having spread the false report that their targets were the Native villages in Michigan bordering Saginaw Bay. Passing north of Lake St. Clair, McArthur used his supply boats to ferry his force across the St. Clair River on October 26, before beginning his campaign of destruction by pillaging and then razing the Baldroon settlement (near present-day Wallaceburg). Riding along the bank of the Bear River (Sydenham River), the Americans continued their wholesale policy of looting and arson at each and every hamlet and isolated farmstead that came in sight or reach, until they came to a point north of the already destroyed community of Moravianstown, whereupon they marched overland to the Thames River, arriving there on October 30. Throughout this advance, McArthur had continued to obsess about keeping his advance toward Burlington Heights a secret and had threatened severe reprisals upon anyone attempting to escape from American custody in order to warn the British. Nevertheless, some enterprising militia officers did succeed in sending word, although at the cost of seeing their homesteads burned to the ground. Ironically, McArthur's obsession with secrecy actually served to impede the American war effort;

for without a full knowledge of the threat this large force posed to his main supply base at Burlington Heights, Drummond kept the bulk of his forces on the Niagara, instead of being forced to split his army and fight on two fronts simultaneously.

Under normal circumstances, General Drummond's failure to defend his open flank would have allowed McArthur the opportunity to take Burlington Heights as planned. However, all was not well within McArthur's own force as dissent arose over precedence of the position of units within the column. In fact, this could more accurately be described as an argument over which unit would benefit from the opportunity to obtain extra plunder while being posted as the advance guard. This disagreement escalated to the point that men of the Michigan Volunteers insisted that their place in the vanguard had been usurped by other units and that if not reinstated they would unilaterally abandon the expedition, as their term of enlistment was due to expire.

In response, McArthur not only met and faced down these dissenters but also informed them that any men who absconded would be ordered hunted down by their own Native contingent. With the incipient mutiny temporarily quelled, McArthur continued his destructive advance through Delaware (November 2). Here the Michigan Volunteers acted upon their previous threat and as a body marched for Detroit, as by now their official term of enlistment had expired. Left with no realistic recourse but to either abandon the campaign and chase after the absconding troops or continue his advance and let the volunteers leave unchallenged and unpunished, McArthur moved on to raze Westminster (November 3), Oxford (November 4), and Burford, near the banks of the Grand River (November 5). Once at the river, he found it greatly swollen by the torrents of rain that had deluged the region over the past two months. In addition, as news of his advance had been leaked to the British (who had received reports that the American force varied from six hundred mounted men to a two-thousand-man force, composed of infantry, cavalry, and three cannon), the local military commander, Major Muir (41st Regiment) had destroyed the river ferry boat near Brantford and with a detachment of regulars, militia, and British Native allies had established a holding position on the far (east) bank of the Grand River, while warnings were dispatched to General Drummond. Following some inconclusive exchanges of fire between the two contending forces as the day waned, both sides established sentries that had little to fear, as neither side could readily cross the intervening torrent to attack its enemy.

By the following morning (November 6), McArthur had come to the conclusion that his attempt to attack Burlington Heights by surprise had failed and with the added news that Izard had retreated back across the Niagara River, it was now obvious that any attempt to press on would only expose his troops to an ever-increasing threat of counterattack by the enemy. Instead, he decided to change his plan and move south to continue his swath of destruction through the Long Point area and then return back toward Detroit along the Talbot settlement road and down the Thames Valley.

Leaving behind a rearguard of around a hundred men to keep the British fixed in place, McArthur and the remainder of his force moved south about ten miles (sixteen kilometers) to Malcolm's Mills, where he had intelligence that a force of Canadian militia had established a defensive position covering the main road.[*3]

CANADIAN MILITIA FORCE: BATTLE OF MALCOLM'S MILLS, NOVEMBER 6, 1814[*3]

1st Oxford County Embodied Militia Regiment
(Lieutenant Colonel Henry Bostwick)
1st Middlesex County Embodied Militia Regiment
(Major John Eakins)
1st Norfolk County Embodied Militia Regiment
(Lieutenant Colonel Joseph Ryerson)
2nd Norfolk County Embodied Militia Regiment
(Major George Salmon)

Estimated Total: 400 All Ranks

At Malcolm's Mills the Canadian troops had spent the previous two days constructing a barricade of tree limbs on a raised point of ground that overlooked the road and also provided an excellent field of fire down the slope and across a rain-swollen creek spanned by a narrow bridge that the militiamen had already destroyed. On the other hand, the men of the militias could only be considered as moderately trained and not capable of any advanced forms of manoeuvre or military combat. In addition, far from having any comprehensive or uniform cache of weapons and ammunition, the Canadians' arsenal consisted only of a motley assortment of military muskets of varying vintages, civilian muskets, rifles, and even shotguns — and all of varying calibres.

The American attack began late in the afternoon by elements of the Ohio State troops and American Native allies, who used the cover of the nearby forest to outflank the Canadian position and attack from the rear. Despite putting up strong initial resistance, the fate of the defenders was all but sealed and the position rendered untenable once the attack upon the rear was reinforced by the Kentucky troops making their own assault from the front. Casualties attributed to this skirmish vary considerably[4] depending on which side is telling the story, but for those Canadians lucky enough to avoid injury and escape capture, their only option was to slip off into the forest and make their way south to re-form their diminished detachments. For those taken, a forced parole effectively ended their further military involvement in the war for the foreseeable future.

With no other opposition in sight, McArthur and his troops continued their passage through the region, destroying or looting everything that came within reach, irrespective of whether it had any military value or was the private, civilian property of men, women, and even children. In this way the small communities at Malcolm's Mills, Sovereign's Mills, and Sayle's Mills (Waterford); Union Mills (Simcoe); and Culver's Tavern all suffered at the hands of the Americans. The only locations that somehow remained untouched were the more isolated Tisdale's Mills (north of Turkey Point) and

ESTIMATE OF CASUALTIES: BATTLE OF MALCOLM'S MILLS, NOVEMBER 6, 1814[4]

Canadian
According to the American account/ (according to the British account)
Killed: 1 Officer, 17 Other Ranks/ (3 Other Ranks)
Wounded: 9 Other Ranks/ (2 Other Ranks)
Prisoners: 8 Officers, 103 Other Ranks/ (not recorded)

American
Killed: 1 All Ranks
Wounded: 6 All Ranks

Backhouse Mill (north of Long Point). Nor were individual farms immune from assault, as the Americans continued west along the Talbot Road and then across country to the Thames Valley, leaving behind them a tract of devastation and human misery the likes of which had not been meted out on such a calculated basis and over such a wide area during any previous point in the war. Although there are a number of references to individuals and small groups of settlers fighting back and even ambushing the Americans during their withdrawal, the details of these events cannot, unfortunately, be detailed with certainty. Arriving back at Detroit on November 17, McArthur not only claimed a victory for the American war effort, but went out of his way to justify his men's directed excesses by blaming them on his Native allies.

> Of private property, no more was destroyed than was absolutely necessary for the support of the troops…. It is much to be regretted that there were some partial abuses produced by the Indians, whose customs in war impel them to plunder after victory; but for this blemish there was some excuse in their correct and gallant conduct before and during battle …[5]

In response to this incursion, Drummond was forced to transfer a number of regular detachments from the Niagara frontier to the Long Point area to bolster the local militias and patrol the Grand River line, resulting in an effective termination of American incursions for the remainder of the year.

With this final threat removed in the west and the Niagara once more firmly in British hands, General Drummond ordered his remaining troops to enter winter quarters, while he passed over command on the Niagara to Major General Stovin and sailed with the fleet to Kingston. Once there, he continued to press Yeo to send his vessels back up the lake with more of the supplies needed to feed the army throughout the forthcoming winter, only to have Yeo remain obdurate and uncooperative until the worsening weather made the point moot and all lake traffic ceased for the year, leaving the all-but-devastated regions of Niagara and southwestern Upper Canada to fend for themselves in the face of an increasingly bad winter.

CHAPTER 12

Planning for the New Year's Campaigns

During the initial months of 1815, both sides engaged in making elaborate and grandiose plans for the upcoming campaign season. The new American secretary of war, James Monroe, in conjunction with General Brown, contemplated making a concerted attack up the Champlain Valley to seize Montreal, while a secondary attack at Prescott would sever the Upper Canada lifeline and prevent any counterattack from Kingston. For this plan, they anticipated using over fifteen thousand regular troops and double that of militia, although how this invasion was to be paid for from the empty American treasury was not explained. Neither was how they expected to conquer the most strongly defended segment of North America, within which an estimated twenty-five thousand British regular and Fencible troops were garrisoned, all backed by series of well-fortified garrison posts, secure supply lines (thanks to the might of the British navy), and the entire as-yet relatively unused militias of Lower Canada.

In a similar fashion, the secretary of the navy, William Jones, looked to substantially enlarge the American fleets, not only at sea, but also on Lake Champlain and throughout the Great Lakes. Sackets Harbor in particular was to become the focus of a huge program of construction that would see, in short order, the launching of a flotilla of mega-warships, backed by a veritable fleet of smaller warships and gunboats that would eliminate the *St. Lawrence* and any other vessel the British dared to send out to challenge for the permanent command of Lake Ontario and the St. Lawrence River.

NAVY HALL ↑   ↑ FORT GEORGE

↓ BUTLER'S BARRACKS

Details from original artwork depicting British locations around Newark (Niagara-on-the-Lake).
(Above) *A View of Fort George, Navy Hall and New Niagara, Taken from the United States Fort of Old Niagara*, E. Walsh, artist, circa 1805.
(Below) *Butler's Barracks*, J.P. Cockburn, artist, 1829.

For the northern territories, Michilimackinac was to be retaken and all communications between the British and the western tribes were to be cut off.

However, behind the scenes, things were far from rosy for the American war effort, because America was effectively bankrupt, to the point where the U.S. treasury secretary, George Campbell, resigned his post in frustration over his inability to finance the government's demands. Furthermore, such was the political opposition to the continuation of the war in certain New England states, that federal attempts to extend taxation and military service measures (aimed at raising new war revenues and the calling out of some forty thousand state militia troops) proved to be all but dead before the bills

were even tabled for consideration. So bad had things become, that there were serious calls in certain parts of New England for its secession from the Union and the making of a separate peace with the British.

On the other side of the border, the British had also envisioned making one of their 1815 winter campaigns through the Lake Champlain corridor with some seven thousand troops under Major General Thomas Brisbane, while a second major incursion would be made by Lieutenant General Drummond across the ice from Kingston to raze Sackets Harbor and destroy the American fleet before it could sail in the spring. On the Niagara frontier, emphasis would be placed upon making it

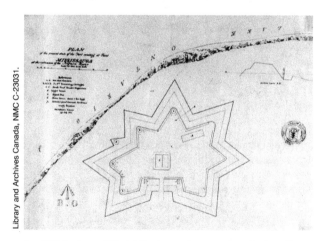

An 1814 plan of Fort Mississauga, constructed on the western bank of the Niagara River where it flows into Lake Ontario.

(Above) *South East View of Sackett's Harbour*. A later undated copy of an engraving created by W. Strickland (1815). (Below) A comparable view in 2012.

into a veritable fortress of defensive positions, military supply bases, and secure lines of communication. To that end, Fort Mississauga was completed, Fort George was extensively repaired, and additional barracks and blockhouses were constructed at Newark (Niagara-on-the-Lake), Queenston, and Chippawa, while plans were in progress for the building of a series of entirely new fortifications that would render the Niagara impregnable.

With the Niagara frontier secured, the next phase of the 1815 plan would be to build up a large force of troops for the retaking of the remainder of Upper Canada to the Detroit River and then crossing into the Michigan Territory to re-establish the lost British control of this officially still-ceded region. (For details see *The Call to Arms*.)

In conjunction with this, it was recognized that the domination and permanent control of the interconnecting waterways would be an essential component of any long-term military strategy for victory. To further this goal, Sir James Yeo prepared plans for a full-scale naval expansion across his command. In Lower Canada, the Île aux Noix shipyard (at the north end of Lake Champlain) would be greatly enlarged so that an entirely new fleet could be constructed to retake control of that strategic waterway. On the St. Lawrence River, new flotillas of gunboats — some of which were to be copies of the steam-powered *Swiftsure* (which

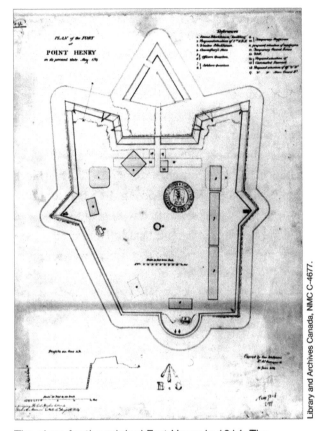

The plans for the original Fort Henry in 1814. The fort was constructed principally by detachments of Canadian militia under the supervision of officers drawn from the Royal Engineers and Royal Sappers and Miners regular regiments. In the postwar era, this fortification was entirely replaced by the massive citadel that exists today. The only surviving feature of the original fort is the well (No. 13 on the map, located at the centre of the main parade square).

Kingston, E.E. Vidal, artist, 1815. A detail from a panoramic view of Kingston in the immediate postwar period, with the British Lake Ontario fleet mothballed ("in ordinary") anchored in the harbour. Fort Frederick and the main dockyard (now the Royal Military College) lies to the left, while Fort Henry sits atop the dominating heights to the right. The details marked on the image are inscribed as:

5. Two ships of the line, building
6. New careening wharf
7. *St Lawrence*. 102 guns on three decks, no poop

8. *Prince Regent*. 60 guns, a beautiful frigate
9. *Princess Charlotte*. 32- gun frigate
10. *Psyche*. 52-gun frigate sent from England in frame, housed for winter.

had regularly sailed between Quebec City and Montreal throughout the war as a troop and supply transport) — would act as escorts for the convoys of cargo boats that would keep Upper Canada supplied with all the essentials of waging war. These would then be backed by the construction of canals and locks to bypass the numerous rapids on the St. Lawrence and all were to be protected by an enlarged series of land fortifications and defendable staging posts.

At Kingston, Yeo planned for the massive enlargement of the already impressive dockyard facilities to accommodate the construction of at least three more warships the size of the *St. Lawrence*, as well as smaller warships, dedicated supply vessels, and additional squadrons of gunboats.

For the upper Great Lakes, too, Yeo's plans were nothing if not ambitious. At Long Point, a new shipbuilding facility, protected by dedicated fortifications and bodies of troops, would create a brand new fleet that could wrest control of Lake Erie and facilitate the British western campaign to recover the Detroit frontier. Finally, the tedious and arduous multistage journey required to move men and supplies from York to Lake Huron and Michilimackinac would soon be greatly eased by the construction of a new road that would connect Lake Simcoe to a brand new custom-built military and naval base called Penetanguishene, located near Matchedash Bay.

Unfortunately for the planners on both sides of the border, all of their strategies and schemes would come to naught, as word arrived in North America in late February that on December 24, 1814, at Ghent (in modern-day Belgium), a peace treaty had been signed by representatives of the United States and Great Britain, technically bringing an end to hostilities. Along with this news came directives for Prevost, Drummond, and Yeo that, apart from certain specific locations, all construction of military emplacements and non-essential expenditures were to immediately cease within Canada. As to the locally raised Canadian militias, they were to be returned to their homes with the grateful thanks of His Majesty's Government and a commitment of a land grant for every soldier, starting with 100 acres to each private and working its way up to 1,200 acres for the senior officers.

Regrettably, while representing a fascinating study in day-to-day political manipulation, international one-upmanship, and just plain bluff and bombast, a detailed examination of the events and details of the negotiations that led to the peace treaty in Ghent lie far beyond the scope of this work. However, a short synopsis would not be out of place to put the aftermath of the war in its context.

CHAPTER 13

Concluding the Peace

From the very onset of the war in 1812, various overtures and exchanges of letters had taken place between the two warring countries but were not pursued with any degree of urgency. Furthermore, apart from some minor input provided by Sir George Prevost and his staff from Quebec, there was effectively no direct inclusion of opinion or recommendation from either the leaders of the colonial legislatures or the Native nations, resulting in a singular London-based point of view being presented by the British to the Americans. In addition, because the initial peace negotiations had adopted a somewhat nomadic existence (as no mutual agreement on a venue could be reached), it was not until August 1814 that true "talks" began in the Flemish town of Ghent. There was also the fact that these negotiations were not the only ones going on in Europe at the time. For following the abdication of Napoleon in April and the effective end of the wars that had devastated most of Europe, the subsequent peace conference, which became known as the Congress of Vienna, had taken on a scale of political importance that dwarfed any other discussions.

There, nothing less than the prospect of a European coalition of empires and the redrawing of the continent's territorial borders was being decided. Both the British prime minister, Robert Jenkinson (the Earl of Liverpool), and his foreign secretary, Robert Stewart (Viscount Castlereagh), were fully occupied in pressing Great Britain's claims at the Congress. This left the negotiations with the Americans in the hands of what can only be described as a B team for the British side,[*1] who were further hampered by a rigid set of instructions that no concessions or changing of positions was to be undertaken without prior consultation or instructions directly from London.

On the other hand, the American delegation[2] was made up of a collection of individuals representing a conflicting diversity of political interests at home, who had the dubious advantage of being located significantly farther from their superiors in Washington. Consequently, due to the excessive time delays that would have been incurred if they required authorization for every detail of the negotiations, the American team, while sometimes being widely divergent or even vehemently opposed in individual viewpoints, was relatively more independent and collectively able to maintain a more determined course during the ensuing negotiations.

Furthermore, because neither side was undertaking these negotiations as clear victors in the conflict (an unusual situation for negotiations at this time in international politics), it is not surprising that both negotiating teams took up an initial extreme position of demanding major concessions from their foes when the first official meeting took place on August 8, 1814.

While the British could be said to have a stronger desire to see peace restored (principally to seize upon improved trade opportunities), they were nonetheless determined to attain certain securities. For example, having already repealed

PEACE TREATY NEGOTIATORS: THE WAR OF 1812–1815

British Delegation[1]
Henry Goulburn (Undersecretary to the Secretary of War and Colonies)
Vice Admiral James Gambier
William Adams (Lawyer with expertise in maritime and naval law)

American Delegation[2]
John Quincy Adams (U.S. Minister to the Court of Tsar Nicholas of Russia)
Albert Gallatin (U.S. Secretary of the Treasury)
Henry Clay (Speaker of the House of Representatives, Kentucky Senator, and anti-British "War Hawk")
James Ashton Bayard (Delaware Senator)
Johnathan Russell (former chargé d'affaires to London and current U.S. Minister to the Court of King Charles XIII of Sweden)

the authorization for their naval search and seizure tactics (which had been loudly touted by the Americans as the official cause of the war), the British saw little reason to make any further concessions on that subject. Similarly, they were particularly determined to maintain their official policy that any individual born under British citizenship had no innate right to renounce it but was, for life, a British subject and required to give allegiance to the Crown.

As to territories, the British position called for a realignment of the disputed border regions between New Brunswick and Maine, along the St. Lawrence River and Great Lakes, with the huge areas of U.S. land that were currently being occupied by British forces being kept by their new "owners." The British also sought to gain new rights of trade and fishing along the East Coast of North America and along the Mississippi River to match these new territorial gains. Most importantly to its initial position though, was the British government's absolute determination to honour its treaties with and promises to its Native allies by calling for the establishment of an independent Native nation's territory in the upper Great Lakes area that in future could act as a buffer zone between the two principal contending powers.

On the other side of the table, because the Americans were the ones who had declared war and then been unable, over a period of more than two years, to achieve a total victory in the field, the political ramifications of failing to "win" at the negotiating table threatened blame and dishonour for the Republican party and, in particular, President Madison and his administration. The American negotiators were therefore instructed to demand that the British issue a virtual admission of guilt for causing the war and an acknowledgement of having been defeated. This was then to be followed by a series of punitive damages, including:

- Admission of wrongdoing and financial compensation for the "illegal" blockade and impressment of American sailors
- The payment of indemnities to American towns damaged or destroyed during the war
- The return of, or payment for, any slaves removed from slavery in the southern States
- The complete ceding of the Canadian colonies to the authority of the United States

They also reacted to the British proposal for an independent Native state by not only making an outright rejection, but by demanding that no further mention of that topic be brought up or referenced in any later negotiations. However, the British continued the matter by pointing out that as both sides had used Natives within their respective armies, and that both had treaty obligations that they were bound to honour with the Native nations, it could hardly be equitable if they were not included as part of the negotiations, or if the final treaty did not specifically refer to their future status within both states. Unmoved, the Americans countered by seeking to conclude a bilateral deal between the United States and Great Britain on the majority of the points, while claiming that anything to do with Native issues was a matter exclusively to be resolved between the United States and the Native tribes and *not* to be included in the present negotiations.

Seeing that matters were going nowhere, the British representatives suspended the talks while instructions were obtained from Whitehall. Upon their return to the negotiating table, the British reiterated their absolute determination to include the Native question in the overall treaty of peace, while the American delegation remained similarly obdurate that it should not. Matters continued in this way throughout September and October, with each round of discussions getting more and more heated and acrimonious. However, external influences that were to shift matters to a new level soon came to bear. These included:

- The military events at Baltimore and Plattsburgh, which undermined the British position by boosting American resolve to continue the war
- The growth of domestic political disruptions and indications of an economic downturn (as British industries turned from a war footing to domestic production), coupled with the spectre of open riots and rebellion as hunger and unemployment soared within Britain's urban centres
- The rise in political unrest within France, as supporters of the exiled Napoleon Bonaparte became increasingly vocal in their opposition to the policies emanating from the restored Bourbon monarchy of Louis XVIII

- The news that negotiations at Vienna were not progressing as well as hoped and were shifting against British interests

As a result, the British government relegated the North American question to such a low priority that word leaked out that it not only wanted peace with the Americans, but that it was prepared to go to great lengths to obtain it, even if it meant abandoning many of its previously claimed irrevocable positions and treaties — and effectively humiliating its negotiators in the process.

Sensing that they had gained a significant edge, the American negotiators pressed home their advantage by digging in their heels over making concessions and pushing for a return of all boundaries and issues to a pre-war condition — "status quo ante bellum." Without the moral authority of the backing of their own government, the British negotiators were now placed in an impossibly weak position, leading to the presentation of a draft treaty on October 31. Knowing they had nothing to lose, the Americans rejected this draft outright and made threats that they would break off all negotiations unless further concessions on details of land boundaries and fishing rights were forthcoming, and unless Britain agreed that the future of the Native nations in North America was the exclusive jurisdiction of the American government to decide.

So vehemently was this demand represented, that on November 25, 1814, the lead British negotiator, Henry Goulburn, wrote to Lord Bathurst:

> 25 November, 1814 … I had till I came here, no idea of the fixed determination which prevails in the breast of every American to extirpate [utterly destroy] the Indians and appropriate their territory; but I am now sure that there is nothing which the people of America would so reluctantly abandon as — what they are pleased to call — their natural right to do so![3]

On November 27, the British delegation submitted a revised draft, effectively capitulating all of its principal demands on the questions of borders, Native issues, and Great Lakes demilitarization, and pressing for concessions only on points of detail on trade issues. Once again, the Americans rebuffed this version and countered with additional demands over the future of British westward expansion, access to the Mississippi River, and fishing rights off the East Coast.

Frustrated to the limits of their endurance, Goulburn and the other British negotiators let it be known that they were prepared to immediately break off negotiations indefinitely unless the Americans relented and accepted what was offered. It appeared the Americans had finally overplayed their hand; instead, the British delegation was forced to eat its own words a few days later when directives arrived from London stipulating that a treaty was to be signed, no matter what.

In this way the Americans succeeded in getting the British to relinquish virtually all of their territorial demands and agree to the restoration of the international border to that which existed prior to the war, a situation that greatly favoured the Americans. The issues of defining a new border, as well as trade and fishing issues, were officially shelved for future negotiations to solve. Most importantly and devastatingly, however, this new version made no provision for Native interests, thus betraying the solemn promises made by the British to their Native allies both to recognize the needs and claims of the Native nations for an independent territory and to gain any safeguards against future American expansionism and aggression — leaving a legitimate legacy of bitterness that soured relations between the two cultures for generations to come.

While the formal signing of the treaty was conducted on December 24, 1814, technically ending the war, the logistics of distance and limitations of communications meant that while the British government was able to ratify the document within days, it was not until February 14, 1815, that the news arrived in the United States, thereafter to be ratified by Congress on February 16, and signed by President Madison on February 17, 1815. The war was officially over.

During this interval, the war in North America and on the high seas had continued on in ignorance, resulting in several engagements between the forces of the two nations, the most famous of which was the Battle of New Orleans, which many modern-day Americans choose to claim as proving that because they won the "last" battle of the war, they won the lot. Unfortunately this ignores the fact that at least two subsequent, albeit smaller, engagements took place in the southern campaign zone, both of which were British victories.

CHAPTER 14

Aftermath

With the end of fighting in the "North American War of 1812–1815," the theory was that all territories and posts that had changed hands during the fighting were to be returned to their original nation's ownership. However, due to bureaucratic delays and logistical difficulties, not to mention the entirely justified anger and foreboding of the British Native allied tribes, it was not until several months after the announcement of peace that the final American posts such as Michilimackinac were finally handed over. The troops of both sides were "returned to barracks" or transferred to other locations, while the respective naval vessels were either sold for civilian use, broken up and sold for parts, or put into "ordinary" (which in modern parlance means put into long-term storage or "mothballed").

From the American point of view, the most pressing problem facing the country was that it had been literally bankrupted by the war. While a new "national" bank of the U.S. was established in 1816 — with the claim that the economy was well on the mend — there were no immediate postwar reductions in either taxes or tariffs, as revenues had to be maintained to pay off incurred debt and finance the new American expansionist dreams. While this continued fiscal drain did not sit well with the opposition Federalist politicians, their attempts to use it as a political electoral weapon against the Republicans effectively backfired, as the Republican administration successfully persuaded the American populace that instead of thinking about the cost of the war, there was a great victory to be celebrated and heroes to fete. The Federalists

Amerique Septentrionale, Pub. E. Ardit, Paris, 1829.

Military Post, Sacketts Harbor. J.G. Milbert, artist, circa 1816–1823. A view of the inner harbour in the years following the war. Across the harbour, the rotting hulks of the once mighty American fleet lie derelict and partially aground. The huge building beyond is the protective boathouse built in 1815–1816 around the unfinished hull of the *New Orleans*. The rotted remnants of this structure were still in existence as late as 1880, when a storm demolished the building, thus exposing the deteriorating shell of the vessel to the elements. In 1883, the *New Orleans* was officially scrapped on the slipway it had never left since 1815.

were therefore painted as simply eating sour grapes and were destined, within a few years, to become effectively politically extinct.

Behind the scenes, however, while the Republicans could be confident of their ability to ride the coattails of "victory" to wield the reins of power for the foreseeable future, there was also the recognition that there was a need to secure the future of the nation, both defensively and offensively (if required). On land this was most clearly seen in the establishment of a proper standing federal army, rather than relying on the pre-war system of maintaining a handful of half-trained regular regiments, backed by an inefficient patchwork of state militias. During the following decades, the new federal U.S. army became an important tool in pushing the government's agenda to expand to the west and south of the existing United States. Similarly, because of the postwar growth that occurred in international maritime trade, an expanded U.S. navy became an important component of American foreign policy, including the maintenance of the occupation and annexation of Spanish West Florida, which had taken place in 1813.

On another level, and entirely in keeping with the American attitude displayed at the peace negotiations, there was a general feeling of having a score to settle with Native tribes in the west, especially those who had fought alongside the British. The "Great Father's" (King George's) protective shadow had been all but eliminated by the capitulation of the British at the negotiating table and the Americans were not about to let it be re-established. To this end, sensationalized American media accounts depicted the threat of further Native aggression as what, in modern terms, could be paraphrased as a "weapon of massive destruction" that needed to be eliminated. In response, the government constructed a series of strategic military posts across the American Midwest and edicts were issued prohibiting any form of trade between the Natives and the British fur-trading interests of the North West Company and Hudson's Bay Company. To back this up, there was also an active promotion of westward expansion through the construction of projects such as the Erie Canal, the opening of previously off-limits Native treaty lands to white settlers, mining interests, buffalo hunters, gold prospectors, et cetera, and the political expedient of expanding the union by rapidly admitting the territories of Indiana, Mississippi, Illinois, Alabama, Maine, and Missouri to statehood between 1815 and 1821. Together these measures helped to secure the American determination to marginalize the Native tribes into insignificance and fulfill the United States' "manifest destiny" to be the pre-eminent nation in the Americas.

At a more individual level, many of the American military commanders and officers used their wartime experiences as foundations for furthering their own military or political careers by writing and often paying for the publication of their wartime reminiscences and memoirs — which at times elevated their roles in mere skirmishes into life-or-death contributions of international consequence. These accounts also frequently criticized or even condemned other senior officers and thereby reignited the personal hostilities and enmities that had shown themselves between these commanders during the war.

Generally speaking, however, in the immediate postwar period and thanks partially to a deliberate governmental publicity campaign of resurrecting the pre-war anglophobia, the North American War of 1812–1815 was transformed from an American war of opportunity (that failed to gain virtually any of its stated objectives), into a nationalistic

(Above) *Kingston*, Sir E.W. Grier, artist, circa 1896 (based on the original painting by Admiral Henry Bayfield, R.N.). A view of the shipyards at Point Frederick (centre) and the town of Kingston (right, distant) as they looked at the end of the war from the hillside alongside Fort Henry (left).
(Below) The same perspective in 2013.

victory and a focus for national pride. The plethora of military biographies and war histories that were published for the American market in the decades that followed fixed the self-justification of going to war over "Sailors' Rights and Free Trade" as fact in the American consciousness. The war was even touted by some nationalist historians as proving that they, as the "victims" of foreign aggression, had just fought a second war of independence from Great Britain. This resulted in battlefields such as Chippawa and Lundy's Lane becoming major tourist attractions for American visitors throughout the following decades. That is, until the American Civil War began, whereupon the battlefields of Gettysburg, Vicksburg, and a hundred other locations became the overwhelming focus of the American national collective military memory. As a result, the earlier sacrifices and very existence of the conflict of the War of 1812–1815 faded from the American consciousness to the point where many of the American tourists who currently visit Canadian heritage sites such as Fort York, Fort George, and Fort Erie are surprised to hear that there was ever a war between the United States and Canada. For those who remember being taught "something" about the war in school, it is the story of "Sailors' Rights," the sanitized version of the writing of the "Stars and Stripes" at Fort McHenry, and the postwar American victory at the Battle of New Orleans that come to mind, leaving them in no doubt that it was they who "won" the war.

In Great Britain, the end of the war with the United States produced mixed feelings within the population. Some forward-thinking individuals took the time to assess the results of the North American war and its implications for the future and made their concerns public:

> As this treaty upon the whole leaves the parties in *statu quo ante belum* and as the war originated with America for pretensions not now secured to her by the treaty, she certainly cannot boast of having attained the object she went to war for: but upon the whole, she sheathes her sword under other advantages, which in our opinion, more than compensate the loss of her primary object. The sword, which was drawn blunt and rusty, is sheathed keen and fit to cut with effect on the first favourable opportunity. From the war she has derived officers and soldiers, and above all a navy, all of which she lacked before; an infant navy it is true, but a Hercules in the cradle, whom she will not neglect nursing into puberty; and in the last campaign she has, to her surprise, seen the possibility

of fighting the undivided strength of England. It has therefore been asserted, that the peace has been made either a campaign too late, or a campaign too soon; but in all probability his Majesty's ministers were induced by the unsettled state of European policies, to wave the trial of another campaign.[1]

— editorial comment, *Ackermann's Repository*, February 1815

However, the majority of Britain's populace, and in particular its political and military leadership, were simply glad to have the North American war over and done with. This became especially true when, in late February 1815, news arrived that Napoleon Bonaparte had escaped from his forced exile on the island of Elba and landed on the south coast of France. By March 20, the return of the "Corsican ogre" had become the emperor's triumphal procession into Paris, precipitating the collapse of the Royalist government and causing France's puppet monarch, Louis XVIII, to decamp from Paris for Ghent with the crown jewels. Seeing the resurrection of its most formidable enemy, the interminable squabbling and political manoeuvring taking place at the multi-national Congress of Vienna was abruptly halted, while Great Britain immediately took the lead in cobbling together a new coalition of nations that was created on March 25. Recalled from Vienna, the Duke of Wellington was made supreme military commander and while Austria, Russia, and the German states gathered their armies and marched toward France, he ordered the immediate recall of every available British regiment to strengthen his own European forces — especially those stationed in a now peaceful North America. However, before the majority of these troops could be brought back into action, Napoleon struck at the armies of Britain and Prussia gathering in the Netherlands (today's Belgium). Thus, in June 1815, the Battles of Quatre Bras, Lingy, Wavre, and Waterloo sealed the fate of the French emperor once and for all.

Once that issue was dealt with, British attention was then fully occupied by the difficult and complicated necessity of integrating huge numbers of soldiers and sailors back into civilian society and converting the British economy from a wartime production centre of arms, uniforms, and military supplies, to a peacetime producer of consumer and trade goods for the domestic and international markets. On the other hand, after the initial euphoria of peace had worn off and the British economy had started to adjust itself, the growing importance of commercialization, industrialization, and world trade — all channelled through Great Britain — made the occupation and expansion of colonial holdings even more vital as sources of raw materials and as captive and expanding markets. In response, the British government became even more determined to maintain and protect its national interests in the Canadas.

As an initial measure, it was deemed vital to ensure the expulsion or exclusion of any settler who had actively gone over to the American side. Those who had remained neutral or tacitly assisted the Americans needed to be marginalized or reduced to an impotent minority. To this end, property of those who were deemed traitors was seized and allocated (for the most part) to those who had not only remained overtly loyal, but also had the social, economic, or political clout to make sure their names were at the top of any list for benefits. The British government also undertook a direct campaign to populate British North America, and Upper Canada in particular, with a more "loyal" population from both the ranks of soldiers who had served in the Canadas and from troops in Europe. Both groups were offered substantial financial incentives and grants of land if they settled in Canada. And the military wasn't the only audience the government sought to attract. The return of the troops to Britain had thrown tens of thousands of "surplus" men onto the streets, all seeking employment, which in turn had driven down the wages of the civilian workers and precipitated a catastrophic slump in the British economy. In response, using a host of broadsides and pamphlets, backed by roving recruiting agents, the British government sought to reduce this social pressure at home and simultaneously boost a loyal population in the colonies by enticing unemployed civilian workers to consider leaving their impoverished homeland for a "guaranteed" better life in the Canadas.

Not content with this relatively passive form of ensuring the future of British North America in the face of potential future American threats of invasion, the British government put into place additional safeguards. Because the naval Rush-Bagot Agreement of 1817 virtually eliminated the establishment of a strong naval presence on the Great Lakes, the British government began a decades-long program of military construction that saw massive "modern" fortifications built at Halifax, Quebec City, and Kingston, while lesser works were developed at Montreal, York, Penetanguishene, Amherstburg, and elsewhere along the Great Lakes system. In addition, the tenuous supply lines of the St. Lawrence and Niagara Rivers were recognized as being particularly vulnerable to attack and disruption by the Americans. In response, the construction of a series of defended transportation corridors was initiated, starting with the Lachine Canal at Montreal, followed shortly thereafter by the first Welland Canal across the Niagara

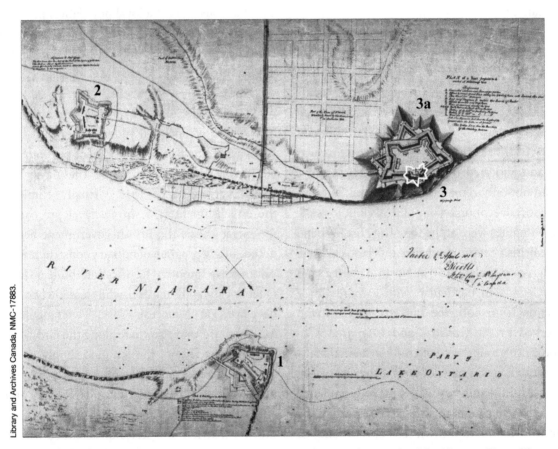

An 1816 map showing the relative positions of the three forts at the mouth of the Niagara River: (1) Fort Niagara; (2) Fort George; and (3) Fort Mississauga (in white outline). It also shows the huge prospective scale of the postwar works (3a) that were intended to be built over the original site of Fort Mississauga but were never developed.

Peninsula, and culminating with the incredibly difficult construction of the Rideau Canal system from Bytown (Ottawa), on the Ottawa River, to Kingston, entirely bypassing the St. Lawrence River above Montreal. However, other than these official governmental initiatives, the North American War of 1812–1815 became effectively forgotten in the minds of the general public of Great Britain and relegated to the footnotes of British military histories — while the simultaneous conflict within Europe filled the chapters of every student's history books. Even at the time, the officers who fought in North America complained of the way their contributions and service were effectively ignored in comparison to those who had served under Wellington in the Spanish Peninsula or at Waterloo.

What should also be noted is that, even after the fighting had ended, the war claimed at least one additional high-profile British victim, in the person of Sir George Prevost. For almost three years Sir George had faithfully followed the dictates of his political and military masters to conduct his war with the Americans at the least possible cost and with the fewest possible resources. Unfortunately, this lacklustre battlefield command skills and inability to conjure up a military victory (that he could claim sole credit for) left him highly vulnerable to criticism for his administration of the war. This was particularly true in the case of Sir James Yeo,

whose personal dislike of Prevost had grown substantially throughout 1814, especially after Prevost criticized Yeo's unwillingness to be a "team player" in his reports to Lord Bathurst. In retaliation, Yeo had used his enhanced position as an independent commander to cast numerous aspersions against Prevost and generally undermine his authority.

As a result, once there was peace, Prevost's tenure as the governor general and commander-in-chief came to an abrupt end when he was recalled to Great Britain to face questions about his conduct during the war, and particularly his decisions during the 1814 Plattsburgh expedition. Despite being in failing health, Prevost was determined to face up to his accusers. However, on January 5, 1816, only a month before the inquiry was to begin, Sir George died in England at the age of forty-eight. As a result, history has not been kind to the memory of this officer, as he was given no opportunity to state his case and the aspersions cast by his detractors became accepted as the "facts" of history.

As for the colonies of British North America, one consequence of the war with America was the development of a distinctly separate, if not yet "Canadian" identity from that of their former enemy and a reaffirmation of their strong allegiance to their mother country. In Lower Canada and the Maritime colonies, any anti-American feelings remained relatively muted, as neither region

NIAGARA.—OLD FORT MISSISAUGA

Above and right: Later nineteenth-century illustrations of the remains of the principal War of 1812–1815 fortifications on the Niagara frontier: Fort Mississauga, *Canadian Illustrated News*, August 23, 1870. Fort Erie, *Canadian Illustrated News*, September 9, 1876. Fort George, *The Illustrated Atlas of Lincoln and Welland Counties*, 1876.

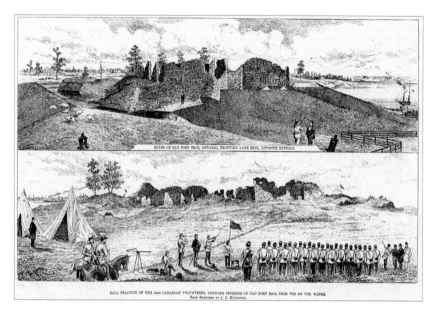

RUINS OF OLD FORT ERIE, ONTARIO, FRONTING LAKE ERIE, OPPOSITE BUFFALO.

BALL PRACTICE OF THE 44TH CANADIAN VOLUNTEERS, SHEWING INTERIOR OF OLD FORT ERIE FROM THE 800 YDS. RANGE.
FROM SKETCHES BY J. C. HOARSTEA.

PRESENT APPEARANCE OF OLD FORT GEORGE AT NIAGARA.

Views in 2013 of the reconstructed Fort George.

had been seriously threatened during the course of the war and both were soon able to simply restore their business and trading links with their pre-war partners. In addition, they were perfectly placed to take advantage of the postwar European (and in particular British) demand for industrial raw materials to rebuild the economies of Europe, such as timber, potash, and minerals, thus cementing their economic advantage (provided by their location on the lower St. Lawrence and Atlantic coast) for the foreseeable future.

In Upper Canada there was no such moderation when it came to feelings about the Americans. Upper Canada had been "preserved" and peace restored, but at what cost? Apart from Kingston, virtually every other community in the colony had suffered attacks from the Americans over the course of the conflict and either been damaged, looted, or razed. The St. Lawrence frontier of Upper Canada was not heavily damaged as far as commercial and agricultural production was concerned, but it remained vulnerable and under threat from any renewed American aggression. Distinctly worse for wear was the Niagara frontier, much of whose infrastructure had been heavily damaged due to the repeated campaigns that had been fought upon its fields. But it was within the vast stretch of territory lying to the west of Burlington Heights, along the Lake Erie shoreline, through the Grand River

and Thames Valleys and throughout the Detroit frontier, that anti-Americanism held the strongest sway. Hardly a grain mill, smithy, or any other trade or production shop still stood intact, and the agricultural infrastructure was all but wiped out. It would take years, if not decades, to restore the economic and agricultural output of Upper Canada to its pre-war levels, putting it at an initial significant economic disadvantage compared to its "lower" compatriot colonies. Feelings of anti-Americanism remained high for generations to come.

With the devastation of Upper Canada by the war, it was expected by many within the population that their own Upper Canada government or the British colonial representatives would be quick to come to their aid. And it must be said that within a year or two, official panels and boards were established with the theoretical mandate of assisting those in distress. However, almost without exception these bodies proved to be anything but helpful. For example:

- The government's offer of compensation for civilian war losses became a nightmare of bureaucratic complexity, as the official requirements for fully itemized and provable documented claims allowed many submissions by claimants to be either dismissed entirely, delayed and postponed while additional demands for information were accommodated, or discounted item-by-item to such a degree that they were all but valueless when they were eventually awarded.

- The boards established to assess the appropriate pensions that should be granted to wounded soldiers of the Upper Canada militias, or awards to the widows of those who were killed, likewise failed in their duty. Many petitioners found that when they submitted their claims to the established regional boards for consideration, they were expected to attend multiple hearings (held at widely differing locations) and subjected to rude and officious demands for additional affidavits, proofs, and medical reports — all of which had to be paid for by the applicant and which served to intimidate many petitioners into abandoning their claims. Others who persisted, meanwhile, saw their cases delayed for up to two decades, by which time a significant number of claimants were no longer in a position to press their cases — by the simple expedient of already being dead.

- The Crown's promise of granting land to every veteran of the war, while initially appearing to be moving ahead in a timely manner, actually fell into an abyss of official delays and procrastination that lasted not mere years, but rather took decades to work through. So protracted were some of these delays that when the commission finally began to process and award grants of land, the best tracts had long since gone to preferred insiders and political cronies, leaving, in many instances, plots totally unsuitable for agriculture or ones in such remote and sometimes uninhabitable locations that they were all but useless to the person to whom they were awarded. Furthermore, even where a tract might have proved suitable, the inordinate delays had left many of the still-living veterans at an age where they were no longer physically capable of undertaking the back-breaking task of clearing the distant virgin forest in accordance with the government-imposed timetable to assure continued permanent ownership. Many claimants were forced instead to accept the payment of government scrip (money) at substantially discounted rates that in no fashion matched the prospective value of their awarded land. Nor were those who accepted the tracts and then attempted to resell them better off, as unscrupulous land speculators, often within the commission itself, bought up these properties at massive discounts before amassing significant fortunes upon their subsequent resale at market value.

Even the recognition of those who had fought for their "country" fell foul of the postwar compli

View in 2013 of preserved War of 1812–1815 locations around Niagara-on-the-Lake (formerly called Newark, later Niagara) that are now under the administration of Parks Canada.

1–2. Fort Mississauga.
3–4. Navy Hall (below Fort George).
5–7. The Butler's Barracks complex.

of the various militia corps to submit the names of men who had distinguished themselves during the course of the war and were therefore deserving of receiving a medal that the society had commissioned. However, the committee was stunned when the total number of men deemed worthy for recognition within the single regiment of the Incorporated Militia of Upper Canada alone far exceeded the total number of medals produced, leading to some bitter infighting within the committee as to what should be done and ultimately resulting in no presentations whatsoever. In fact, after two decades of an increasing public scandal over the non-issuance of the medals and questions being raised within the press as to the whereabouts of the publically raised associated funds, it is generally believed that all but three of the originals were deliberately scrapped in 1840, leaving only the image and motto of this "Upper Canada Preserved" medallion to be reproduced on the covers of the books in this series.

Nonetheless, the survival of British North America and especially Upper Canada was initially something to be hailed as a grand victory. The authors of the multitude of early war autobiographies and Upper Canada's "impartial histories" lost no time in creating a Canadian myth that "victory" had been achieved principally by the superior efforts of the loyal Upper Canada militia, backed by the efforts of a mere

cations, as seen in the efforts of the Loyal and Patriotic Society of Upper Canada.

This organization had already been providing charitable support for Upper Canada militiamen and their families during the course of the war. But once the war ended, its Committee for the Distribution of Medals put out a request for commanding officers

The design for the medal produced by the Loyal and Patriotic Society, which was never officially issued.

handful of British troops. Furthermore, like their American counterparts, many Canadian militia officers used their wartime connections to solicit government and civil posts, not to mention ranks within the reorganized militia system and high-ranking political and judicial offices.

Unfortunately, this also led to instances of political manipulation, nepotism, and insider-trading taking place, especially when the social, military, and political elite of the pre-war era sought to turn back the clock and restore the status quo of their hold on the reins of power. Inevitably, those who had been previously excluded and to whom the war had given credibility, author-ity, and influence, resented any attempt by what would later be referred to as the "Family Compact" to suppress these gains and re-establish control of Upper Canada for their own self-interests. As a result, the seeds were sown for more than

twenty years of political, economic, and social infighting amongst the more influential families of Upper Canada, while disgruntled excluded individuals and groups nursed their grievances with less and less patience until matters came to a head in the rebellion of 1837.

Finally, while all of the other participants within the war can be said to have had gains and losses, the true losers in this conflict were the Native nations. Before the war they existed not only as individual tribes but also as a collective culture. True, this was under increasing pressure from "foreign" incursions into their homelands — be that American or British — but they still had their roots in their tribal lands, resources to survive on, and firm assurances from both Great Britain and the United States that their rights and lands would be guaranteed forever. However, following the war, their culture, lands, resources, and hopes for a homeland were lost as these solemn treaties were ignored or broken by one government after another and by the remorseless encroachment of the white man on both sides of the border. Not a happy way to conclude the official story, but a point that cannot be ignored or forgotten as the bicenten-nial of this event has been celebrated.

On a more positive note, this two-hundredth anniversary has given us the opportunity to not only re-examine the tumultuous events that took place two hundred years ago with new eyes and discover new facts in our researching but also to reassess these events in the context of how they unquestionably shaped the destiny and relationships of four nations and three countries for two centuries. Not bad for what some military historians have dismissed as a forgotten little war fought in the middle of nowhere.

AFTERWORD

Thirty-five years ago, I participated in a historical re-enactment that led to my becoming part of the Living History community portraying the War of 1812, or what I prefer to call the North American War of 1812–1815. When people ask why I do it, I simply reply that it began as an interest, developed into a hobby, graduated through a passion into an obsession, and then became the far more comfortable stage of being a lifestyle, one that my wife and I have enjoyed sharing, first with our children and now our grandchildren, who I am pleased to say have definitely caught the "bug."

As part of this hobby, and because I am also a professional museum curator and historian, I wanted to do things right and so began to do background research and reading into an increasingly diverse range of topics — but entirely for my own interest. I accumulated what later became a library of references and a virtual archive of copies of documentation and papers, which I used as the foundation for my discussions with the public and other re-enactors about various aspects of the war and our re-enactment presentations. As a corollary, I inadvertently became regarded as something of an "expert" on the war. This, in turn, led to additional research to answer inquiries about specific aspects of the conflict, published articles and papers, public talks, media interviews, and even a published regimental history about the unit I have sought to recreate in my re-enactments. But I never dreamed that it would end up becoming a three-year marathon of writing an entire series of books in conjunction with the bicentennial of those momentous original events.

Such, however, are the dangers of what used to be called (and were frequently frowned upon as) "enthusiasms." My only hope is that you, dear reader, will feel that the end result was worth it, and that it may spark you into following up a trail of inquiry of your own interests and enthusiasms.

Richard Feltoe
March 2014

NOTES

A star (*) indicates the note refers to a sidebar.

Abbreviations:

LAC: Library and Archives Canada

AOO: Archives of Ontario

CRDH: Ernest Cruikshank, *The Documentary History of the Campaigns upon the Niagara Frontier 1812–1814*, 9 Volumes (Welland, ON: Tribune Press, 1896–1908).

CGMC: Buffalo and Erie County Historical Society Archives, B00-11, A. Conger Goodyear, War of 1812 Manuscripts, 1779–1862.

SBD1812:   William C.H. Wood, *Select British Documents of the War of 1812* (Toronto: Champlain Society of Canada, 1920).

Le Couteur: Graves, D.E., ed., *Merry Hearts Make Light Days: The Journal of Lieutenant John Le Couteur, 104th Foot* (Ottawa: Carleton University Press, 1993).

CHAPTER 1: INTRODUCTION

1. Government of the United States, *Causes of the Failure of the Army on the Northern Frontier*, Report to the House of Representatives, February 2, 1814, 13th Congress, 2nd Session, Military Affairs, Vol. 1.

CHAPTER 2: WAR ON THE NIAGARA FRONTIER: WHEN FORTUNE TURNS THE WHEEL

1. David B. Douglass, "An Original Narrative of the Niagara Campaign in 1814," *The Historical Magazine*, 3rd ser., Vol. 2, (1873): 23–24.

CHAPTER 3: THE SIEGE OF FORT ERIE: ENCIRCLEMENT

1. Major Jacob Hindman. Original letter, Lilly Library, Indiana University.
2. SBD1812, Vol. 3, Part 1, 174.
*3. Ibid.
*4. Composite of CRDH, Vol. 1, 120–23 and CRDH, Vol. 2, 428.
5. SBD1812, Vol. 3, Part 1, 177.

6. Le Couteur, 184.
7. CRDH, Vol. 1, 121–22.
8. Le Couteur, 184.
9. Orderly Book of General Jacob Brown, April–August 1814, CGMC, Vol. 5.
10. Carl F. Klinck, ed., *Journal of Major John Norton*, Champlain Society, Publication No. 46, 360–61.
11. Le Couteur, 185.
12. Orderly Book of General Jacob Brown, April–August 1814, CGMC, Vol. 5.
13. Le Couteur, 186–87.
14. CRDH, Vol. 1, 137.
*15. CRDH, Vol. 1, 134–35.
*16. CRDH, Vol. 1, 135–36.
17. CRDH, Vol. 1, 177.
18. General James Brown, memorandum of occurrences attending the campaign on the Niagara, 1814, CGMC, Vol. 3.
19. David B. Douglass, "Attack on Fort Erie," *The Portfolio*, 4th ser., Vol. 1, No. 2 (February 1816): 99–101.
20. Ernest Cruikshank, "Documents Relating to the Invasion of the Niagara Peninsula by the United States Army, Commanded by General Jacob Brown in July and August 1814," Niagara Historical Society Papers, No. 33 (1921), Vol. 2, 438.
21. CRDH, Vol. 1, 176.
22. CRDH, Vol. 1, 129–30.

CHAPTER 4: ASSAULT AND DISASTER: AUGUST 14/15, 1814

1. Douglass, "An Original Narrative," 26–28.
*2. United States National Archives, Morning Reports, United States Army, Fort Erie August 10–14, 1814, Papers K2-560-569.
*3. SBD1812, Vol. 3, Part 1, 183.
4. CRDH, Vol. 1, 138–39.
5. CRDH, Vol. 1, 140.
6. Ibid.

7. CRDH, Vol. 1, 138.
8. CRDH, Vol. 1, 140.
9. Douglass, "Attack on Fort Erie," 101.
10. United States National Archives, Copy of Original Testimony Notes, Court Martial of General Gaines (1816), General Ripley, 122, Major Marston, 144.
11. Ibid.
12. CRDH, Vol. 1, 156–57.
13. CRDH, Vol. 1, 144–45.
14. SBD1812, Vol. 3, Part 1, 186.
15. United States National Archives, Copy of Original Testimony Notes, Court Martial of General Gaines (1816), Captain Eben Childs, 330–31.
16. Ibid.
17. Douglass, "An Original Narrative," 29.
18. Le Couteur, 190.
19. Douglass, "An Original Narrative," 29.
20. John Kearsley (lieutenant in 1814), original handwritten memoir by Major John Kearsley, Clement Library, University of Michigan, 20–21.
*21. CRDH, Vol. 1, 148–49.
*22. United States National Archives, Copy of Original Testimony Notes, Court Martial of General Gaines (1816), Appendix and CRDH, Vol. 1, 150–51.
23. CRDH, Vol. 1, 55.

CHAPTER 5: STALEMATE: AUGUST 17–SEPTEMBER 16, 1814

1. Douglass, "An Original Narrative," 30–32.
2. CRDH, Vol. 1, 147.
3. Douglass, "An Original Narrative," 32–34.
4. Klinck, ed., *Journal of Major John Norton*, 364.
5. Kearsley, original handwritten memoir, 21–22.
6. Le Couteur, 194.
7. LAC, RG8-I, British Military and Naval Records, 1757–1903, Vol. 1219, 274.
8. LAC, RG8-I, British Military and Naval Records, 1757–1903, Vol. 1219, 277–78.

9. CRDH, Vol. 1, 179.
10. CRDH, Vol. 1, 187.
11. David B. Douglass, "Attack on Fort Erie," 108–09.
12. Cruikshank, "Documents Relating to the Invasion," No. 33 (1921).
13. Ibid.
14. Orderly Book of General Jacob Brown, April–August 1814, CRDH, Vol.2 and CGMC, Vol. 5.
15. CRDH, Vol. 1, 194.
16. CRDH, Vol. 2, 220–21.
17. Winston Johnston,. *The Glengarry Light Infantry, 1812–1816: Who Were They and What Did They Do in the War?* (Self-published, 2011), 159.

CHAPTER 6: THE AMERICAN SORTIE: SEPTEMBER 17, 1814

*1. Composite of CRDH, Vol. 1, 208–210 and CRDH, Vol. 2, 223–24.
2. Letters and map regarding battles of Fort Erie and Niagara, CGMC, Vol. 16.
*3. Composite of LAC, RG8-I, British Military and Naval Records, 1757–1903, Vol. 1219, 296 and CRDH, Vol. 1, 213.
4. CRDH, Vol. 1, 225–26.
5. LAC, RG8-I, British Military and Naval Records, 1757–1903, Vol. 685, 261.
*6. CRDH, Vol. 1, 214.
7. CRDH, Vol. 1, 206.
8. CRDH, Vol. 1, 207.
9. Douglass, "Attack on Fort Erie," 111.
10. Public Records Office, Kew, U.K. PRO Admiralty I, Vol. 507, 171.

CHAPTER 7: AN EXERCISE IN FUTILITY AND FRUSTRATION: THE AMERICAN EXPEDITION TO RECAPTURE MICHILIMACKINAC

1. Orderly Book of General Jacob Brown, April–August 1814, CGMC, Vol. 5.

*2. Composite of references including Brian Dunnigan, *The British Army At Mackinac, 1812–1815*, Reports in Mackinac History and Archaeology, No. 7 (Mackinac Island State Park Commission, 1980), 20–21, and Journal of Usher Parsons, CGMC, Vol.11.
3. Journal of Usher Parson, CGMC, Vol.11.
4. Dunnigan, *The British Army At Mackinac*, 22–23.
*5. Ibid.
6. Journal of Usher Parsons, CGMC, Vol.11.
7. Ibid.
8. Michael J. Crawford, ed., *The Naval War of 1812: A Documentary History*, Vol. 3, (Washington: Naval Historical Center, Department of the Navy, 2002), 565.

CHAPTER 8: ALL FOR NOTHING: THE BATTLE OF MICHILIMACKINAC ISLAND, AUGUST 4, 1814

1. Journal of Usher Parsons, CGMC, Vol. 11.
*2. Dunnigan, *The British Army At Mackinac*, 23–25.
3. Ernest Cruikshank, "An Episode of the War of 1812: The Story of the Schooner *Nancy*," Ontario Historical Society Papers and Records, Vol. 9 (1910), 108.
*4. Report of Captain N.H. Moore, August 11, 1814, in John R. Bailey, "Mackinaw, Formerly Michilimackinac" (Tradesman Co.: 1895), 176–77 and Cruikshank, "An Episode of the War of 1812," 105.
5. Crawford, ed., *The Naval War of 1812*, 568–70.

CHAPTER 9: THE *NANCY*: LOSS AND RETRIBUTION, JUNE–OCTOBER, 1814

1. Barry Gough, *Through Water, Ice & Fire: Schooner* Nancy *of the War of 1812* (Toronto: Dundurn Press, 2006), 127.
2. United States National Archives, RG45, CL 1814, Vol. 6, 10.
3. Ibid., and Cruikshank, "An Episode of the War of 1812," 106.
4. Crawford, ed., *The Naval War of 1812*, 570–71.

*5. Dunnigan, *The British Army At Mackinac*, 26.
6. Gough, *Through Water, Ice & Fire*, 146.
7. SBD1812, Vol. 3, Part 1, 273.
8. Gough, *Through Water, Ice & Fire*, 148.

CHAPTER 10: FINALE ON THE CHIPPAWA RIVER

1. CRDH, Vol. 2, 238.
2. CRDH, Vol. 2, 235.
3. CRDH, Vol. 2, 240.
*4. "Official Correspondence with the Department of War relative to the Military Operations of the American Army under the Command of Major General Izard of the Northern Frontier of the United States in the Years 1814 and 1815" (Philadelphia: Thomas Dobson1816), 100–01.
5. Ibid., and CRDH, Vol. 2, 242–43.
6. Ibid.
7. CRDH, Vol. 2, 257.
*8. Composite of SBD1812, Vol. 3, Part 1, 222–25 and CRDH, Vol. 2, 263.
*9. SBD1812, Vol. 3, Part 1, 225, 270.
*10. CRDH, Vol. 2, 260–61, 275.
11. "Official Correspondence with the Department of War", 103–04.
12. LAC, RG8-I, British Military and Naval Records, 1757–1903, Vol. 1219, 307.

CHAPTER 11: DESOLATION AND SCORCHED EARTH: "TOTAL WAR" COMES TO UPPER CANADA, OCTOBER 1814

1. Glenn Stott, *Greater Evils: The War of 1812 in Southwestern Ontario* (Self-published: 2001), 165.
*2. CRDH, Vol. 2, 308–09.
*3. Stott, *Greater Evils*, 170–73.
*4. Ibid.
5. Stott, *Greater Evils*, 176.

CHAPTER 12: PLANNING FOR THE NEW YEAR'S CAMPAIGNS

No notes

CHAPTER 13: CONCLUDING THE PEACE

*1. Mark Zuehlke, *For Honour's Sake: The War of 1812 and the Brokering of an Uneasy Peace* (Alfred A. Knopf, Canada, 2006), 297–305.
*2. Ibid.
3. Zuehlke, *For Honour's Sake*, 359.

CHAPTER 14: AFTERMATH

1. Editorial comment, "Ackermann's Repository," February 1815.

GLOSSARY

The following is a list of terms used in the series.

NB The terms as used here may not always coincide exactly with other dictionary definitions.

FORTIFICATIONS

Abattis (abatis/abbatis): A temporary defensive structure, equivalent to modern barbed wire. Constructed of felled tree branches and limbs piled into an intermeshed linear obstacle. Usually with the branched or "pointed" ends of the branches placed facing to the outside of the formation.

Bastion: A multi-sided defensive structure or earthwork (usually with two front faces and two flanks) connected to and projecting from adjacent fortifications, such as a curtain wall.

Breastwork: A linear defensive structure or earthwork embankment that is erected chest-high, to enable firing over the top, but is without additional protective additions or an internal raised firing step.

Counterscarp: The outer face of a ditch.

Curtain wall: A linear defensive structure or earthwork that is erected above head height and that connects two other defensive structures, such as bastions.

Demi-bastion: A multi-sided defensive structure or earthwork (usually with only one main face) that is connected to and projecting from adjacent fortifications, such as a curtain wall.

Epaulement: A linear defensive structure or earthwork embankment that projects out at a distinctive angle from a main fortification without connecting to any similar structure on the outer flank.

Gorge: The narrow opening or passage that connects the interior space of a bastion or similar projected work and the main interior space of a defensive position.

Merlons and embrasures: Defensive embellishments on a parapet, consisting of interspersed raised sections (merlons) and gaps (embrasures).

Parapet: A vertical extension of a wider wall or earthwork, placed along the outer side to provide protection to the troops manning it.

Picket wall: A defensive structure, usually above head height, made up of a wall of wooden posts erected to create a linear protective barrier or stockade.

Ravelin: A V-shaped outer defensive structure or independent earthwork, usually erected to mask or protect an exposed wall or gateway from enemy fire.

Redan: A V-shaped defensive structure or earthwork connected to and projecting from adjacent fortifications such as a curtain wall.

Redoubt: A defensive structure or earthwork located separately from and defended independently of other parts of the fortifications.

Sally port: A small gateway in a defensive line, principally designed to allow defenders a means of exiting their positions to make sorties or attacks on their enemies.

Scarp: The inner face of a ditch or one directly attached to the defence line.

Traverse: A linear defensive structure or earthwork embankment that projects out or runs at an approximate right angle to the main line of defences.

MILITARY UNITS

Rank and file: The troops forming the core linear formation of a company or regiment and who do the firing (e.g., privates and corporals).

Other ranks: The troops consisting of the rank and file and non-commissioned officers (e.g., privates, corporals, sergeants, colour sergeants, et cetera) but not officers.

All ranks: The entire body of troops, including other ranks and officers.

Detachment: An unspecified but usually small unit of men acting independently from their main formation.

Company: The main internal division of a military unit such as a regiment. In the British army this usually consisted of ten companies per regiment or battalion.

Grenadier company: An elite or specialist company within a regiment. Traditionally but not necessarily exclusively consisting of the taller and bigger men, with additional training for assault and specialized combat duties. Usually placed on the right-hand end of a regimental line on parade.

Light company: An elite or specialist company. Traditionally but not necessarily exclusively consisting of the shorter or smaller men in a regiment. With additional training for skirmishing and specialized combat duties. Usually placed on the left-hand end of a regimental line on parade.

Flank company: A detached formation of troops, consisting of the union of the Grenadier and Light companies into a combined elite formation. Sometimes the flank companies of several regiments would be temporarily brigaded together to form a "Light" or "Flank" brigade.

Forlorn Hope: A detachment or formation of troops assigned the extremely hazardous duty of spearheading or leading an attack. The expectation being that they would suffer extremely high casualties and thereby have only a "forlorn" hope of survival. However, for those who survived, fame and promotion often followed.

Line or Centre company: The backbone or core companies of a regiment. (There were usually eight within a standard British regiment.) Generally formed in a two-deep, shoulder-to-shoulder formation of companies and trained to fight in a structured line or column formation. Usually placed at the middle of a regimental line.

Battalion/Regiment: These terms are often used interchangeably, but regiments sometimes are composed of two or more battalions. The standard administrative or formational unit of an army.

Picket (piquet/picquet): A detachment of men assigned scouting or sentry duties along the perimeter of a larger formation of troops, encampment, or fortification.

ARTILLERY

Gun: The generic term for an artillery piece.

Bore/Calibre: The inside measurement of a gun's barrel, which determines the size or weight of shot that can be fired. Thus 6-pounder, 18-pounder, 24-pounder, 8½-inch, et cetera.

Cannon/Long gun: An artillery piece, generally with a long barrel length compared to its bore. Designed to be mobile and to fire shot at longer ranges and at relatively flat trajectories.

Carronade: An artillery piece with a short barrel length compared to its bore. Designed to be mobile and to fire larger-sized shot at shorter ranges and at relatively flat trajectories.

Howitzer: An artillery piece with a relatively short barrel length compared to its bore. Generally designed to be mobile and fire shot at a medium- to high-arced "lobbed" trajectory.

Mortar: An artillery piece with an extremely short barrel length compared to its bore. Generally designed to fire from a static position (no wheels) and firing larger-sized shot in an extreme high-arc "plunging" trajectory.

En-barbette: An artillery piece "gun" that is mounted on a platform for firing without any additional surrounding form of defensive protection.

SELECTED BIBLIOGRAPHY

PRIMARY SOURCES

Archival

1. Library and Archives Canada
   Manuscript Groups (MG)
   MG10A: U.S. Department of State, War of 1812 Records.
   MG11(CO42): British Colonial Office, Original Correspondence, Canada.
   MG11(CO47): Upper Canada Records, 1764–1836, Miscellaneous.
   MG13 (WO62): Commissariat Department, Miscellaneous Records 1809–1814.
   MG19, A39: Duncan Clark Papers.
   MG24, A9: Sir George Prevost Papers.
   MG24, I3: Archibald McLean Papers.
   Research Groups (RG)
   RG5-A1: Civil Secretary's Office, Upper Canada Sundries, 1791–1867.
   RG8-I: British Military and Naval Records, 1757–1903.
   RG9-I: Pre-Confederation Records, Military.
   RG10: Indian Department Records.
   RG19/E5A: Department of Finance, War of 1812, Losses Board.

2. Archives Ontario
   MS35/1: Strachan Papers.
   MS74/R5: Merritt Papers.
   MS501: Thorburn Papers.
   MS58: Band Papers.
   MS500: Street Papers.
   MS502/B Series: Nelles Papers.
   MU2099: A.A. Rapelje Papers.
   MU527: Duncan Clark Papers.
   MS74.R5: Henry Ruttan Papers.

3. Metro Toronto Reference Library
   Hagerman, C.: Journal of Christopher Hagerman.
   Prevost Papers, 7 Volumes, S108, Cub 7.

4. Detroit Public Library Archives
   Kirby, J.: James Kirby Papers.

5. Buffalo and Erie County Historical Society Archives, A. Conger Goodyear War of 1812 Manuscripts, 1779–1862, Mss. BOO-11. 16 Volumes.

6. Burton Historical Library, Detroit, MI. Diary of Ensign Andrew Wharffe.

7. Lilly Library, Indiana University. 1812 manuscript collection.

Early Secondary Publications

Armstrong, J. *Notices of the War of 1812*. New York: Wiley & Putnam, 1840.

Boyd, J.P. *Documents and Facts Relative to Military Events During the Late War*. Private publication, 1816.

Brackenridge, Henry. M. *History of the Late War Between the United States and Great Britain*. Cushing & Jewett, 1817.

Brannan, J. *Official Letters of the Military and Naval Officers of the United States, during the War with Great Britain in the years 1812, 13, 14, & 15*. Washington City: Way & Gideon, 1823.

Chapin, C. *Chapin's Review of Armstrong's Notices of the War of 1812*. Black Rock: Private publication, 1836.

Congreve, Colonel Sir W. *The Details of the Rocket System, shewing the various applications of this weapon, both for sea and land service, and its different uses in the field and in sieges*. London: J. Whiting, 1814.

Davis, Paris M. *An Authentick History of the Late War Between the United States and Great Britain*. Ithaca, NY: Mack & Andrus, 1829.

_____. *The Four Principal Battles of the Late War Between the United States and Great Britain*. Harrisburg, NY: Jacob Baab, 1832.

Gilleland, J.C. *History of the Late War Between the United States and Great Britain*. Baltimore: Schaeffer & Maund, 1817.

Hitsman, J.M. *History of the American War of Eighteen Hundred and Twelve*. Philadelphia: W. McCarty, 1816.

James, W. *A Full and Correct Account of the Military Occurrences of the Late War Between Great Britain and the United States of America*. London: William James, 1818.

McCarty, W. *History of the American War of 1812*. Philadelphia: William McCarty & Davis, 1817.

Merritt, William Hamilton. *Journal of Events: Principally on the Detroit & Niagara Frontiers During the War of 1812*. St. Catharines, CW: Canada West Historical Society, 1863.

Morgan, J.C. *The Emigrant's Guide, With Recollections of Upper and Lower Canada During the Late War Between the United States of America and Great Britain*. London: Longman, Hurst, Rees, Orme & Brown, 1824.

Official Correspondence with the Department of War relative to the Military Operations of the American Army under the Command of Major General Izard of the Northern Frontier of the United States in the Years 1814 and 1815. Philadelphia: Thomas Dobson, 1816.

O'Connor, T. *An Impartial and Correct History of the War Between the United States of America and Great Britain*. Belfast: Joseph Smyth, 1816. Reprint of the John Low edition, New York, 1815.

Perkins, S. *A History of the Political and Military events of the Late war between the United States and Great Britain*. New Haven: S. Converse, 1825.

"Proceedings and Debates of the House of Representatives of the United States." 12th Congress, 1st Session (1812). U.S. Government Records.

Ripley, E.A. *Facts Relative to the Campaign on the Niagara in 1814*. Boston: Self-published, 1815.

Thomson, J.L. *Historical Sketches of the Late War between the United States and Great Britain*. Philadelphia: Thomas Delsilver, 1816.

Sturtevant, I. *Barbarities of the Enemy Exposed in a report of the Committee of the House of Representatives of the United States*. Worcester, MA: 1814.

Wilkinson, J. *Diagrams and Plans Illustrative of the Principal Battles of the War of 1812*. Philadelphia: Self-published, 1815.

_____. *Memoirs of my Own Times*. Philadelphia: Abraham Small, 1816.

SECONDARY SOURCES

Later Secondary Publications

Baylies, N. *Eleazer Wheellock Ripley of the War of 1812*. Des Moines, 1890.

Buell, W. *Military Movements in Eastern Ontario During the War of 1812*. Ontario Historical Society Papers and

Records, Vol. 10 (1913) and Vol. 17 (1919).

Cannon, R. *Historical Record of the Eighth or the Kings Regiment of Foot.* London, 1844.

_____. *Historical Record of the 1st or Royal Regiment of Foot.* London, 1847.

Carnochan, Janet. *Reminiscences of Niagara and St. David's.* Niagara Historical Society Papers, No. 20 (1911).

Cruickshank, Ernest. *Campaigns of 1812–1814.* Niagara Historical Society Papers, No. 9 (1902).

_____. *Letters of 1812 from the Dominion Archives.* Niagara Historical Society Papers, No. 23 (1913).

_____. *Documents Relating to the Invasion of the Niagara Peninsula by the United States Army, Commanded by General Jacob Brown in July and August 1814.* Niagara Historical Society Papers, No. 33 (1921).

_____. *A Memoir of Colonel the Honourable James Kerby, His Life in Letters.* Welland County Historical Society, Papers and Records, No. 4, 1931.

Douglass, David B. "An Original Narrative of the Niagara Campaign in 1814." *The Historical Magazine,* 3rd ser., Vol. 2 (1873).

Edgar, M. Ten Years in Upper Canada in Peace & War, 1805–1815.

_____. *Being the Ridout Letters with Annotations by Matilda Edgar,* Toronto: William Brigs, 1890.

Family History and Reminiscences of Early Settlers and Recollections of the War of 1812. Niagara Historical Society Papers, No. 28, 1915.

Government of the United States. *Causes of the Failure of the Army on the Northern Frontier.* Report to the House of Representatives, February 2, 1814, 13th Congress, 2nd Session, Military Affairs.

Illustrated Historical Atlas of the Counties of Northumberland and Durham. Toronto: H. Belden & Co., 1877.

Illustrated Historical Atlas of the Counties of Stormont, Dundas & Glengarry. Toronto: Belden & Co. Toronto, 1879.

Illustrated Historical Atlas of Norfolk County. Toronto: H. Belden & Co., 1877.

Illustrated Historical Atlas of the Counties of Frontenac, Lennox and Addington. Toronto: J.H. Meachan & Co., 1878.

Illustrated Historical Atlas of the Counties of Hastings & Prince Edward. Toronto: H. Belden & Co., 1878.

Illustrated Historical Atlas of the Counties of Lincoln and Welland. Toronto: H.R. Page, 1876.

Johnson, Frederick H. *A Guide for Every Visitor to Niagara Falls.* Niagara Falls: Self-published, 1852.

Kearsley, John (Major). *Memoir of Major John Kearsley.* Clement Library, University of Michigan.

Kilborn, John. "Accounts of the War of 1812." In Thaddeus W.H. Leavitt. *History of Leeds and Grenville Counties from 1749 to 1879.* Brockville, ON: Recorder Press, 1879.

Leavitt. T.W.H. *History of Leeds and Grenville Counties from 1749 to 1879.* Brockville, ON: Recorder Press, 1879.

Lossing, Benson. *Pictorial Field Book of the War of 1812.* New York: Harper and Brothers, 1868.

Recollections of the Late Hon. James Crooks. Niagara Historical Society Papers, No. 28, (1916).

Reminiscences of Arthur Galloway. Cornell University Library.

Scott, Winfield. *Memoirs of Lieut. General Scott.* Sheldon & Co., 1864.

State Historical Monographs, Historical Literature Collection, Anonymous collection, *circa* 1850.

Reminiscences of Niagara. Niagara Historical Society Papers, No. 11 (1904).

Severence, F.H., ed. *Papers Relating to the War of 1812 on the Niagara Frontier.* Buffalo Historical Society Publications, No. 5 (1902).

_____. "The War of 1812 on the Niagara Frontier." Buffalo Historical Society Publications, Vol. 29 (1927).

Warner, Robert I. *Memoirs of Capt. John Lampman and His Wife Mary Secord.* Welland County Historical Society, Papers and Records. Vol. 3. (1927).

BOOKS

Adams, Henry. *History of the United States of America During the Administrations of Madison.* New York: Library of America, 1986. Reprint of original 1891 edition.

Auchinleck, George. *A History of the War Between Great Britain and the United States of America During the Years 1812,*

1813 & 1814. Toronto: Thomas Maclear, 1853. Reprint by Arms & Armour Press and Pendragon House, 1972.

Babcock, Louis L. *The War of 1812 on the Niagara Frontier, Volume 29.* Buffalo: Buffalo Historical Society Publications, 1927.

Benn, Carl. *The Iroquois in the War of 1812.* Toronto: University of Toronto Press, 1998.

Bingham, Robert W. *The Cradle of the Queen City: A History of Buffalo to the Incorporation of the City, Volume 31.* Buffalo: Buffalo Historical Society Publications, 1931.

Blakeley, B., and C. McDonald. *Norfolk, Haldimand and the war of 1812, including the Six Nations.* Nanticoke, ON: Heronwood Enterprises, 2008.

Bowler, R. Arthur, ed. *War Along the Niagara, Essays on the War of 1812 and Its Legacy.* Youngstown, NY: Old Fort Niagara Association, 1991.

Brant, Irving, *The Fourth President: A Life of James Madison.* Indianapolis & New York: The Bobbs Merrill Company, 1970.

Casselman, Alexander C., ed. *Richardson's War of 1812.* Toronto: Historical Publishing Co., 1902. Facsimile edition by Coles Publishing Co., Toronto, 1974.

Contest for the Command of Lake Ontario in 1812 & 1813. Transactions of the Royal Society of Canada, SEC II, 3rd ser., Vol. 10.

Cruikshank, Ernest. *The Documentary History of the Campaigns upon the Niagara Frontier in 1812–1814.* Welland, ON: Tribune Press, 1896–1908. 9 volumes.

Dunlop, William (Tiger). *Tiger Dunlop's Upper Canada.* Ottawa: Carleton University Press, 1967.

Dunnigan, B. *The British Army at Mackinac, 1812–1815.* Reports in Mackinac History and Archaeology, No 7. Mackinac Island State Park Commission, 1980.

Elliott, C. *Winfield Scott, the Soldier and the Man.* Toronto: The Macmillan Company of Canada Ltd. 1937.

Fredriksen, J. *Green Coats and Glory, The United States Regiment of Riflemen, 1808–1821.* Youngstown, NY: Old Fort Niagara Association, 2000.

Gardiner, Robert, ed. *The Naval War of 1812.* U.K.: Caxton Publishing Group, 2001.

Gayler, Hugh J., ed. *Niagara's Changing Landscapes.* Ottawa: Carleton University Press, 1994.

Gough, B. *Through Water, Ice & Fire: Schooner Nancy of the War of 1812.* Toronto: Dundurn Press, 2006.

Graves, D.E. *Fix Bayonets! A Royal Welch Fusilier at War 1796–1815.* Montreal: Robin Brass Studio, 2006.

_____. ed. *Merry Hearts Make Light Days: The Journal of Lieutenant John Le Couteur, 104th Foot.* Ottawa: Carleton University Press, 1993.

_____. ed. *The Battle of Lundy's Lane on the Niagara in 1814.* Baltimore: The Nautical & Aviation Publishing Company of America, 1993.

_____. ed. *Soldiers of 1814: American Enlisted Men's Memoirs of the Niagara Campaign.* Youngstown, NY. Old Fort Niagara Association Inc. Lawrenceville, NJ: Princeton Academic Press, 1995.

_____. *And All Their Glory Past: Fort Erie, Plattsburgh and the Final Battles in the North, 1814.* Montreal: Robin Brass Studio Inc. 2013.

Gourlay, Robert. *Statistical Account of Upper Canada Compiled with a View to a Grand System of Emigration.* London: Simpkin and Marshall, 1822. 2 volumes. Republished by the Social Science Research Council of Canada, S.R. Publishers Ltd., Johnson Reprint Corp. 1966.

Gray, W. *Soldiers of the King.* Erin, ON: Boston Mills Press, 1995.

Hill, P. *Napoleon's Troublesome Americans, Franco-American Relations, 1804–1815.* Dulles, VA: Potomac Books, Inc. 2005.

Hitsman, J. Mackay. *The Incredible War of 1812: A Military History.* Toronto: Robin Brass Studio, 1999. Revised edition, updated by Donald Graves.

Horsman, R. *The Causes of the War of 1812.* New York: A.S. Barnes and Co., 1962.

Illustrated Historical Atlas of the Counties of Lincoln and Welland. Toronto: H.R. Page, 1876.

Irving, L.H. *Officers of the British Forces in Canada during the War of 1812.* Toronto: Canadian Military Institute, 1908.

Jarvis Papers. Women's Canadian Historical Society of Toronto Papers and Transactions, Transaction No. 5 (1902), 3–9.

Jay, W. *Table of the Killed and wounded in the War of 1812*. New York State, Historical Monographs, Historical Literature Collection, Cornell University Library.

Johnston, Winston. *The Glengarry Light Infantry, 1812–1816. Who Were They and What Did They Do in the War?* Self-published, 2011.

Klinck, Carl F. *Journal of Major John Norton*. Toronto: Champlain Society of Canada, Publication No. 46. 1970.

Mackay, J. *The Incredible War of 1812*. Toronto: University of Toronto, 1965.

Malcomson, Robert. *Lords of the Lake: The Naval War on Lake Ontario, 1812–1814*. Toronto: Robin Brass Studio, 1998.

——————. *Warships of the Great Lakes, 1754–1834*. Rochester, U.K.: Chatham Publishing, 2001.

Niagara Historical Society Papers, Nos. 2, 3, 4, 5, 9, 11, 20, 22, 23, 28, 30, 31, 33.

Pfeiffer S. and Williamson, R., eds. *Snake Hill, An Investigation of a Military Cemetery from the War of 1812*. Toronto: Dundurn Press Limited, 1991.

Ruttan, Henry. *Reminiscences of the Hon. Henry Ruttan: Loyalist Narratives from Upper Canada*. Toronto: Champlain Society, 1946.

Stagg, J.C.A. *Mr. Madison's War: Politics, Diplomacy, and Warfare in the Early American Republic 1783–1830*. Princeton, NJ: Princeton University Press, 1983.

Stanley, George F.G. *The War of 1812: Land Operations*. Toronto: Macmillan of Canada and the Canadian War Museum 1983.

Stott, G. *Greater Evils: The War of 1812 in Southwestern Ontario*. Self-published, 2001.

Whitehorn, J. *While Washington Burned*. Baltimore, MD: Nautical and Aviation Publishing Company of America Inc., 1992.

Wood, William C.H. *Select British Documents of the War of 1812*. Three volumes. Toronto: Champlain Society of Canada, 1920.

Zuehlke, M. *For Honour's Sake: The War of 1812 and the Brokering of an Uneasy Peace*. Alfred A. Knopf Canada, 2006.

INDEX

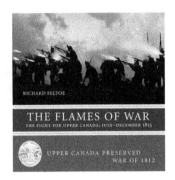

The Flames of War
The 1812 Invasions of Upper Canada
Richard Feltoe

In April 1813 the Americans launched a new campaign to conquer Upper Canada, after their failure to do so in 1812. However, following initial victories, the U.S. assault stalled as a combined force of British regulars, Canadian militia, and Native allies counterattacked, throwing the Americans entirely onto the defensive by the end of June. During the next six months, this seesaw of military advantage was repeated again and again as each side escalated its commitment of men and resources and fought to gain the "final" victory. Unfortunately, this also brought with it an increasing level of destruction and hardship suffered by armies and civilian populations on both sides of the border.

Numerous images of locations at the time are counterpointed with modern pictures taken from the same perspective to give a true then-and-now effect. Maps are also included to trace the course of individual battles stage by stage, while placing and moving the shifting formations of troops across a geographically accurate battlefield.

This third volume in the six-part series Upper Canada Preserved — War of 1812 recounts the dramatic and destructive campaigns in the last six months of 1813 as the Americans continued their remounted attack on Upper Canada.

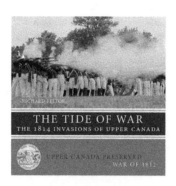

The Tide of War

The 1812 Invasions of Upper Canada

Richard Feltoe

Book four in the Upper Canada Preserved — War of 1812 series. Throughout 1812 and 1813, Upper Canada had been the principle target for a succession of American invasions and attacks. Fortunately they all had been repulsed, but at a high cost in lives and the devastation of property on both sides of the border. By the beginning of 1814, both sides were determined to bring the war to an end with a decisive victory through an escalated commitment of men and military resources.

Continuing the story already detailed in *The Call to Arms*, *The Pendulum of War*, and *The Flames of War*, *The Tide of War* documents the first six months of 1814 and the ongoing fight for the domination and control of Upper Canada.

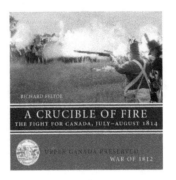

A Crucible of Fire
The 1812 Invasions of Upper Canada
Richard Feltoe

Following their invasion at Fort Erie and decisive victory at the Battle of Chippawa, an American army of over 5,000 men seemed poised to sweep across the Niagara frontier to Lake Ontario, link up with the American fleet, and complete the final expulsion of the British allied forces from Upper Canada. However, only a month later, the shattered remnants of this force were firmly on the defensive and feverishly digging in as the British advanced to begin the siege of Fort Erie.

The fifth book in the Upper Canada Preserved series examines this pivotal period in the course of the War of 1812–1815 with particular emphasis on the events that led up to and took place at the Battle of Lundy's Lane on July 25, 1814.

Excerpts from original accounts, letters, and diaries and a series of new highly-detailed maps place readers on the field where they can follow the action as each phase of this decisive combat took place in the darkness of the night and within earshot of the Great Falls of Niagara.

Available at your favourite bookseller

Visit us at

Dundurn.com | @dundurnpress | Facebook.com/dundurnpress | Pinterest.com/dundurnpress

Printed in the USA
CPSIA information can be obtained
at www.ICGtesting.com
JSHW052016140824
68134JS00027B/2504

9 781459 722835